81-199

Y0-AVS-333

81-199

Architecture and
the Microprocessor

Architecture and the Microprocessor

John Paterson
Department of Construction Management
University of Reading

Illustrations by Pamela Paterson

A Wiley-Interscience Publication

John Wiley & Sons
Chichester · New York · Brisbane · Toronto

By the same author: *Information methods for Design and Construction*

British Library Cataloguing in Publication Data:

Paterson, John
  Architecture and the microprocessor.
  1. Architecture—Data processing
  2. Microprocessors
  I. Title
  720'.28'54044 NA2728 79–41210

ISBN 0 471 27680 4

Text set in 10/12 pt VIP Optima, printed and bound in Great Britain at The Pitman Press, Bath

ACKNOWLEDGEMENTS TO
AUTHORS AND PUBLISHERS

I wish to acknowledge the following for granting permission for diagrams, tables, and passages of text to be used from their various publications:

The Architectural Association. Illustrations from CERDA exhibition brochure 7–25/2/78 (Figure 6); (see caption for credit to artist). Illustration, p. 31, *A.A.Q.* vol. 7, no. 1. (Figure 26), Illustration, p. 51, *A.A.Q.* vol. 7, no. 3. (Figure 28(c))

Architectural Design, vol. XLVI, 11/76. Extracts from p. 667 and illustrations on pp. 668 and 669. (Figure 50)

Architectural Press Ltd. (Figure 22)

Angela Bates. Reproduction of prize-winning photograph. (Figure 5)

M. Bedford. Unit for Architectural Studies, School of Environmental Studies, University College London. Extracts and illustrations from article in *Environmental Planning B*, 1976, vol. 3, p. 155, and illustration p. 178. (Figure 52)

Thomas L. Blair, 'Habitat: Key issues for Debate and Action in the United Kingdom', *Habitat International Journal*, vol. 1, No. 3/4, 1976, pp. 251–257. Reproduced by permission of Professor Thomas L. Blair, Habitat Forum, The Polytechnic of Central London. [pp. 1, 2, 3]

Christo. Photographs by Wolfgang Volz of Wrapped Reichstag and Christo and Brandt in Brandt's office. (Figures 2, 3(a), and 3(b)).

Edinburgh University Press, Extracts from Report on BOXES by D. Michie, Figure 8, p. 148, and Figure 6, p. 146. (Figures 69 and 70)

Environmental Planning B, Extracts and illustrations on pp. 155 and 176. (Figures 52, 53(a), and 53(b))

Faber and Faber Ltd., *Fine Buildings*, Figures 1a and 1b on pp. 30 and 31. *The Modulor*, 1954. Illustration p. 51. (Figures 25(a) and 25(b)).

B. Hillier, Unit for Architectural Studies, School of Environmental Studies, University College London. Extracts and illustrations from article in *Environmental Planning B*, 1976, vol. 3, p. 155, and illustration p. 178. (Figure 52)

The Controller, HMSO. Extract from Building Research Establishment Current Paper CP28/77. Crown copyright.

The Journal Press. Figure 7 and Figure 8 of H. J. Eysenck, 'An experimental study of aesthetic preference for polygonal figures', *Journal of General Psychology*, Vol. 79, 3–17 (1968). (Figure 54)

A. Leaman, Unit for Architectural Studies, School of Environmental Studies, University College London. Extracts and illustrations from article in *Environmental Planning B*, 1976, vol. 3, p. 155, and illustration p. 178. (Figure 52)

Arthur D. Little Inc. Diagram of Evolution of Microprocessor technology. (Figure 86)

Loeb Classical Library (Harvard University Press; William Heinemann). Extracts from *Vitruvius on Architecture* by Frank Granger, reprinted by permission. Book 1, pp. 3, 7 and 35. Book 1c, pp. 9 and 23.

W. D. C. Lyddon. Extracts from articles in *Habitat*, vol. 1, no. 3/4, p. 263. Crown copyright.

D. Michie and Edinburgh University Press. Illustrations from *BOXES: an experiment in adaptive control*. (Figures 69 and 70)

Middle East Photographic Archive. Photograph of The Treasury, Petra, Jordan. (Figure 13)

The National Gallery. Reproduction of painting of the *Martyrdom of St. Sebastian* by Antonio Pollaiuolo. (Figure 20)

Netherlands Government Information Service. Reproduction of photograph of the Vondelschool, Hilversum, Holland (photograph Rousel). (Figure 24)

Oxford University Press. R. Dawkins, *The Selfish Gene*, pp. 163 and 164.

Ewart Parkinson. Extracts from article in *Habitat*, vol. 1, no. 3/4, p. 280.

Pergamon Press Inc. Extracts from *Habitat*, vol. 1, no. 3/4, pp. 251, 252, 263 and 280.

Pion Limited, London. *Environmental Planning B*, Extracts and illustrations on pp. 155 and 176. (Figure 52)

Pitman Publishing Ltd. Taylor, *Expansions and Catastrophes* (1976), Figure 3.6. (Figure 55)

Plenum Publishing Corporation. Illustrations from Eye Movements and Vision (1967) by A. L. Yarbus. © Plenum. (Figures 33 and 34)

Jean Robert, Reproduction of photographs from *Pentagram Papers 4*. (Figures 35 and 36)

SITE (Emilio Sousa, Alison Sky, Michelle Stone, James Wines). Photographs of Indeterminate Facade, Houston, and Peeling Project, Richmond, USA. (Figures 28(a) and (b))

P. Stansall, Unit for Architectural Studies, School of Environmental Studies, University College London. Extracts and illustrations from article in *Environmental Planning B*, 1976, vol. 3, p. 155, and illustration p. 178. (Figure 52)

The Sunday Times. Illustration, teletext/viewdata, © *The Sunday Times* (Figure 77)

University of London/Royal Institute of British Architects/The Athlone Press. *A History of Architecture*, Figure E, p. 853, p. 1310, Figure C, p. 54, Figure A and B, p. 730. (Figures 7, 21, 37, 38, 72, 73 and 74)

University of Reading. (Figure 62)

Weidenfeld and Nicolson. Illustrations from *Eye and Brain*, 2nd edn. (Figures 4(a), 4(b), 4(c), 39(a), and 39(b))

West Sussex County Council. Photographs, Old People's Home, Horsham, and School at Eastergate. (Figures 82 and 83)

John Wiley and Sons Ltd. *Design Methods* (1970), p. 76, Figure 1. p. 77, Figures 6.3, 6.4, 6.5,, p. 294, Figure 4 and 4.1. (Figures 40, 41, 42, 43, 49) *Information Methods* (1977), p. 34, Figure 10, pp. 148, 151, p. 102 Figure 34, p. 68 Figure 26, p. 67, Figure 25. (Figures 46, 58, 59, 67, 80 (part))

CONTENTS

PREFACE

The path of computers in architecture has been a bumpy one with a surprisingly small impact considering the amount of time and resources which have been expended on the subject.

At a time when even the most conservative layman is beginning to lose his prejudices and enjoy the fruits of computer technology it seemed to be worth considering why there has been such a slow development in architecture and how the inevitable use of microprocessors and computers will eventually happen.

Although it seems to be a gross affectation to write even one book, let alone attempt a second, interest in such a book was further encouraged by the fact that when writing *Information Methods* it became increasingly difficult to restrain expansion into areas which had by necessity to be omitted. One was the concept of art and architecture and the other was the potential, limited or otherwise, of the computer as an aid to creative design. In the case of the former, it was necessary to restrict the chapter on design because the architect (although he may not think so) and his view of architecture already dominates the construction industry, and it was therefore important not to let this happen when talking of a total integrated system.

The potential use of computers in the creative process was not within the scope of that book, but as the development of the cheap microprocessor has now brought the potential of computing not only to the smallest units within the industry but to the layman himself, it is necessary to consider what we seek from architecture before the processes are again encapsulated in systems and establishment.

Already a lot of work on 'computer-aided design' has been based upon traditional processes which have been developed over hundreds of years, and so we might be in the danger of falling into the 'mechanizing the horse' syndrome if we do not rexamine our objectives in the light of latest developments.

Whilst it is true that there has been a lot of heart searching in the architectural profession in recent decades, this has usually been done from the predetermined viewpoint of the architect–patron relationship developed in earlier times. But these heart searchings have done little to paper over the very large cracks which have developed between the architect and society. Perhaps by taking the surgeon's knife a little deeper the cure may not be found to be as bad as imagined. In any case something has to be done, particularly when people all over the world now believe that they have rights as strong as any other human rights to make decisions about their environment. The United Nations conference on Human Settlements in 1976 confirmed these rights, but there is still a great deal of work to be done before they become a reality.

We now have the technology to bring the fundamental building needs of people to even the smallest community, but will it be possible for them to apply these with what we have come to know as the art of architecture? What is art anyway?

In an age when even the most intimate sexual details can be discussed openly and publicly, and religion can be researched as though it was an historical or social subject, the existence of art and art in architecture is taken for granted, and any questioning is taken as philistinism requiring courage. The existence of the universe, this planet, or even our own existence is questioned by philosophers, and yet art is taken as a basic assumption. This may seem to be an extreme statement, but substantiation can be found everywhere. Even if we go to that fountainhead of enquiry, the philosophers, we find that over and over again they pass over the subject without question. For example, Popper (1972) states:

> I know that the beauty of Rembrandt's self portraits is not in my eye, nor that of Bach's Passion in my ear. On the contrary, I can establish to my satisfaction, by opening and closing my eyes and ears, that my eyes and ears are not good enough to take in all the beauty that is there. Also *that there are other people who are better judges and better able than I to appreciate the beauty of pictures and music* (my italics)!

On what basis can he make such an assumption? This is not at all untypical of most people's views, and it is only surprising that such blind acceptance should come from a philosopher. If everyone adopts the attitude that 'I don't understand but somebody else does', how can we be sure that there is such a thing as the art of architecture? What is more, how can we have user participation if that art is restrictive?

Whilst it is the intention of this book to explain some of the uses and effects of microprocessors on architecture, it is essential that this must be viewed in context. The pattern of the future may be created as much in the early days of microprocessors as it was with railway engines, motorcars, and radios, which quickly developed an establishment that was difficult to change later. Who, for example, would be brave enough to set about changing the railway gauge now?

Since writing and circulating the draft of this book in 1977–78, there has been an increased amount of discussion on some of the issues discussed here. This will undoubtedly further increase. Furthermore, having tried to rectify omissions of the earlier book, it has now not been possible to deal adequately with the language of vision and computer modelling in this one.

I should like to thank Professor Bennett, Harry Atherton, John Worthington, Jon and Pru Amner, and the many others who made such valuable comments on the draft, and in particular to thank Peter and Christina Goodacre for their help and encouragement.

Finally, my greatest appreciation to my wife, who not only gave so much assistance with the research but made such a personal contribution with her illustrations.

May 1979   John Paterson
                                                              Privett, Hampshire, England

INTRODUCTION

Everyone is a philosopher in one degree or another, but very often a personal view of what is right and what is wrong is sacrificed to one which seems to carry greater weight, either because it has been around for a long time, or because it was printed in a book, or was taught at school or university. Sadly these stronger views do not always turn out to be the right ones, but it is the fashionable ideas which persist at any one time. These fashionable ideas often create violent swings of taste which impose considerable strains on heavy industries such as the construction industry. In the light industries and those producing short-life products the problem is less serious and, in fact, for them fashion acts as a stimulus in the market-place.

However, violent swings of taste in architecture leave nations with vast stocks of outmoded buildings. Very often a high proportion of the national budget is still being spent on projects under construction which have already become obsolescent. Fashionable 'all glass' architecture, for example, was still being built long after the energy crisis had become a reality.

Our traditional concepts of art in architecture also leave us with another problem in these rapidly changing times. All over the world, individuals are fighting for human rights and personal freedom; but this must create a difficulty if we assume, as in the past, that there is an art in architecture and that only a small proportion in any society have the natural gift or the training, and sometimes the right, to design the environment for the rest.

In addition to the many reports, such as Skeffington, recommending user participation, the United Nations Habitat Conference on Human Settlements at Vancouver, Canada, in 1976 included the following principles in its Declaration, which was endorsed by its members:

> Adequate shelter and services are a basic human right which places an obligation on Governments to ensure their attainment by all people, beginning with direct assistance to the least advantaged through guided programmes of self-help and community action . . .
> and
> Basic human dignity is the right of people, individually and

collectively, to participate directly in shaping the policies and programmes affecting their lives. The process of choosing and carrying out a given course of action for human settlement improvement should be designed expressly to fulfil that right. Effective human settlement policies require a continuous co-operative relationship between Government and its people at all levels . . .
and again,
All persons have the right and duty to participate, individually and collectively, in the elaboration and implementation of the policies and programmes of their human settlements.

The microprocessor might now provide us with the means to achieve these ends in the constructional sense. But how do we account for the art in such environments? Art has now become not just a matter of taste but a matter of morality—at least in architecture and planning. It is not just our traditional views of art which shape our environment but the structure of society and the structure of the industry, both of which have undergone and will continue to undergo changes. What effect will the microprocessor have on that change? It will probably be very substantial, but in order to see this potential for change in perspective, it is necessary to have some knowledge of how we arrived where we are. Any history is selective in the items chosen to create a single strand out of the multiplicity of available strands, and a single chapter must be even more prejudiced in its selection. Nevertheless, there are some signposts in our history which stand out as major points of change in society, and this review sets out to do no more than highlight these significant points. In recent times we have also learnt a great deal more about ourselves, about our processes of design, and what we see, all of which must be considered in setting up systems for the future. The computing industry will be affected by our views and their products in turn will affect our views. We do not know where this journey of interaction will end but we must at least recognize our starting point and begin to get involved.

No matter how much we may desire personal freedom, user participation, and decision making at a local level, it is inevitable that the trend is for much of our decision to be made at higher and higher levels in national, international, and global bureaucracies. The decisions of any community must take into account such things as national and international communications or global problems of energy and resources about which they must be relatively ignorant. It is for this reason that we must consider the impact of the microprocessor on society at the strategic as well as the tactical level.

At a follow-up conference to the Vancouver one, the conference chairman said:

It is now much clearer after Vancouver that human settlement issues are not really only about housing and technology, but about politics and social change as well. Those who ask what the United Nations can do to resolve all the enormous and complex issues of human settlements will, I fear, be doomed to frustration and disappointment. These are basically issues of the organisation and structure of societies, and can only be solved by reforms and new initiatives within each society at the local, regional and national level. It is obvious that the United Nations and other international bodies can undertake certain initiatives and provide an arena for discussions, but the basic motivation and effort for change must come from within each society itself to create the appropriate national human settlement policies and the new institutional forms to implement them.

The greatest problems will undoubtedly lie at the interfaces of these local, regional, national, and international policies. For this we must have an understanding of the human mind and the way it works in the light of present-day knowledge, so that we can learn to use the methods and tools we have developed to the best advantage. Very often emotive descriptions of the environment are made which only contribute prejudice and ignorance to a situation in which real knowledge is available. Sometimes it seems as though architectural comment and criticism is made in the most obscure manner either as a defence of or as a cover for ignorance. Whilst it is impossible to cover all those areas where knowledge of how the brain reacts to its environment has made rapid development, at least it is hoped to show that these areas are worthy of architectural interest for the student. Furthermore, it is the increased understanding of the working of the brain, both human and animal, which has contributed to the development of an enormous range of methods. At the present time, methodologies are extremely unpopular with architects, many of whom have returned to 'seat of the pants' management systems and 2B pencils for their salvation, somehow believing that art is despoiled if it comes into contact with science or modern management tools. Even many of the originators of design methodologies have recanted and expressed disillusionment. This is particularly unfortunate at a time when such methods are being transferred to computing systems without the participation of those who will undoubtedly have to use them.

It is the effect of the microprocessor on computing which will make this inevitable, because it has reduced the cost of computing to bring it within everybody's price range. The dramatic drop in price to give wide availability is reminiscent of the position with motor cars at the time of the 1930 depression. Until that time, motor cars had been expensive and rather rare. Suddenly, through mass production, Henry Ford produced his £100 car, which was immediately followed by other competitors. This sudden reduction in price created enormous sales, even in a period of recession. The expansion of the motor industry spilled over into every aspect of society. New roads gave an access to hitherto inaccessible areas which in turn had an impact on town and country which is still reverberating today. In addition, it created a whole new outlook for society. People used their motor cars as a means of escape from their everyday environment and more recently, with the increased use of tents and caravans, they have found a capacity to organize their own environment. The microprocessor will probably have an even greater impact on future society and its environment and therefore the tool and its power will be discussed.

The microprocessor and its effect through the computer of using new methodologies and modelling techniques will be discussed in its relevance to the larger and the smaller organization. Obviously many of the applications will not be solely applicable to just the one or the other, but the implications for the organization may be different. The future will see the development of applications which cannot yet even be envisaged, but a range is given for organizations concerned with the environment to start what will probably be a long journey.

Finally, there is the impact of these new methods and tools on the environment itself. There are many who would like to ignore these new technologies and try to maintain things as they are, or better still, to go back to the eighteenth century. Whilst we may sympathize with the dream, with the world's population increasing at the present rate it would probably prove to be a terrible nightmare. We have no choice but to change and move into the future, if not with the naive hopes of the past, at least with a firm resolve to help solve some of the problems of human need.

Chapter 1
WHAT ARE WE TRYING TO DO?

Once upon a time, man lived a happy and natural bucolic existence in a beautiful world created by nature in which art was a normal and intrinsic part. More recently he lived in a Constable-type landscape designed by famous artists and lived in architectural masterpieces, whether they were mansion or bijou cottage. As industrialization grew, because of the extreme greed of a few, the environment became more and more intolerable in spite of efforts by architects and planners. Now the future can only be viewed with extreme gloom.

This is the picture which is explicitly or implicitly portrayed, not only in books on the history of art and architecture but also in most books on the environment surveying the past and present or even forecasting the future. Anyone who doubts this need only try to find a recent book with either an optimistic view of the future or a pleasurable view of the present to discover how rare they are by comparison with the confidence and optimism of the past.

Le Corbusier (1947) described 'a series of dimensions (a, b, c, d, e, e^1, e^2, e^3) which could and should have filled the sky with the radiance of mathematics'. It would not be an exaggeration to say that few people today would share this sort of excitement for the future of the environment, whereas there were many at that time. Earlier still, the architects and patrons of the great Renaissance houses must have found the future exciting as the landscape was transformed to provide vistas and lakes, even though it is doubtful whether the villagers who were dispossessed and their homes demolished as nature was tidied up felt any more sense of joy in this artistic creation than the suburban householder does today as he watches a motorway being constructed over his house. It is also doubtful whether the architecture was appreciated by the vast numbers of servants who had to toil all day to make up for the functional deficiences of the buildings. Time and nostalgia cure many sores. Whilst the past is portrayed as a happy and artistic time, the picture which is generally built up about today and the future is usually based on a different set of assumed and often unequestioned *facts*. For example:

(1) Life is worse today than ever before.
(2) Catastrophes and the potential for catastrophes are greater than ever before.

1

(3) Man faces a shortage of resources for the first time.
(4) Man has been forced into the indignity of urban living by the greed of a few.
(5) Life in the country is happiness whilst life in urban or suburban area is hell.
(6) Art exists and, although it cannot be described or prescribed, could make the environment beautiful again if it were not for controls and regulations.

We could continue with this list of well-established assumptions just as we could make a list of the 'facts' of science which we believe we *know* and for which in fact we have no explanation. Whilst our prejudices are extremely strong our knowledge is extremely weak; the evidence for this is considerable. Apart from Feyerabend (1975), who strikes at the very roots of our ignorance, there are innumerable others who have tried to illustrate the limits of our knowledge. For example, Lyttleton (1977) states: 'It seems to be a common defect in human minds that they tend to crave for complete certainty of belief or disbelief in anything. Not only is this undesirable scientifically, but it must be recognized that no such state is attainable in science.'

Rowan-Robinson (1977) states: 'In extra galactic astrophysics we suffer from three types of ignorance: ignorance in principle, ignorance due to observational limitations and ignorance due to inadequacy of theory and observation.' That is a pretty all-embracing statement of ignorance for a society sending spaceships into orbit and embarking on the exploration of the solar system. As the area of our search for knowledge increases it only illustrates with ever-increasing clarity the extent of our ignorance and the fact that we exist on prejudices. It might therefore be worth looking at some of those prejudices which affect architecture, to see whether they should be replaced by new prejudices if we cannot find anything more substantial.

Take for example the first of the assumptions given above, that life today is worse than ever before. This very common type of statement is usually made by someone enjoying the benefits of the modern industrial world such as plentiful food, car, central heating, holidays with pay, and so on, whilst decrying some of the side-effects such as noise. But the obvious question must be that if the primitive life of earlier times is so much better than our modern industrialized life, why is there not a rush to join the majority of the world's population still enjoying a primitive life instead of the other way round? Why is man throughout the world leaving the rural life to become an urban dweller at an ever-increasing rate? The United Nations estimates that by the year 2000 more people will live in urban areas than in rural areas. At the present time the growth rate is 4.5 per cent per annum in urban areas but only 2.5 per cent in rural areas—a pattern which has persisted for a long time. Figure 1 illustrates the changing pattern over a short time in the United Kingdom, where the point at which more people lived in towns rather than the country arrived in 1851.

This movement was once blamed upon industrialists who were accused of dragging people from the fields into the terrible conditions of

Figure 1(a) Map showing 18th-century population

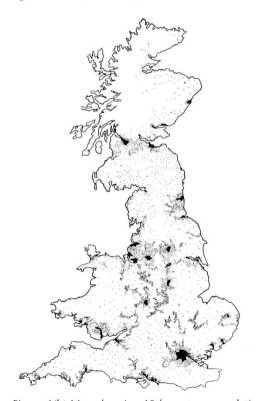

Figure 1(b) Map showing 19th-century population

the factory, but even today when there is greater freedom of choice the pattern is still the same. Mechanization of agriculture has proceeded at a considerable pace due to the shortage of labour caused by the movement to towns. This movement can no longer be entirely put down to low wages and land ownership because the pattern is the same in countries of every political and economic persuasion.

It is easy to judge industry and housing of the nineteenth century by present standards but it is necessary to remember the harsh world of the country at the time to see why the towns must have looked so attractive. It is also easy for townsmen not to appreciate the reasons why people today also move to the urban centres. One of the reasons, of course, is that the people who actually work in the fields, can find the work physically demanding and often mentally boring as well as having a twenty-four hour involvement. It is not only the wages but also the boredom of repetition and the physical demands on the agricultural worker which have helped the drift or flood into the cities. But the dream persists of the country idyll, and the architect and the planner has always been particularly prone to the idea that everyone should live and work in the country. Morris and Le Corbusier are only two of a long line who have exalted country life, but the mass of people keep choosing the gregarious life of the towns.

When we look at the second assumption—that catastrophes are getting worse—there are similar complications through oversimplification. First, we have to consider whether we are evaluating this in general terms or the individual's reaction to the catastrophe. If we talk of general statistics it is obvious that as the global population increases there is a likelihood that the numbers involved in any catastrophe will increase. However, even bearing this in mind, many of the disasters befalling mankind reduce in terms of human deaths rather than increase. The further we go back in history the more horrific the death toll becomes, particularly when we consider the numbers as a percentage of the world population at the time.

For example, Cottrell (1960) says of the battle of Cannae (216 BC) that of 80,000 Roman infantry, only about one man in ten was alive at the end of one day's fighting; 70,000 Romans and their allies died, and in addition there were 4,000 Celts and 1,500 Spaniards and Africans who died. Nearly 80,000 men dead in one day! In the 1939–1945 war, RAF casualties for the whole period were 70,000, and in the battle of Passchendaele in the First World War, usually considered as one of the worst of modern slaughters, about 60,000 men were killed over four months. The battle of Cannae only lasted for a few hours!

But in any case, in spite of the catastrophes, wars, and pestilences which have occurred over the centuries, the global population has continued to expand and seems likely to do so exponentially for some time at least. It took the whole period from the arrival of man until 1850 to produce one thousand million persons simultaneously alive. To reach two thousand million people simultaneously alive only took another 75 years (reached in 1925), for three thousand million only 37 years (reached in 1962), and four thousand million only 15 years (reached in 1977). It is anticipated that it will be less than ten years from 1977 to produce an extra thousand million people simultaneously alive. The majority of the world is already inadequately housed or not housed at all. What about housing an extra thousand million in ten years time? Or in five hundred weeks time? And by the present processes?

The next assumption is that man faces a shortage of resources for the first time. But all through history he has had to cope with the continual disappearance of one resource after another. Even when man was a hunter food was a diminishing resource, which led to the development of agriculture; this in time created a society which caused further shortages. A man in Hampshire, for example, during the period of the Napoleonic wars, saw the forests already ravaged by the brick makers and their kilns finally destroyed by the need to build ships, and must have felt that this was the end for mankind as far as he was concerned. Not only was his natural fuel gone but also the material with which he built and made the necessities of his life—his home, his furniture, and even his transport. But of course, as we know, with the development of coal, the iron and steel industry, and new forms of transport, his horizons actually widened rather than narrowed. This is just one example of the disappearing resources in the past which have made whole communities reorganize and redistribute themselves with what is later seen to be an advantage. There will no doubt be many more crises in the future which man will overcome and turn to his advantage. The trouble is that, because we are what we are, we can only see ourselves uniquely in our present situation with the limitations of today's knowledge or perhaps more precisely today's beliefs.

A further argument today is, of course, that we have now reached the end of discovering new resources, but the indications are that we are becoming more adept at conjuring up new resources from the constituents of this planet, its atmosphere, and soon the solar system.

In case we might become a little optimistic about the future, we are now sometimes confronted with the problem of a greenhouse effect in which the earth's atmosphere prevents the dispersal of the products of burning fossil fuel, thus causing a rise in world temperature. Heilbroner (1975) states: 'The limit on industrial growth . . . depends in the end on the tolerance of the ecosphere for the absorption of heat.' Ayres and Kneese (1972) write: '. . . if the present rate of growth continued for 250 years, emission would reach 100% of the absorbed solar flux. The resulting increase in the earth's temperature would be about 50°C. . . .' This type of forecasting is then used as an argument to halt technology and promote the simple life.

The problem is that the people in the industrialized world show no signs of wanting to give up their sybaritic ways. This then leaves the possibility, sometimes argued, that the rest of the world should be dissuaded from aspiring to Western standards. Apart from the morality of the argument, it is not even conceivable that such ideas could be promoted amongst those who quite rightly wish to share some of the benefits which the West takes for granted. It is maintained that 20 per cent of the world's population uses 80 per cent of the world's resources and that 6 per cent command 30 per cent of the world's energy. However, in these high consumption populations the population increase has declined or stopped and the demand for energy has flattened out.

5

Therefore it is the major part of the world's population which will cause the demand for energy to increase enormously, for even small per capita increases. Thus the answer cannot lie in conservation and primitive technology alone. We must continue to exploit new technologies if man is to have any hope for the future. Already we have the technology, if required, to put huge solar panels several miles square into orbit which can transmit energy to the earth by microwaves, thereby not only supplying our energy needs but avoiding the dangers of the greenhouse effect, even if such dangers exist.

From time to time we are also threatened with world famine, but at the present time only 2.6 billion acres of the backward areas of the planet are cultivated. This is a minute amount when we consider that the Sahara alone occupies 3,500,000 square miles or 500,000 square miles more than the whole of the United States of America. Not only that, but only 7 per cent of these backward areas is planted with modern varieties of seed. As we have seen in parts of Asia, for example, quite small improvements in organization and technology can reduce or abolish the famines so common in the past, and this freedom from famine starts a demand for the living standards of the industrial world. These assumptions have been discussed, not only because they have a direct relevance to our view of the global environment which should be the concern of architecture but also to suggest that industrialized societies might regain their confidence in new technology. This will help them and the underdeveloped world as well.

It is well known that only bad news sells newspapers; in addition, there is a tendency for people with a lot of money but few active interests to become pessimistic and neurotic. Could it be that the rich urban societies—rich in terms of low physical output—gradually achieve the same pessimistic state for very similar reasons? The more we are free from the continuous battle to survive in the physical world, the more we are able to retreat into a world of pessimism and dream of some far-off idyllic life.

It is this retreat from the realities of life which brings us to the last assumption in the list—art. Whichever way we look at it, art is elusive whilst at the same time appearing to fulfil a human need. As architecture nowadays is considered to be an art, it is worth considering whether we have prejudices on this subject as well and what they might be. Probably most people without a vested interest in art have had severe misgivings as to whether art is just a big confidence trick manipulated by dealers and financiers. Even some artists like Beecham, when he said that 'the arts in America are a gigantic racket run by unscrupulous men for unhealthy women', must have had similar doubts at times. Yet when confronted with the possible loss of an 'old master', the public will not only mourn with emotion but also contribute large sums of money for its salvation. Andre's brick sculpture at the Tate Gallery, London, brought a storm of protest when it was purchased, but now attracts a lot of visitors. Duchamp, in trying to ridicule the art scene by submitting an old urinal as an exhibit, made the mistake of signing it, even though not with his own name, thereby guaranteeing its increasing cash value. His doubts about the art scene from which he retired to spend the rest of his life playing chess has been shared by many other artists. J. M. W. Turner declared 'it's a rummy business', a statement to be echoed later by Vaughan Williams. Oscar Wilde declared that 'all art was quite useless' and that 'there are moments when art attains almost to the dignity of manual labour'. Not only did artists such as these hold little respect for art, but artists generally seem to be rather poor at recognizing a fellow artist. When Tchaikovsky said 'I played over the music of that scoundrel Brahms. What a giftless bastard!', he was plainly out of tune with posterity. Ruskin, a favourite philosopher with architects, declared that James McNeil Whistler's Symphony in Grey and Green was 'a daub professing to be a "harmony in pink and white" (or some such nonsense): absolute rubbish, and which had taken about a quarter of an hour to scrawl or daub . . .'. Here Ruskin seemed to think that production time was a factor in artistic value.

Not only can artists not always recognize their peers or works of art as defined later by posterity, but a Rembrandt would not automatically be recognized as beautiful by an Eskimo or an Aborigine until he or she had been educated in art appreciation. Furthermore, few people would recognize works of art if they were left in second-hand shops or jumble sales. Many items considered as important works of art have neither intrinsic value nor exceptional craftsmanship.

Much, if not most, of the art which is now admired was, at the time of its creation, greatly denigrated and very far from being instantly recognized as art. Some of the artists even had strange histories. Michelangelo started his career as a successful 'faker' of drawings and statues, trying to make them look like antiques. Gauguin deliberately misrepresented the source of his work. Sincerity and the search for truth is often held to be the basis of all art, but these and many other great artists managed quite well at times without it. Even though art when Plato was alive had not achieved the status it has done in recent centuries, he, as well as people before him, were already concerned about whether art could or should exist. In fact, in The Republic, Plato condemns art and poetry as being both misleading and dangerous in the pursuit of the good. Murdoch's (1977) arguments do not materially change the obvious interpretation in spite of her spirited defence of art. Since his time, Plato has been followed by others such as Kierkegaard and Wittgenstein, but all follow their investigations with greater reverence for the subject than we normally examine our beliefs today. This seems to be the key to the problem—reverence, both as individuals and collectively as a society. Like superstition it can be ridiculed but not completely denied. Hogarth (1753) recognized this reverence in his Analysis of Beauty when he said: 'For though beauty is seen and confessed by all, yet, from the many fruitless attempts to account for the cause of its being so, inquiries on this head have almost been given up: and the subject generally thought to be a matter of too high and too delicate a nature to admit of any true or intelligible discourse.' Popper has already been quoted as having this unquestioning reverence.

As life itself may be said to be an illusion and our knowledge only a collection of prejudices it could be argued quite reasonably that it does not matter anyway. It is true that except to the artists themselves, it does not matter whether a painting, a piece of music, or a sculpture is or is not a work of art, as the beauty can be in the eye of the beholder or not, as the case may be. We can look or listen as we please without a great disruption to society. But when art is applied to architecture, something quite different happens. If a building or a group of buildings or a town is designed with a belief that it is an art form, then the building or buildings will be constrained by our understanding of art. As we cannot walk away from these buildings in the way that we can from a painting, it therefore follows that we should be very clear about what we mean by the art of architecture.

If we look back at the six assumptions which were selected earlier, it can easily be seen that all of these, and many more, have a considerable influence on the environment in which we live and therefore, by definition, our architecture. As even a superficial examination of these suggests that strongly held tenets are not always what they seem, it would seem sensible to examine our understanding of architecture before we try to computerize it.

Examination of the dictionary definition of architecture shows a consistent stress laid on skill and craft but no reference to any undefined aesthetic. Certainly the Greeks saw architecture as a craft rather than an art—even the word for architect (ἀρχόστέκτων, architekton) meant master carpenter for them. But skill and craft alone would certainly not satisfy the criteria of present-day critics. We find that writers from Plato to Heidegger worried about the use of words when considering art and continuously fell back to the view that it was something that is felt. This, of course, is the way out of any scientific investigation and has been greatly supported by Cartesian philosophy, commonly used to bolster the egocentricity of human thought.

Unless we can find a better understanding of art in architecture we are confronted with two problems:

(1) If architecture is a craft or skill, it should be within the skill of the ordinary layman and probably capable of being produced by machines and computers.
(2) If it is something special involving an aesthetic sense which is held by a few, then we should use this elite to design the environment for the rest and forget participation by the user.

Most architects would reject the idea that architecture was just a craft, but at the same time would not be happy with the charge of being elitist and undemocratic. Furthermore, the elitist view would not only make talk of user participation an hypocrisy but also make nonsense of planning committees, for how can an untrained committee be better at selection than other artists?

The architect is obviously left in an invidious situation in which enthusiastic creativity, which would bring praise in another art, puts him into the elitist position of dominating the lives of his fellow men. On the other hand, a self-effacing retreat into carrying out the wishes of a community brings charges of 'designing camels by committee'. Beck (1976) attributes this duality to the Modern Movement:

> Although the antecedents of egalitarian philosophy of architecture can be traced back to the 1850s and earlier, it first

gained significance during the Modern Movement's heroic period after the First World War. . . . This New Architecture with its stripped aesthetic, however, failed to resolve two fundamental oppositions to its moral purpose. First, that the new technology could also support the prevailing social order—which in time substituted technocrats for aristocrats; and second, that architects by definition were found to join this new aristocracy of the technological society. How could it be otherwise? Thus New Architecture proposed an egalitarian ideology that could only be practised by those initiated into its esoteric theory—by an elite. All architects who now accept the Modern Movement's social ideology are trapped in this double bind. For to avoid the charge of 'elitist', they must deny their profession and so be prevented from practicing as architects: or, in accepting the theory and realising its inherent contradiction choose not to practice.

In an effort to short circuit this dilemma a few architects are seeking new interpretations of the theory. Others have chosen to call themselves architects—but their commitment to architecture's . . . ideology has led them instead into Alternative Technology, Appropriate Technology, Public Participation, Self Help, Community Action, Urbanology, and so on.

If we are to make any headway in solving this problem of art versus democracy there are a number of facets of the problem to be examined:

(1) If architecture is an art can it be left to individuals without training and selection?
(2) Could we conceive a system for the ownership of land which would make personal expression possible?
(3) Is it possible to create a mechanism in which individuals can not only create their own environment but also interact with their neighbours doing the same?
(4) How could the major strategies mesh with the local tactics?
(5) If these were all possible, what would we feel about the environment which resulted?

The first question brings us back to the problem of art and whether architecture is an art.

Let us start with an example—the Parthenon in Athens. Most architects would agree that this is a perfect example of art in architecture, and most laymen, at least in the West, would feel ennobled by seeing it. Few would doubt its importance to architecture and society. So much so that during the Second World War both sides agreed not to damage it (and a few other pieces of architecture) and to confine themselves to the slaughter of other human beings. Yet, the Parthenon as a whole building has never been seen by a living human being; nobody has ever seen more than an open ruin. But architecture is surely supposed to be the art of enclosing space! How many visitors, however, have even seen the drawings or the model? Even for those who have, do these qualify as architecture? It is true that we can admire the craftsmanship of the pieces such as those in the British Museum, but again, do the components, no matter how well made, necessarily come together to make architecture? If this is so, then why does system building not achieve the same status? Surely it must be because we know of the subtle mathematical basis which was used to deceive the eye. This would be more understandable if we could actually see the total result of such use of mathematics. Furthermore, if it is the mathematics which makes it art, then it should be simple to use a computer to make art. Not only that, but do the fascinating calculations of a box-girder bridge turn that into a work of art? The fact that Ictinus and Callicrates used the optical corrections, which were a standard of the time, would seem to give no greater reason for calling the Parthenon a work of art than using the calculations for daylight factors would make all schools works of art. Furthermore, it was a team design as opposed to one single artist's creation. Meanwhile, the specialists, as described by Summerson (1964), have wrangled over the relative purity of Roman Doric or the Greek Doric, based upon which came first.

As the standards by which we might expect to be able to select a work of art do not seem to give much help, it might be worth considering some non-architectural factors to see whether there are other things which give art status to certain buildings:

Uniqueness	e.g. the Pyramids, the Parthenon, etc.
Important or large building	e.g. the Pantheon, Rome
Historically notorious	e.g. the Colosseum, Rome
Very old	e.g. Stonehenge
Having some peculiarity	e.g. the Parthenon—mathematical illusion
	Tower of Pisa—leaning
	Stately Homes—Queen Elizabeth slept there
	Wren's buildings—usually relate to calendar measurements

This may sound outrageously cynical and simplistic but it is surprising how many 'works of art' are on tourist routes for these very reasons. First comes intellectual discovery by the few followed by promotion. Byron and others 'discovered' the Parthenon, for example; this discovery then gained reinforcement as indoctrination began to place an image in the forefront of the public eye. Each new publication reinforced the image.

We can see the process at work at the present time. Many buildings which were denigrated by architects at the time of building are gradually acquiring respectability and are included in the standard works as well as the tourist routes. One example is County Hall, London, where even now tourists are given the lengths of its corridors and other statistical details, and is even described by Banister Fletcher as having a strong free-classical design showing French Renaissance influence—whatever that means. And yet this building was generally dismissed as being of poor architecture at the time of its erection.

Publicity certainly cannot be ruled out as a factor. Even in the days of Alexander the Great, Dinokrates brought himself from obscurity to become the architect/planner for Alexandria by making the outrageous proposition to Alexander that he shape Mount Athos into the figure of a man holding a fortified city in one hand and a huge vase in the other to collect all the waters from the mountain streams. How similar this extravagant conception is to Christo IV's proposal to parcel up the

January 1977—Willy Brandt (SPD Chairman) and Christo in Brandt's office, Bundeshaus, Bonn.

Figure 2

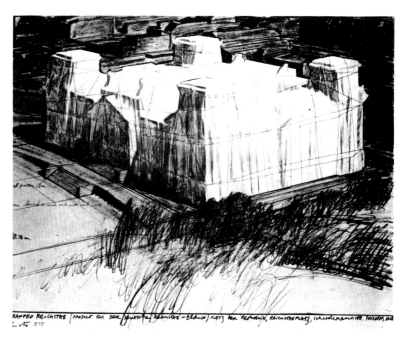

Figure 3

11

Reichstag, Berlin, for which he too gained the interest of statesmen. His mile-long wall cannot fail to be resurrected over and over again by future researchers as it will so often be put before them just as, for example, Wright's Falling Waters. This is quite irrespective of any other merits. However, how many people have ever seen any of the other sides or the inside of Wright's house, and how much fun is it living on top of the noise of a waterfall? These questions become irrelevant to the image.

Once the publicity starts, it is self-perpetuating and, furthermore, becomes self-indoctrinating. Few people in the West have not seen a travel brochure with the standard viewpoint photograph of the white Parthenon against a blue sky. The image is immediately recognized by everyone—but yet the building is rarely seen, let alone appreciated. For all we know, it need be no more than a standard Pavlov reaction— Parthenon = Athens = Greece = Sun = Holiday.

Even such unfortunate piles as the Palazzo Pitti in Florence are absorbed into the realms of art and fortunately, like the Palace of Versailles and so many others, have the advantage of good parking facilities. But is indoctrination to be accepted as the reason for architecture? If it is, perhaps anything can become an acquired taste. After all, how many people liked their first beer, whisky, cigarette, and so on? Because it is socially acceptable we work hard to acquire the taste, but that does not make them become art—or does it?

Berenson (1952), the famous art critic, describes his view of art:

> Many see pictures without knowing what to look at. They are asked to admire works of pretended art and they do not know enough to say, like the child in Anderson's tale, 'look, the Emperor has nothing on'.
> Vaguely the public feels that it is not being fed, perhaps taken in, possibly being made fun of. It is as if suddenly they were cut off from familiar food and told to eat dishes utterly unknown, with queer tastes, foreboding perhaps that they were poisonous.
> In a long experience humanity has learnt what beasts of the field, what fowl of the air, what creeping things, what fishes, what vegetables and fruits it can feed on. In the course of thousands of years it has learnt how to cook them so as to appeal to smell, palate and teeth, to be toothsome.
> In the same way *some few of us have learnt* in the course of ages what works of art, what paintings, what sculpture, *what architecture feed the spirit* . . .
> Just as all of us have learnt what is best as food, *some of us think we have learnt what is best in art* (my italics).

At the same time as he is making a case for elitism he is arguing that art is a matter of indoctrination or acquired taste. If we are to have an understanding of art we must look further than this sort of attitude, which is the common one, even though it is uncommon in science. What is the gulf between those who *know* and buy the workmen's cottages of yesterday, and those who *don't know* and buy semi-detached houses in suburbia with geese flying up the wall? How does this latter choice made by an uneducated mass become artistically acceptable, given time, after its earlier degradation? It is curious that painters, musicians, mistresses, etc., who were notorious in their time become idolized and idealized, given time. Canal boat art and Victorian memorabilia gradually achieves the level of art even though it may have been used as an ordinary commodity by ordinary people. Why do they have to be denigrated by the intellectuals first before they themselves become the discoverers? Is it that there is a group of people in any society who feel that they have to be different and try to convert the world to their beliefs, but when the world is converted and the masses follow their fashion, they then find it necessary to discover something else which is different? If this is so, the power behind art could simply be megalomania.

This again must be oversimplistic. There must be some fundamental qualities which are recognizable by every human being. What about value?

Paintings, for example, quite clearly have a commodity value which equally clearly is affected by uniqueness. Portrait painting also has a memorial value—the value to perpetuate man beyond his life span has always been important to him. Sculpture is even better for this purpose and evidence of this use is seen everywhere. Architecture is different again. It can be ideal for a monument (very often a working monument) and has always been used for this. What better to perpetuate one's own name, dynasty, or even business name than to erect a pyramid, hospital, university college, or even a business tower. This value is quite independent of any art content which in this context is not necessarily important. Monumentality is often very close to using architecture for advertising, which has again always been used as a means of promotion from early Egyptian temples to office tower blocks. Sometimes, however, the 'art' content in the case of advertising can increase the intrinsic value of the building, but this is rare. In painting the 'art' content is the important factor in the value of the item. The canvas and paint have no value, whereas in architecture the material form contains the value and any art content is incidental and valueless in financial terms. A recent court case was fought on the question of whether the value of a building was altered by the name of the architect, but this only served to illustrate the rarity of such a situation. One of the most important factors relating to value in architecture is of course the land upon which it stands and sometimes the ingenuity with which the maximum accommodation is placed on the land. But this is not art. Architecture is also different in the manner in which it is financed. It is alone among the so-called fine arts in being indivisible from finance at the creative stage. This alone sets it apart from the other arts.

Music and poetry have little monumental value and no intrinsic value except for the sale of the copyright.

So far there has been little sale of architectural drawings, although this is likely to change. Therefore, just as the Greeks thought, there is at least one sort of difference between music and drama and the rest; that is their intrinsic value.

Since their time, the activities which have been included under the heading of art have increased enormously. Ballet and opera, for example, are quite modern inventions with rather poor beginnings. Opera emerged in the Renaissance with the Florentines staging plays as they thought the Greeks had done, with a singer delivering the lines in a more or less natural inflection. Sometimes these singers would break out into flowery vocal displays which became known as arias. The ballet emerged from the Renaissance masque with the help of Louis XIV's predilection for dancing. Rhyming poetry, such as Betjeman's, only became popular in Europe in the seventeenth century and before that, was considered rather vulgar. Greek and Roman poetry did not rhyme.

A further difficulty in trying to find an absolute, is the fact that art is not automatically recognized across the cultures. For example, the West has to acquire a taste for Eastern music, and vice versa. Perhaps there are some fundamental material characteristics if one searches deeper and considers shape itself; but immediately there is another problem. Tests on the Muller Leyer diagram have cast doubts on even this as an absolute. Gregory (1966) describes how tests on Zulus living in a non-rectangular world showed that the common effect, known in the rectangular world, of one set of arrows seeming to be longer than the other, did not apply to them. He attributes this to the fact that they have not learned to read external and internal corners into these shapes. We do, and we then try to correct, and in overcorrecting, give ourselves an illusion. This is because we are indoctrinated by a square world (Figure 4a, b, and c).

There is still further evidence that what we see is affected by indoctrination. Stratton for example displaced the image reaching his retina (normally upside-down) by using lens and mirror systems so that the image fell the right way up, thus giving the illusion that his world was upside-down. After eight days he could behave quite normally in this self-created upside-down world, because his brain changed it back to what he expected, i.e. the right way up, proving that the brain has an enormous capacity for indoctrination. However, it might be argued that these are tricks and that things like scale, one of the basic cornerstones of the art of architecture, is beyond illusion. But again this would be wrong. There are many examples of how people under differing conditions see objects at a different scale. Gregory (1966) describes how studies of people living in dense forests show that they do not experience distant objects because there are only small clearings in the forest. When they are taken out of their forest and shown distant objects, they see these not as distant but small. Turnbull (1961) relates how a pigmy, brought out of the forest and shown some distant buffalo several miles away said, 'What insects are those?'

Even in the modern home one frequently finds evidence of distortions of shape on television sets, caused by incorrect adjustments but rapidly accepted by viewers, the necessary compensations being made.

But, apart from not recognizing an absolute scale or shape, there is a

14

grave doubt about what we see at all. Apart from the variability with which we react according to our health, we know that objectivity can be varied by drugs, alcohol, and, perhaps as hallucinatory as anything, hunger. Is it coincidence that so many artists have done their most acclaimed work when they were starving? Perhaps the hallucinations caused by hunger were the source of their inspiration. We also know that,

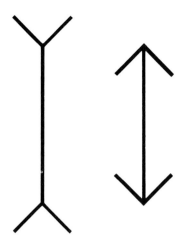

Figure 4(a)

Figure 4(b)

Figure 4(c)

apart from colour blindness, there is quite a difference in the way individuals see colour. Therefore, if shape, scale and colour can all be subject to individual interpretations, indoctrination, or manipulation, how can there be any absolute basis for art in architecture?

If there are no recognizable absolutes the door is open to indoctrination and once that door opens, there is the opportunity either for everyone to say 'I know what I like and my view is as good as the next person's, or for the alternative, where some may decide what is best for the rest, and impose it. Art then becomes a political decision. If the latter prevails, there is no reason why a politically activated elite should not set about educating society to enjoy a convenient standard. This has already been done many times and the computer could help to do it again. If this were done there would only be a need for a few architects to design the approved standard. If this proposition seems absurd we have only to look back to the much-admired and much vaunted grandeur that was Rome where there was a standard architecture, standard plans, and layouts which were maintained for long periods. The alternative is one in which everyone does their own thing; everyone becomes their own architect. But this brings a whole lot of new problems, amongst which are the problems of control and land ownership.

Figure 5

16

Proudhon (1898) after a meticulous and exhaustive examination of property which must still stand as a model, gives a moral and logical argument for the non-existence of property. However, a glimpse of any beach will show that the claim to territory is a very human and fundamental need in mankind.

In the post-war period, buildings such as office blocks became a means of making capital profits, hedges against speculation, and income. In this case, once again, the 'artistic' content of the building was usually completely irrelevant to the intrinsic property value of the building. Only the ingenuity of gaining the last square metre of usable office space out of the building site area was important. In housing, we have seen that the design of buildings can be influenced by those who supply the money, such as building societies who, since their inception, have helped the dramatic change from rental to home ownership. In 1918 only ten out of every hundred homes in England and Wales were owned by the families living in them by comparison with fifty-five out of every hundred homes in 1978. Both forms put restrictions on the form of the building. Almost everyone is either influenced in what they do with their own house by the effect it might have on the sale of the property or by the constraints imposed by the landlord. With squatters, on the other hand, the demands are different. These are only a few examples of the effects that concepts of property have upon architecture and the difficulties which have to be encountered when considering how far we can have personal freedom in our own environment. In spite of the multifaceted view of architecture/planning which is forced upon us, we still try to find simple global solutions. Quantrill (1975) brings out this point in planning:

> In relation to the urban environment, our planning theories are at once determinate and incomplete. Town planning theory, since Camillo Sitte and Ebenezer Howard, has been consistently concerned with only a partial view of human reality. That view may have been historical, as was that of Sitte, or romantic, as was Howard's, or purely statistical, as with the planning theorists of the 1960s. Unfortunately a tradition has been established whereby each of these partial views of urban reality has been taken and acted on as the exclusive and correct one.

Meanwhile, the hordes of homeless people gather around the cities all over the world—in the Barriadas and Urbanizaciones Populares of Peru, the Callampas of Chile, the Barrios of Colombia, the Ranchos of Venezuela, the Favelos of Brazil, and the Villa Miserias of Argentina. Furthermore, we should not feel complacent that these few extreme examples are in South America, because the same problem occurs in varying degrees in most European countries, as the transient labour camps and illegal caravan sites around the cities of Europe and elsewhere show.

These people, and the millions yet to come, will not wait for global artistic solutions. Everywhere the 'have nots' are trying to break out of environments which can no longer contain them whilst the 'haves' concentrate on conservation. How long can the problem be ignored before even the conservation is engulfed—*vide* Acropolis? Through the ages, architects/planners have tried to find universal geometric solutions, often using a single aspect of nature to support their theses for a total and immediate solution to the world's problems. Doxiades is not at all untypical in choosing crystalline formations as a representation of life which he then used to build up Ekistic Logarithmic Scale which was then converted into a hexagonal system. Le Corbusier used Le Modulor to produce his rectangular grid. Prior to this, Cerda had produced another rectangular system from apparently non-rectangular components to produce what he called an egalitarian city.

Equality has often been used as a reason by architects for producing one version or another of a grid-iron plan (Figure 6) which is more convenient for drainage than for human beings. How can one argue for egalitarianism in a plan containing multistorey rectangular blocks in which, to give only a small example, some units get plenty of sun and some get no sun at all? This mathematical neatness, although helpful for the architect to impose his will and very convenient for the use of tee-square and set-square, cannot in any way be ascribed to having any relationship with nature as is usually portrayed. Nature very rarely ties itself to such simplistic solutions and even the apparent tidiness of some

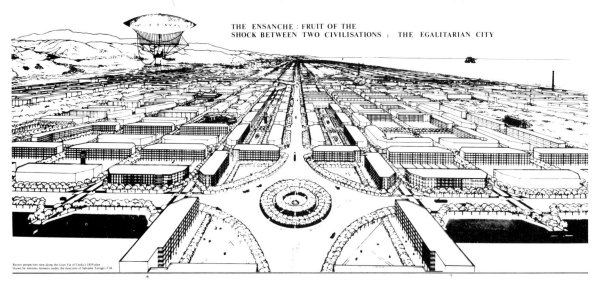

THE ENSANCHE : FRUIT OF THE
SHOCK BETWEEN TWO CIVILISATIONS : THE EGALITARIAN CITY

Figure 6 Recent perpsective view along the Gran Via of Cerda's 1859 plan. Drawn by Antonio Armesto under the direction of Salvador Tarrago i Cid

aspects disappears on closer investigation. Every single human being is different and consists of a high asymmetrical set of organisms not conforming to such a neat mathematical layout. Yet even the great da Vinci, who knew this from personal experience as well as from drawing it, produced his architectural engineering works on a geometrical basis.

Perhaps this is because there are two aspects of creativity in architecture which are not present in the other arts. For man the user, architecture is the constraint which is placed upon his activities. For man the creator, there is an immense joy in wrestling with self-imposed rationalized constraints of what he sees or knows. It is bringing great diversities under one control which gives such enormous satisfaction. But, in architecture, this great illumination can put others in chains. Everything is tidied up into one grand rationale—but are people that tidy? Strangely enough, the designers themselves are often the last people to conform to the regime they propose. Plans for Accra, Chandigarh, and Barcelona are typical of how architects/planners are able to lay out cities, towns, or parts of towns with their own idealized concepts, decide whether hundreds, if not thousands, of people will live in long terraces, tower blocks, or patio houses, how they will live and how far they will be from shops, or even whether they should go upstairs to bed, etc. They even dictate the architectural style in the name of art. The President or Prime Minister of a democratic country would not dare impose such rules except by endorsing the art of an architect/planner.

At the community level, local authority building proposals go to committees representing the community both as the client, for the type of development, and the planning authority, for its artistic and technical merit. If the building is a private development then the local community will only be represented in the latter capacity. Therefore, it could be said that the local community and the occupants are protected. But the introduction of architecture as an art tends to automatically reduce the area upon which comment is made for fear of accusations of philistinism. How many people disliked tower blocks or flat roofs but were afraid to say so because they felt they would be going against the current aesthetic knowledge? Furthermore, even an architect, let alone a lay committee, cannot be certain how another architect's drawings will turn out as a building. There are so many factors which can alter the appearance of buildings as subsequent design decisions are made. But perhaps most of all is the problem of whether a committee is capable of making creative decisions. Jones (1970) comments on the difference between committees and design teams:

> Our distrust of committees of designers seems to owe something to the myth makers such as Northcote Parkinson and to such wisecracks as 'a camel is a horse designed by committee'. It is doubtful if this view fits the facts. There are plenty of complicated things such as automobiles, hospitals and missile systems for which major design decisions have been successfully taken by a committee and could not have been taken by one person. Perhaps we have not learnt to distinguish between the ineffectual majority of committees, in which the chairman and the members are unskilled at collaborative decision making, and the minority of highly influential committees in which the chairman and members have been selected for the relevance of their knowledge, for their understanding of each other's spheres of interest and for their ability to collaborate. Committees of the second kind are particularly to be found within large international corporations, technical agencies and military planning groups in which everyone is

committed to a common interest which makes him an 'organ-isation man'.

A local authority committee, by its very nature of being a part-time group of people from different walks of life gathered together for short sessions, can only critize proposals put before it. It very rarely creates anything—even a policy. Almost all proposals emanate from their officers and/or professionals, and these proposals are then commented upon by the representatives in a critical rather than a constructive design process. There is a big difference between this type of organization and, say, a design team, and this alone should raise issues regarding representation and participation.

The local government committee is organized for political decision and is therefore not necessarily constructed for the design of the environmental needs of the community in the traditional form. The design of city centres and community housing are too complex to be left to the conventional process. Better techniques are needed to help solve these problems. Even the design team approach (without the client user or contractor) has often been condemned by architects although its importance in other areas, such as designing Concorde, has been accepted. But this resistance seems to have little historic justification.

Take the history of St. Peter's in Rome, for example. Briefly, it started as an architectural competition won by Bramante. After seven years he was superseded by da Sangallo, Fra Giocondo, and Raphael. After the other two died, Raphael continued on his own; when he died, Peruzzi took over. After Peruzzi died, da Sangallo the Younger took over, and when he died in 1546, Michelangelo (seventy-two years old at the time) took over until his death eighteen years later. After this, Vignola made additions and Maderna lengthened the nave and added the present facade, to which Bernini subsequently added the entrance piazza. The building, which started on the basis of a competition in 1506, was finally completed in 1626. Would this building classify as team design or design by committee, and who was the artist?

Unless we can find a means of organizing the desires of the individual to that of the community and that of the community to the global strategies and of integrating the whole into an understanding of art, we are faced with a fundamental moral problem. Fromm (1978) believes that as man can no longer rely upon instinct to guide him, he needs a frame of orientation and an object of devotion. If architecture is to be of any help at all in providing such a framework, which it should, it ought to be clear that much more investigation is needed. This examination of simply a few aspects of architecture and the environment which are often taken for granted is not for the purpose of replacing old dogmas with a new dogma: it is to show how necessary it is for us to start searching much deeper than we have done so far for new views to help us in the future and also to dispose of some of the ill-thought-out reasons why the purity of human judgement cannot be supplemented. We should do this before we start rushing into the computer age as we rushed, belatedly and unprepared, into the technological age.

20

Chapter 2
THE BACKGROUND

Any new invention or process is always affected by that which has gone before. The early motorcar, for example, was influenced by the earlier horse and carriage, and the early cast-iron bridges tried to replicate timber bridges. In each case the means had obscured the objective. It is therefore necessary for us to look at the background of architecture before hurtling into the computer age. But here we meet problems. First, the earliest beginnings when man began to create a built environment for himself are unknown to us, and therefore we can only choose an arbitrary starting point. Second, as this is one of the oldest activities of man, the quantity of data which could be explored would be beyond the capacity of all the historians that ever lived to coordinate. Therefore it is necessary to make a selection from this great panorama and obviously this choice can only be made on the basis of personal prejudice. This prejudicial choice must inevitably be a simple selection of existing knowledge contained in one short chapter, but nevertheless it is necessary in order to make comparisons with the present. The selection is like selecting stones (from a vast heap of stones) to make stepping stones to cross a river (the water of which is for ever changing).

Early man clearly began to create for himself his own environment in order to provide shelter and defence, not only from animals but also from his own kind. There are examples of this type of building all over the world. It is when man changes from being a hunter to being a farmer that there is a real change from these two simple and personal needs. The leader of the hunting pack becomes the leader of the tribe and at that moment he takes on a new significance. The leadership is soon identified with a supernatural being, and through this he obtains *ownership* of his people and the lands of his people. The dawn of history already sees this remarkable achievement already accomplished.

The ownership of parts of the earth's surface can be understood as an extension of the consciousness of territory of most animal species. But to take the big leap to owning others of the same species, as well as their lands as property, was a remarkable step which still permeates the very basis of architecture, for architects need this concept of property in order to practise their art. Leadership is very common in herds and packs and it is possible that the leadership which man might have exhibited in hunting was transferred when the pack took to the land and became an agrarian society. It might be expected that a more normal course would have been to form democratic communes once the science of food growing had been mastered, but, for a reason lost in time, the developing civilizations chose the route of forming slave societies.

Throughout the growth of the slave societies of the Sumerian civilizations, an architecture for this type of social struccture was developed and has become embedded in Western culture today. Whilst the structure may have changed, the symbols remain. In these agrarian societies, it appears that two threats were exploited to enable the old leader of the pack to retain his power. First, there was the threat from the nomadic hunters who had not yet become settled and agrarian; second, and more importantly, the big threat to survival was now nature itself. Changes in natural conditions had an immediate effect upon crops and therefore survival. Instead of being mobile as the hunter had been and able to move on to fresh grounds when natural disasters occurred, the farmer now had to accept every catastrophy nature produced. It seems fairly natural that he should begin to hope that there was somebody somewhere who could come to his aid and avert these disasters by controlling nature—mother or father figures emerge in every civilization. The next step was for the leader to claim that he could intercede, and with his chosen priest(s) developed both knowledge and magic. Even today in primitive societies such as the Azande in the Sudan, where this situation still applies, it is sometimes difficult to detect where knowledge finishes and magic begins. Gradually this new knowledge/magic becomes symbolized which, in the case of architecture, took the form of the house of god and the house of the king. The temptation at this point is obvious. Children on the beach build a castle as high as their technology will allow, stand on top, and claim to be king of the castle. It is a very human attribute. The early ziggurats of Mesopotamia (see Figure 7) look surprisingly like children's sand castles.

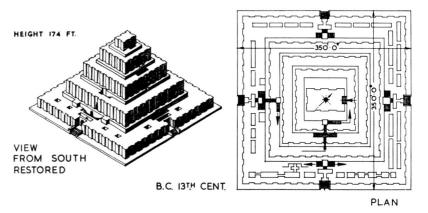

Figure 7 Ziggurat at Tchoga-Zanbil, Elam

With freedom from work, through having a slave labour force, the leader and a few friends and cohorts had the time to spare to develop the sciences of astronomy, astrology, oneiric fantasies, and, of course, the art or science of architecture. (This type of society also developed quickly among educated people from different walks of life in concentration camps during the Second World War.) Very quickly an increasing faith was placed upon necromancy and astrology. An elite (not necessarily the most intelligent) rapidly took over control of the masses. This elite had little else to do but try to make a rationale for the data which was fed to them through their senses.

Everyone has experienced this need to keep making sense of any available data as the mind makes constant demands for stimulation during waking hours. If one experiences enforced confinement in bed or spends an idle day on the beach, etc., one either becomes neurotic or tries, for example, to make a pattern out of other people's behaviour, the stones on the beach, or tries to make faces out of the patterns in the wallpaper. It is only to be expected that 'demi-gods', with time on their hands, should start to rationalize and make figures out of the star patterns in the sky and to build up a religion to give a *raison d'être* for living. Before this new-found leisure, the *raison d'être* was plainly staying alive, as it is with animal life generally.

In the Egyptian civilization the same process continued, but in a more sophisticated fashion. The mass of people lived in pragmatically designed dwellings, even though these were built within a fairly sophisticated framework of service systems such as drainage and water supply, etc. There is probably little difference between these communities and communities still in existence such as Fez, Morocco, which was founded in the twelfth century and has changed little over the centuries. In this type of community the art of architecture is only applied to those buildings requiring prestige. The rest are created

(1) to give the best environmental conditions within the economic limits available and
(2) to provide a means of inhabiting by common agreement contiguous pieces of land.

For them there was no thought for architecture in the academic sense and yet modern-day examples are fascinating to modern eyes because of the excitement of an environment formed by human activity rather than self-conscious design.

Already we have the split between architecture and building which continues through the centuries. The king and/or priests now concentrated on perpetuating themselves and their name or dynasty whilst architecture became identified with their desire for monumentality. This is the step towards the use of architecture for monumentality which takes us, though history, from Imhotep's design for the step pyramid of Zoser, through Le Vau and Mansart with the palace and grounds of Versailles to exalt 'Le Roi Soleil', to Seifert's design of the Nat. West. Tower in London. But architecture is now also identified with something else—knowledge. The knowledge for designing these special buildings, as they were developed through the centuries, was a jealously guarded secret, as was all other knowledge—for knowledge is power. So tight was the rein held on this knowledge that it was often the leader himself who was the architect. It is the association of power and knowledge with architecture

King   Priest

Sumerian

Figure 8

which now seems to become so significant through the centuries. The knowledge of the time, and therefore the power, was concentrated among a very few people who held the balance against a huge uneducated mass.

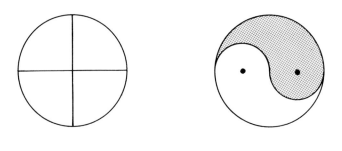

MANDALA

Figure 9

Such knowledge was largely based on mathematics and symbolized in the mystical symbol of the Mandala, which was alleged to express the philosophy that man was at the centre of the universe. This symbolism and philosophy continued right through to the Renaissance (the symbolism itself even to Jung, Moholy-Nagy, and Le Corbusier). An example of its use in planning can be seen in the Roman town plan of Chichester in Sussex. To this symbol, which again is the sort of thing which might be automatically doodled in wet sand, was added the mathematics of other symbols which acquired magical status. The flat-topped and stepped mastabas gradually gave way to the pyramid which used the square and triangle and to early trabeated forms which used the rectangle. Arcuated forms were only used in ordinary buildings for the masses.

24

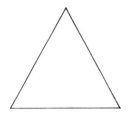 

EGYPTIAN
GREEK

Figure 10

All sorts of sexual and other powers were attributed to such symbols, and it is only natural that the Greeks, when developing their architecture, should have incorporated these geometries, as further developed by Euclid and others, into their architecture. It is curious that the Greeks did not also use the arch, which involved the circle, or even develop the triangulation of trusses, etc., of which they were quite capable. It is as curious as the fact that the Bronze Age should precede the Iron Age, when bronze is more complicated to make and tin and copper are rarer than iron. This shows that the direction of civilization is much more chance than the optimum choice we would like to believe. Also, we ourselves restrict our potentialities. Anyway, an architecture was developed in Greece which seemed to bring out two important characteristics. One was the development of an internal mathematical game played against a set of mathematical rules as rigid as any other game. The other was the process put forward by Broadbent (1973) as the means by which a style evolves. Briefly these are:

Pragmatic	where the designer takes whatever materials are to hand and develops a method of building by trial and error
Iconic	where the pragmatic design has become established as the mental image of what that building should look like and incorporated into the culture
Analogic	where the established idea of what the building should look like is now translated into different materials
Canonic	where the style is further abstracted to become a canon or mathematical principle

Indeed, as a canon we hold today the whole concept of the 'Glory that was Greece' and its democracy which allowed such great architecture to flower. In fact, that which was called the democracy lasted, as one critic has said, for a shorter period than the empire of Boots the chemist, and, even then, it was run on the backs of nine-tenths of the population who were slaves. The leisured one-tenth who survived the oligarchic, tyrannic, or democratic governments, dismissed anything which had to do with labour, and therefore did not include architecture among their arts. Nevertheless, their architects were among the privileged classes,

25

designing a somewhat standard architecture with limited variation for other privileged people. Early Greek architects—Trophonius, Agamedes, Callimachus, Ctesiphon, Metagines, and Andronicus, as well as Ictinus and Callicrates—all seem to have been men of consequence, which meant that knowledge of building was retained by the ruling class. During the great periods of emigrations to Italy, Sicily, and so on, the Greeks took their standard architecture with them. Just as modern buildings have been designed in the same international style, whether they are sited in the tropics or the arctic, so did the Greeks use the same design rules irrespective of site, as did the Romans who followed them. Once an idea has been established in architecture, all follow the same style, only playing variations on the theme but never breaking out of the system until the style has run its full course and degenerated into boredom. A strange phenomenon! The great contribution of the Greeks to architecture was the rationalization of mathematical language. There had been regular shapes for centuries, but the Greeks gave them rules which were probably developed from musical harmony. Just as a lyre string could be stopped in the middle to get an octave higher and at two-thirds to get a further octave, so architectural rules based on intervals were evolved by mathematicians and architects. Proportion and rhythm (periodicy) were developed. Clearly, the adoption of the golden section must have been seen as a representation of the 'harmony of the world' as suggested, for example, by Plato in the *Timaeus*. The golden section is where a line ac is divided into two parts by b so that $bc:ab::ab:ac$ and $bc = ab(\pm\sqrt{5}/2 - 1)$. To this was added the five regular solids which, with the square and triangle, formed the basis of the new language (Figure 11).

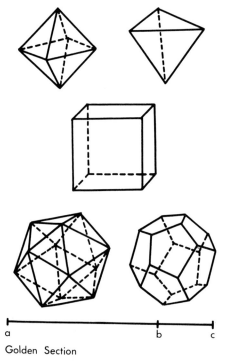

Golden Section

Figure 11

The strange thing was that in spite of their great philosophical discussions on freedom and democracy, which we still hold in esteem today, not only was all property owned by a few but the ownership of some human beings by others was considered to be so natural as not to need discussion. Today we still idealize a 'democracy' in which nine-tenths of the population were slaves. Whilst great architecture developed, the majority lived in pragmatically designed buildings. As far back as the first half of the fourth century BC these buildings were controlled by building by-laws and building inspectors, as at Pergamon, for example, where the by-laws included clauses relating to party walls, dangerous structures, and damp penetration. There were also penalties for building designers whose 'extras' exceeded the contract. There was a symbolic architecture for an elite and there was the rest. Knowledge in the Greek civilization eventually spread a little wider to include an aristocracy, causing a small change in the balance of power.

Greek

Figure 12

By the time the Romans occupied the stage with their great commercial vitality, there began to be new demands on building. The increase in the size of the population which contributed to larger urban environments created a need for large communal spaces which could not be accomplished by using the post and beam techniques used so far. Therefore the arch and dome became a functional necessity and the circle was added to the mathematical repertoire. But the 'image' of what a building should look like died hard, and therefore much of the language and symbolism of Greek architecture persisted into the classical Roman period. This image or symbolization of their culture can be seen all over the Roman world, irrespective of its functional deficiencies. The Romans built more or less identical buildings and town plans whether they were in the Middle East, North Africa, or Northumberland. There are two reasons for this:

(1) The limitations of education made it vital that a standard constructional knowledge was used enabling training to take place in any

country. Only limited variations could be accepted as the craft had to be passed on intact.

(2) The symbol of the building or the city could be recognized wherever a Roman went, in the same way and for the same reason that the national flag was paraded before soldiers and mercenaries in later empires.

The importance of this symbol to the Romans can particularly be seen in Petra, Jordan. From earliest times, man had carved himself caves in the soft rock for somewhere to live, and gradually the Edomites and the Nabataeans living in these caves developed a rich community because of their position on the trade routes. The Romans in due course 'incorporated' them into their empire and used the caves. However, not content with using the caves cut out of the rock, they carved elevations to these caves which were a replica of the architecture they would have built (Figure 13). This was architecture being carved from the solid as one would carve a sculpture, rather than building it up from components, and here at least it is possible to separate, quite clearly, the function from the style. The style was, for them, a necessary addition.

One architect who is known to everybody from the Roman classical period is of course Marcus Vitruvius Pollio, who lived in the century before Christ. Normally we would pass over him as with the other architects, but because he influences all subsequent discussion of architecture he must be dealt with in some detail, particularly as he is quoted so glibly and so incorrectly. Few architectural conferences pass, even today, without a reference to him and his alleged prescription for architecture—firmness, commodity, and delight. As is well known, Vitruvius wrote a set of manuals on the education and practice of architecture which have been used either directly or by implication, with some breaks, right through to this century. His book is a great insight into the ways and attitudes of his time as well as of himself as a man.

He starts his work with a tribute to his major client Augustus Caesar:

> When your Highness's divine mind and power, O Caesar, gained the empire of the world, Rome gloried in your triumph and victory. For all her enemies were crushed by your invincible courage and all mankind obeyed your bidding. . . . Amid such affairs I shrank from publishing my writings on architecture in which I displayed designs made to a large scale, for I feared lest by interrupting at an inconvenient time, I should be found a hindrance to your thoughts. But I observed that you cared not only about the common life of all men . . . but also about the provision of suitable public buildings; so that the state was not only made greater through you by its new provinces, but the majesty of the empire also was expressed through the eminent dignity of its public buildings. . . . (Here he is portraying the importance or architecture as a symbol.)

Poor Vitruvius! In reading his writings it becomes very clear how sycophantic someone needed to be to get work and how that work was largely under the control of one man.

Figure 13

He goes on to set down what he thinks an architect should be:

> He should be a man of letters, a skilful draughtsman, a
> mathematician, familiar with scientific enquiries, a diligent
> student of philosophy, acquainted with music; not ignorant of
> medicine, learned in the responses of jurisconsults, familiar
> with astronomy and astronomical calculations.

and what he should do:

> The reasons why this should be so are these. An architect must
> be a man of letters that he may keep a record of useful
> precedents. By his skill in draughtsmanship he will find it easy
> by coloured drawings to represent the effect desired.
> Mathematics again furnishes many resources to architecture.
> It teaches the use of rule and compass and thus facilitates the
> laying out of buildings on their sites by the use of set-squares,
> levels and alignments. By optics, in buildings, lighting is duly
> drawn from certain aspects of the sky. By arithmetic, the cost
> of building is summed up; the methods of mensuration are
> indicated; while the difficult problems of symmetry are solved
> by geometrical rules and methods. Architects ought to be
> familiar with history because in their works they often design
> many ornaments about which they ought to render an account
> to enquirers.

One gets the impression that if he had lived today he might have been a
computer enthusiast, particularly when he goes on to describe what an
architect should do in detail.

> His personal service consists in craftsmanship and technol-
> ogy. Craftsmanship is continued and familiar practice, which
> is carried out by the hands in such material as is necessary for
> the purpose of a design. Technology sets forth and explains
> things wrought in accordance with technical skill and
> method.

He might have been interested today not only in computers but also in
system building, and would also probably have had some comments to
make on education today:

> So architects who without culture aim at manual skill cannot
> gain a prestige corresponding to their labours, while those
> who trust to theory and literature obviously follow a shadow
> and not reality. But those who have mastered both, like men
> equipped in full armour, soon acquire influence and attain
> their purpose.

It is interesting that in this architect's equivalent to the Hippocratic oath
for the medical profession, Vitruvius seems to suggest that one would

only lack prestige if one were manually skilful in architecture; not of course that the product would be worse. He goes on to say, however, that philosophy is necessary to make an architect high-minded and not arrogant, but urbane, fairminded, loyal, and most important without avarice. He describes how other architects beg and wrangle to obtain commissions, and how he does not seek employment but rather waits to be sought out. Nevertheless, he does publish a book of his designs addressed to the Emperor in hopeful anticipation. He also hopes that in publishing his book his name will also reach 'to after times', which it certainly did.

Whilst his work historically is extremely interesting and he himself is found to be a very human person, it is very difficult to see why he has been considered to be so relevant right through to the present time. First, his technology, whilst being set down in a good methodological form, was very much a product of his time. For selecting sites, for example, he recommends sacrificing beasts on the proposed site and inspecting their livers, continuing the process until satisfactory livers were obtained. This was good science for that time but hardly relevant for today. Second, his scientific knowledge was obviously limited by the times in which he lived:

> Now whether we see the impression of images upon the eye, or by *the effusion of rays from the eyes*, as the natural philosphers teach us, both explanations suggest that the vision of the eyes gives false judgements (my italics).

Even at that time he had doubts about what he was seeing. But it is the words with which he is most firmly associated, firmness, commodity, and delight, that cause the greatest problem, particularly as these are usually used to denote the necessary qualities of a building to raise it to the level of architecture. It is worth quoting his words in full:

> Now these should be so carried out that account is taken of strength, utility, grace. Account will be taken of *strength* when the foundations are carried down to the solid ground, and when from each material there is a choice of supplies without parsimony: of *utility*, when the sites are arranged without mistake and impediment to their use, and a fit and convenient disposition for the aspect of each kind: of *grace*, when the appearance of the work shall be pleasing and elegant, and the scale of the constituent parts is justly calculated for symmetry.

Sir Henry Wooton in the seventeenth century translated *firmitatis*, *utilitatis*, and *venustatis* variously into strength, utility, and beauty and then solidity, use, and beauty; then handsomely, solidly, and usefully and finally firmness, commodity, and delight, which has since been used by public speakers and authors as the criteria of architecture. What do the words mean? How can they be used as a criteria when even Wooton found so many interpretations?

31

Whatever Vitruvius had in mind, he believed that the achievement was

> ... not granted to nations as a whole, but only to a few individuals, to have such genius owing to their natural endowment.

He also gives some rules for the selection of these chosen few:

> Therefore our forefathers used to entrust commissions to architects of approved descent in the first place; in the second place they inquired if they were well brought up. . . .

Architecture in the time of Vitruvius was not only to be practised by a few from an upper class (Vitruvius was of sufficient class to write to the Emperor) but also for the few. Vitruvius was a man who dedicated his life to his work and who expected other chosen men to practise it as diligently as he did himself. A lot of space has been devoted to Vitruvius already, but there is one more quotation which would appear to have great relevance to our present problems:

> But while I observe that an art of such magnificence is professed by persons without training and experience, by those who are ignorant not only of architecture but even of construction, I cannot refrain from praising those owners of estates who, fortified by confidence in their own erudition, build for themselves, judging that if inexperienced persons are to be employed, they themselves are entitled to spend their own capital to their own liking rather than to that of anyone else. For no one attempts to practise any other calling at home, such as shoemaking or fulling or any other easy occupation, with the one exception of architecture, because persons who profess it are falsely called architects in the absence of a genuine training. And so I considered it a duty to compile with care a system and method of architecture, imagining it would serve a purpose generally acceptable.

Vitruvius is here going far beyond a design guide, and producing in effect a do-it-yourself architecture kit; and that is precisely how it was used for centuries to come. Encapsulated in this quotation is a problem which is relevant today. He raises the question of the rights of people to spend their money as they wish on their own environment. In 1979 a large group of architects gathered at the Royal Institution, London, to hear a debate on 'This house moves that the architect should put the requirements of his client before the good sense of the public and his own sensibilities as an artist', and they rejected the proposal wholeheartedly.

Vitruvius' treatise laying down the rules of architecture was handed down in manuscript form until it was eventually published in Rome about AD 1488. His rules, whilst giving a great similarity of building to that of Greek architecture, were formed less upon the harmonic proportions of divine order, than upon the idealized idea of man. His 'proof' for this was the development of the Greek idea for squaring the circle and placing the ideal man inside, using his navel for the compass point of a circle. This symbol has been used and developed by other famous artists up to the present time, even being used as a television symbol.

Figure 14

Soon after the death of Vitruvius came the birth of Jesus Christ. But even as Christianity spread, the mass of people and the land they used still remained the property of the few. Knowledge and power had spread a little wider but no matter whether the political environment was tyrannic, dynastic, or republican, they were both always concentrated within a small minority. This pattern continued through the heptarchies which followed the collapse of the Roman Empire and into the Middle Ages, except that slaves were now called serfs, even though their position had scarcely changed. They did, however, have a little more hope now that Jesus could be identified with the poorest of men (as did other prophets emerging at this time) rather than the earlier conception where all gods were wealthy men living in celestial palaces and definitely on the side of the aristocracy.

Even with this new concept of religion, however, it was still the Church and State that held all the knowledge and therefore maintained the power of the few. Architecture was clearly identified with this few. It could hardly be otherwise when all of the land, apart from common land, was owned by the King, Church, and a few barons, who granted tenancies or fiefs to the rest in return for work and military service. Even the later development of frank tenement or freeholder still required service to the overlord. St Thomas Aquinas (1225–1274) affirmed the case for such laws of property and thereby gave offical blessing to the situation.

It was only the King and his acolytes or the Church which commissioned anything more than the simple dwellings of the masses. As their building programmes increased, groups of specialists in all industries began to form themselves into groups to protect their own 'know-how' and therefore their employment. These became the Guilds which, in the case of building, moved around the country as a design and construction team carrying out projects for what were, in effect, only two clients. Whilst away from home, in their 'Lodges', they had time to consider further ways of protecting themselves. Knowledge of their craft had to be kept a secret and only apprentices who had seven years of training and initiation could become privy to those secrets, even though they did not

33

become a master until they had presented a work thesis two years later. In this way the first closed-shop unions were established. The power that this brought them was enhanced by the tremendous reduction of manpower brought about by the Black Death earlier and the enormous demand created later by military and ecclesiastical building programmes. The barons had shown the power of collective bargaining at Runnymede in the thirteenth century and now the Guilds used the same power to confront the State and Church. The Regensberg Convention of 1459 stated that 'no workman, nor master, nor journeyman shall teach anyone, whatever he may be called, not being one of our handicraft and never having done mason work, how to take the elevation from the ground plan'. This was a confirmation of what had been going on for a long time. Guildsmen must have felt secure for all time as they even challenged the State and Church for power. The exuberance and vitality of the cathedrals of the time, usually ascribed to their devout belief in God, may also have been due, in part at least, to the exciting position they now held.

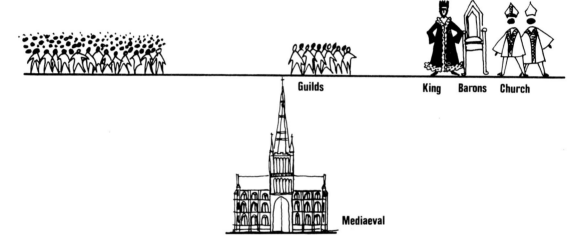

Figure 15

But, as so often with power, just at the point of ultimate exploitation everything began to go wrong. So many things happened over a relatively short period that only a selection can be made of some of those things that eventually destroyed the power and the mystique of the Guildsmen. They had wielded their knowledge as a mystique just as much as the Babylonian priests had done and how it was to collapse. Europe was about to develop new technologies and new wealth and yet they were unable to take advantage of it.

Their mathematics or mystique had included the *Vesica Piscis* which formed the basis of the Gothic arch, as well as having many other remarkable geometric properties. (Figure 16):

(1) The figure enables a pentagon to be formed and the centre of a circle to be pinpointed by describing three similar circles with their centres at the angles of an equilateral triangle which, in turn, form three further *Vesica Piscis*. This creates both a pentagon and an arch form.

34

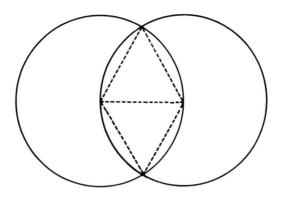

Vesica Piscis

Figure 16

(2) The rectangle can be subdivided indefinitely without changing its form.

(3) The diagonal of the rectangle is exactly double its shorter side, enabling the length of the rectangle to be the base of an elevation from which an equilateral triangle can be created of equal and known sides. A line from the apex of this triangle is a true plumb-line and therefore at a perfect right angle with the base, thereby creating a useful tool for setting out, for example, a cathedral.

(4) There are further useful properties of trisections and subdivisions.

The mystique of earlier architectures had also persisted, as did the 'old religion'. The Christian Church had learnt to live with both, where it had to, whilst at the same time trying to expunge anything which constituted a real threat. From the old religion may have been derived the symbolism expressed in their geometry of nature. Gothic symbols represented the structure of the forests. The Guildsmen could carve the symbols of their old religion high up on their buildings, but threats to power such as visionaries, knowledge of lays, and so on, had to be destroyed. It is probable that the old religion had developed telekinesis and other 'spiritual' powers to an advanced degree, but they were stamped out with such vigour that even today there is some residual fear in such things as hypnosis, water divining, and other obvious extrasensory perceptions. However, this closed shop of knowledge (or prejudice) was jealously guarded by the State, Church, and Guild until suddenly all three came under threat from knowledge itself. Although some of the Greeks understood the relationship between the sun and earth, for many centuries the established belief was that man was at the centre of the universe and everything revolved around him. Further investigation was to be dissuaded. But then one after the other, Copernicus (1473–1543), Galileo (1564–1642), Kepler (1571–1630), and Newton (1642–1727) gradually destroyed all the previously held spatial concepts.

To get some idea of how traumatic this change in thinking was at this time we have to remember that before Copernicus the earth was known to be flat and seemed to be the foundation and centre of the whole universe.

35

On the basis of this belief, the movement of the heavenly bodies had to be defined from a viewpoint on earth; this meant that the planets appeared to move in such incredible epicycles that the cosmologist had to try and devise an extraordinary complexity of spheres within spheres to try to make sense of it all. Even Kepler, before finding that the solution to the problem was to locate the centre for the ellipses elsewhere, thought that the planets were moved around by angels. The conceptual leap from the idea of a flat earth at the centre of the universe to a round earth going round the sun with the other planets must have been even greater for them to grasp than the idea of negative space is for us. However, changing the viewpoint did not apply only to cosmological space but also to terrestrial space. The search was now on for new knowledge and absolute truth.

Michelangelo (1475–1564) and da Vinci (1452–1519) were only two of many who dissected the human body to find out how it worked, thereby starting a train of events which led to the design of machines to replicate our physical labours; this in turn eventually led to the Industrial Revolution.

With the development of printing by Caxton (1422–1491) and others came the means of disseminating this new knowledge to a wider and wider body of people. In a comparatively short time the knowledge of the Guilds was not only becoming outdated by new science but their monopoly on its dissemination was being broken as well.

But worse was yet to come. Not only was new scientific knowledge being created but concepts were changing, and part of those changing concepts was the loss of power by the Church. Just like the Guilds, their monopoly over knowledge and/or mystique was now undermined and God and religion began to be seen in a new way. Science had given man a much greater control of his world and therefore he was able to take God into a new partnership.

Whereas Lorenzetti (1319–1347) had painted the Madonna as a remote stylized Ikon, Titian (1477–1576) was now painting her like the girl next door. Everyman was closer to his God than ever before and he also had more power. Serfdom disappeared and a new wealthy class of merchants was created by the new technologies which were being developed and exploited. They wanted paintings of themselves and their families and they wanted an architecture to express their power and wealth; for this they needed land. But land was monopolized by the Church, the King, and his acolytes. They also needed architects and builders who were also under the same control.

This problem for the 'nouveau-riche' was resolved by the changes of concepts which finally resulted in the Reformation. Similar religious changes were occurring all over Europe, but in varying forms.

The concepts of property was also changing. With the rise of Protestantism, Melanchthon (1497–1560) and Luther (1483–1546) were advocating the delineation of property, asserting that the fall of man denied the common use of property and that it was necessary to divide property to keep peace among men. The Book of Common Prayer (thirty-eighth article) stated that 'the goods of Christians are not to be had in common . . .'. Denman (1978) crystallizes their view as seeing 'common property as a dream from the paradise of man's early origin in a sinless Eden, a state of being of which he is now unworthy and incapable of expression'.

By the time of Locke (1632–1704) a new theory of property had developed:

> Every man has a property in his own 'person'. This nobody has any right to but himself. The 'labour' of his body and 'work' of his hands, we may say properly are his. Whatsoever, then, he removes out of the state that nature hath provided and left it in, he hath mixed his labour with it and joined to it something that is his own and thereby makes it his property. . . . Thus labour in the beginning gave a right to property.

Locke was trying to support both a natural theory and conventional property right.

With the restoration of Charles II in 1660, the feudal system of land ownership was finally and officially dismantled.

The Reformation and the dissolution of the monasteries in the sixteenth century meant that Henry VIII was left with a vast amount of land on his hands whilst he himself was greatly in need of money. He therefore sold the land to the nouveau-riche who were now ready to build. But who was to do it? The Guilds were not only reeling under the collapse of their monopoly but had just lost their major client—the Church. Furthermore, not only were they inexperienced in building large houses but their traditional methods were far too slow for the new and fast-developing economy. New building methods had to be found, new craftsmen had to be trained, and, most of all, new designers had to be found.

Some might recognize a similarity with many of these changes to the recent past:

(1) Changes in land ownership and concepts of property.
(2) Changes in patronage
(3) Changes in building organization to meet new demands
(4) Changes in scientific knowledge and spatial concepts
(5) Changes in communication technology

But there was one further change which was not only similar to the one experienced in the last few years but which was to have a dramatic effect on the practice of architecture and the structure of the construction industry until the present day.

All over Europe, the monopoly of education was being removed from the Church and Guilds. The monopoly probably began to be broken by the flood of Greek scholars into Western Europe after the fall of Constantinople in 1453, and then gradually developed over a period interactively with other factors such as the development of printing.

In England, the grammar schools were created and the Universities were expanded. The disillusionment of the Guildsmen in their loss of control became so great that it is believed that a high proportion of the 20,000 Puritans who left for America between 1629 and 1640 were disillusioned Guildsmen.

In Spain, during the reign of Philip II, master builders were displaced by architects who were imported from Italy where artist architects had already separated themselves from other craftsmen. In France, for example, Colbert, advisor to Louis XIV between 1660 and 1685, destroyed the power of the Guilds by transferring education for everything but the mechanical arts to the Academies. Instead of training as an apprentice craftsman for the Guild, a boy could now train as a young gentleman at the Academy without having to become involved with the process of construction. It is interesting to note, and be warned, that governments

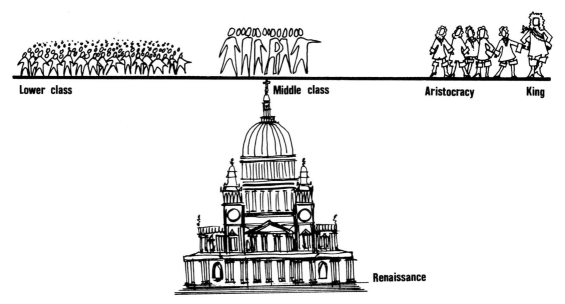

Lower class   Middle class   Aristocracy   King

Renaissance

Figure 17

did not immediately confront the Guilds, but emasculated them first. It was not until 1791 that Le Proclamation de la Liberté du Travail finally dissolved the Guild system, but by that time it had no power to resist.

The separation of design from construction was now complete. The time was ripe for the entry of a new type of designer—the architect—who may not always have come from the wealthier classes but nevertheless had not only been educated in the new manner but often had travelled to see the excavations of the classical world. The new-style architect and the new-style patron came together to develop the newly freed land on which they created the great houses we know today. Man was now very confident of himself in every field.

Not only the wealthy but also the poor sought the benefits of the new technologies—a movement which continued from the time of the Renaissance until today and which was exemplified in the hopes of the Great Exhibition of 1851 and the Festival of Britain Exhibition of 1951.

But the strange thing is that whereas art and science found an exhilaration in their new freedom, which was exemplified in their creativity and explorations over the next three hundreds years, architecture after a few early exciting experiments looked back to the architecture of classical Greece and Rome. Just like the Egyptians, Greeks, and

38

Romans before, Renaissance man looked to the past for his architecture, whilst the other arts and sciences looked to the future. *A significant fact.*

To the earlier list of similarities with the present can now be added architectural expression.

The great fires of London of the seventeenth century finally built up to the Great Fire of London in 1666 when new building regulations became imperative. More and more building regulations had been imposed since the *Domesday Book* was prepared on William I's instructions as a basis of taxation in 1085. In 1189, for example, Fitz-Ailwyn's assize of buildings laid down rules for party walls and ancient lights, and in 1562 Elizabeth I passed an act to restrict wages of servants and workmen, etc. Building workers from this time began to receive wages rather than getting a reward in kind as villeins. To these examples of control of building construction and pay restraint can also be added the Act of 1589 which laid down minimum site areas for new country houses, and the Ordinance of 1607 restricting the erection of new buildings in or near the city of London.

These clearly show that architects were already having to work within tighter and tighter planning and building controls. But the Great Fire meant that a far more comprehensive set of regulations were now required, and so interim measures proclaimed on 13th September 1666 were followed by the Act for the rebuilding of the City of London 1667. This act defined four building categories, thickness of walls and number of storeys for each category, floor to ceiling heights, rules for inspection, and employment of workmen, and demanded the use of brick or stone for the outside of all buildings.

The Building Act of 1774 continued this pattern by creating rates of building, the first four of which were related to domestic buildings and a further three to non-domestic buildings. These rules were so precisely defined that it would be almost impossible to produce anything other than what we know as a Georgian house. The standardization was so exact that the firemen's hook ladder, used until recently, could be expected to hook over one cill whilst the 'toe' would rest on the cill below, as can be seen on firemen's drill towers today. The effect of the regulations can also be seen in many so-called Georgian towns where the new regulation front was put on to many existing timber-framed buildings.

The Renaissance had brought about

(1) separation of design from construction in that class of building known as architecture,
(2) the creation of a new building industry which gradually replaced the Guilds,
(3) a need for new building techniques to cope with a huge building demand caused by a rise in population and demand for higher housing standards through increased wealth (the sash window was introduced from Holland and new forms of brick construction from Flanders),
(4) increased building constraint on building design by new and increasing building and planning legislation, and

(5) changes in education and wealth distribution and therefore power, causing new demands of the built environment and property.

The built environment continued to be created by two separate groups operating almost independently of each other. There were architects who were using classical architecture and the mathematical or design rules associated with it as a set of basic rules on which to play different variations on the theme. For example, the simplicity of Inigo Jones' work developed into the Baroque of Wren and still further into the work of Hawksmoor, Vanbrugh, etc. Then Palladio with his own personal interpretation of classical architecture began to influence a new school of architects. The other group were builders who seldom used architects themselves but were adept at using their design books and adapting them

Figure 18

to the needs of fast economic production. Both groups also used some form of mathematical discipline. The architects used various classical modular systems which had been based on Roman numbers but which now had to be converted to the arabic number systems which had been introduced to cope with the increased complexity and speed of the new mathematics. They also used permutations and variations of standard symbols which had been developed from the rectangle, triangle, and circle. The symbols were used in different ways for giving repetition, rhythm, and so on (Figures 18 and 19).

Figure 19

This is not the place to describe in detail the mathematical and design disciplines which were self-imposed by architects, but the development of the rules of perspective (which had been lost for some centuries) by Brunelleschi (1377–1446) in architecture and Masaccio (1401–1428) in painting recreated a fascination with the mathematics of design which had been held by architects throughout history but which had been kept as a secret mystique during the Middle Ages.

The mathematics and the concept came together in all the arts. In

Figure 20 Martyrdom of St. Sebastian —— *Antonio Pollaiuolo*

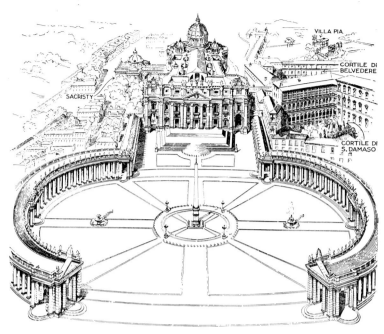

Figure 21 St. Peters, Rome

Figures 20 and 21 the fascination with the triangle can be seen; this was symbolic of the belief which lasted for almost four centuries that the universe was balanced and symmetrical. In Roman times it had been a divine harmony but now it was a symmetrical machine with man at the centre. Even in plays and literature the same sense of absoluteness was present in their climatic form. After all, nature was gradually being brought under scientific control as shown by the laws of gravity, thermodynamics, etc. The architect felt confident to apply the rules of geometry not only to his buildings but also to the landscape.

In this period of great confidence even nature was to be tidied up. Released from the secrecy imposed by the Guilds and encouraged by the increasing development of printing, architects began to publish their own interpretations of classical principles. Serlio, Palladio, and many others were later followed by Kent, Campbell, Gibbs, and Burlington. Their books, which were often more influential than their architecture, were pattern books illustrating current aristocratic taste.

Meanwhile the builder was left to produce the mass housing and factories which were in such great demand due to the increase in wealth and development of technology. Based on his early anatomical researches, man was now learning how to produce machines which could not only replicate human activities but do it cheaper and faster. The builder was not only constrained by all the same factors as the architect but in addition had to produce his buildings as cheaply as possible. He took advantage of the new technologies of mass production by machine as well as by people. The new middle class, as with all nouveau-riche, desired for themselves what the aristocracy had already got—but at a price they could afford. Therefore, builders like Nicholas Barbon who developed Soho became the forerunners of today's speculative house builders by learning how to acquire land and to lease the buildings they erected. The construction was controlled by regulations (even if they did take short-cuts) and their designs were pared-down versions of those produced by architects for the aristocracy, as shown in the humble

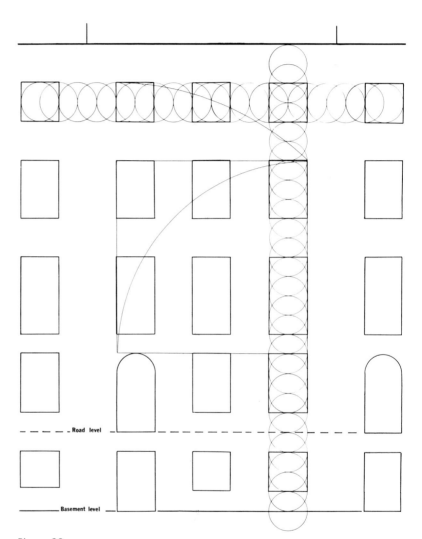

Figure 22

manuals of Batty Langley and William Halfpenny. Nevertheless, the builder also worked to a clearly laid down set of rule-of-thumb mathematical design rules (Figure 22). Not only were areas and heights clearly laid down by regulation and the openings agreed by convention

44

but also the spaces between the voids were controlled by the dimension of the brick. Just as in Roman times, the post-Renaissance architect and builder worked within a very tightly coordinated dimensional system, and with a set of standard design symbols. Even the spaces between the buildings were similarly controlled and coordinated.

Although it was not always appreciated at the time, it is now almost universally accepted that this incredibly disciplined system has become a highly desirable environment. This was the Age of Reason. Here was a total environmental design system which could today so easily be produced by computer that one wonders why architects have so far spurned not only the computer but also dimensional and design control. To understand this we must consider the developments which occurred in the nineteenth and twentieth centuries.

As with all aspects of human taste, a stable fashion gradually becomes boring, and a search begins for a new attraction. Again, instead of looking for an expression of the new materials and new technologies to meet the demands of a society which had become different from any other in the history of mankind, architects looked to the past for their inspiration. Although the Romans or Renaissance man could not have begun to make a steam engine or a spinning jenny or the many other inventions which brought wealth to the new society, it would have been difficult to find a building erected before the mid-nineteenth century that they could not have built.

Rigidly disciplined architecture gradually gave way to a more romantic approach which in turn engendered a nostalgia for the Middle Ages. Even though mass production was the source of so much wealth and the mass production of building materials and components was affecting the building processes, architects chose to hope for a return to the 'old days' when knights were chivalrous (or so it was portrayed) and craftsmen were happy (or so it was believed). Ruskin (1855) in the *Seven Lamps of Architecture* who was then, and to some extent still is, a great influence on architects, said, 'There are only two fine arts possible to the human race, sculpture and painting. What we call architecture is only the association of these in noble masses, or the placing of them in fit places. All architecture other than this is, in fact mere building. . . .' He believed that a building was not architecture when it fulfilled a function and also that there was an *absolute truth* and an *absolute beauty* based on *natural forms*.

It can clearly be seen that this was a shift from the earlier absoluteness of science and mathematics to the absoluteness of nature, but was, nevertheless, still a belief in the absolute values of the world. These absolute values Ruskin listed and identified with various characteristics of architecture as follows:

Sacrifice
Truth
Power
Beauty
Life
Memory
Obedience

By the moral standards of today they seem rather old-fashioned and reminiscent of the Empire and the old public school tradition, and particularly tortured when applied to architecture. However, it was upon this type of ethic that the institutions were formed.

Ruskin was not alone. Scott said that 'architecture as distinguished from mere building is the decoration of construction'. Morris, too, clearly shows his escapist desires in his poem *Earthly Paradise*. Thus, at a time when the professions were being formed—Civil Engineers in 1818, Mechanical Engineers 1847, Architects 1854, and Surveyors 1868, the architect, already divorced from the construction processes, now proceeded to divorce himself from the problems of the measurement, the structural design, and the environmental engineering design of building. (This decision to divorce himself from measurement was due in part to the poor reputation he had gained because of the implications of corruption. Architects therefore emphasized their concern for design standards to the exclusion of all else, which has persisted to this day.) Just when there was a need for a new approach to building because of the demand for new types such as railway stations, large communal spaces for entertainment, exhibition centres, and so on, the architect decided to concentrate on being an artist and hope for a return to a past idyll in architecture and planning. The tug of war between the writhing forms of nature and the regular geometries of the classical past, which was encompassed by Art Nouveau, began to engulf and to influence the work of architects until comparatively recently. It is easier to understand in retrospect the dilemma in which an architect found himself, and which broke out in the controversy at the RIBA in 1891, on whether architecture was a profession or an art—a controversy which has never been resolved. Several problems probably came together over a short period:

(1) Scientists, engineers, and industrialists pressed on rapidly with their new developments.
(2) Artists, benefiting rather less from the wealth created, dreamt of the old days of patronage.
(3) Architects had to choose between art or science, and chose art and nostalgia, thereby handing over a large part of the control of the built environment to others—mainly engineers.
(4) Their identification with the Middle Ages also made them identify themselves with a privileged elite. Even into the twentieth century it was not considered respectable for architects to work for industry, commerce, or local government.
(5) They developed an educational system rather similar to that of the Guilds—articled pupilage. Also like the Guilds, they obtained for themselves a monopoly to call themselves architects.

Unfortunately, they ignored the growing and very real comparisons with the past. On top of this, they set about discarding all the mathematical disciplines from the past without considering the new spatial concepts and mathematics which were emerging.

Already, there were the same warning signs that there had been for the Guilds before the Renaissance. In 1687 Newton had helped to change the concepts of space and society with his Law of Universal Gravitation when he gave gravity a force of

$$\frac{G.\,mm'}{d^2}$$

In 1905 Einstein amended the force to

$$\frac{G.\,mm'}{d^{2.00000016}}$$

This is a small difference, but an absolute world now became a relative world. Classical physics had used a three-dimensional space and a universal one-dimensional time. Einstein now developed his Special Theory of Relativity in which there is one universal four-dimensional 'flat' space-time, but which he then developed into his General Theory of Relativity in which he used four-dimensional Riemannian curved space-time. At this point, space and time can no longer be viewed independently. All truths were now only relative and although some absolutes like the speed of light remained, even these were redefined by Heisenberg's Uncertainty Principle, among others.

From the mid-nineteenth century onwards, education was made available to an increasing proportion of the population, culminating in the post-Second-World-War Education Acts which made university education a possibility for all. The Education Act of 1870 made elementary education compulsory. Establishment of Boards of Education in 1907 was followed by increasing responsibilities for local authorities and the raising of the school-leaving age, culminating in the far-reaching changes of the 1944 Education Act. This not only destroyed the articled pupil system, and to some extent cheap labour, but also made architecture an even more academic subject. This same process of generalizing education meant, as always in the past, that with knowledge went power. A massive interacting shift of power, education, and wealth started and still continues.

Out of this came several problems for the architect, but they took some time to develop and to be recognized. Women, released from the domination of child bearing, increasingly attained equal rights with men which had a dramatic effect on the structure of society, many aspects of which are still emerging. Concepts of God and morality changed. There

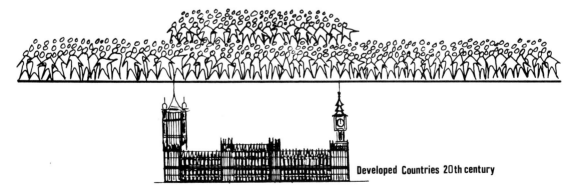

Developed Countries 20th century

Figure 23

47

was the universal franchise causing a major redistribution of power which in turn created a shift in wealth and therefore patronage. Instead of a wealthy aristocracy, there were now powerful bureaucracies, trades unions, and action groups fighting for universal human rights. Having spent four hundred years of concentrated effort releasing himself from the strain of using his muscles for anything other than leisure, man now started to replicate his mental activities.

Land ownership patterns were also changing. Until the 1920s a limited number of people owned land whilst the rest occupied leasehold and rented properties. With the introduction of the Building Societies there was a massive swing to home ownership which was helped by the breaking up of large estates due to political changes and taxation. Later, the Community Land Act created new attitudes to land values and ownership. Now land development is no longer within the province of a single owner to do with as he wishes; nor even are the resources of any single nation completely within its own disposal.

The problem of land ownership and property has changed but has not been resolved. Since the nineteenth century there have been many propositions but none resolve all the problems. They range from Hegel believing in personal rights to property to Prudhon who most persuasively produced a logical case for social rights of property in land and the means of production. The choice became one of allowing a free market to operate, creating a managed economy, or hoping that technology would resolve the problem. This is still the position as politicians swing from one side to the other.

Meanwhile, the Building Societies and the speculative builder emerged from the First World War as powerful forces which caused and were products of the massive upsurge of home ownership. The speculative builder set about building a world 'fit for heroes' by producing a fairly standardized range of houses which were personalized by alterations to the front elevation—the traditional solution. Sometimes he employed architects like N. Shaw and C. A. Voysey, but on the whole he made up the designs for himself from construction books as his eighteenth and nineteenth century predecessors had done. The depression of 1929/30 strangely further increased his control of the housing market as many people, particularly in the south, surprisingly became richer and sought to move to the suburbs to bring up their children in a cleaner and healthier environment. Factories, offices, shops, and cinemas also went to the suburbs with the housing. Some of the more purist architects lambasted these developments, which were often being carried out by their hard-pressed colleagues, to such a degree that they built up a pressure which eventually led to the Post-war Planning Acts. Recently, of course, much of this earlier despised building has been brought back under the cloak of architecture and conservation whilst the Planning Acts went on to highlight still further the problem of art in architecture.

For many architects in the 1930s, architecture was a very hard business, trying to maintain professional standards whilst seeking work in an atmosphere in which fee cutting was prevalent because of the competition for work. Even though classical architecture was getting rarer, drawings of the classical orders of architecture were still recognized as a test of knowledge and competence as part of the examination for RIBA membership. In this climate, few architects or their assistants and articled pupils had the time or interest to bother with the words of Le Corbusier or the buildings of Wright and van der Rohe. They were more likely to be influenced by the Busby Berkeley film-sets and the skyscrapers they saw at the local cinema. (Indeed, was Port Grimaud influenced by Portmeirion through the internationally acclaimed television series *The Prisoner?*) The film industry was becoming an educational force, and, in disseminating ideas, a creator of fashion. The twin bed, for example, required under the morality regulations of the American censors, started a fashion that continues to this day. Le Corbusier has been accredited with, or blamed for, far more than was attributable to him at the time.

The loss of faith in absolutism meant a loss of faith in symmetry, and this had been increasingly expressed in the architecture of architects such as Oud and Dudok (Figure 24) and other members of the de Stijl group who gradually influenced the design of factories, cinemas, etc. The balance of masses was now more important than the symmetry which had been a fundamental architectural expression of absolutism up until this time. In painting and photography importance was laid upon the third. The climax of a picture had to be at a third of a rectangle instead of the apex of a triangle. Soon, even this rule was to go.

Figure 24

The few architects who were trained at full-time schools became increasingly involved with the work of Le Corbusier who, recognizing the need for a new mathematical conceptual structure, tried to produce one on the basis of traditional mathematics. He called it Le Modulor (Figure 25).

In the Renaissance, da Vinci produced a drawing which is very popular today in which he developed Vitruvius' squaring of the circle. This is a surprisingly unsatisfactory product of his phenomenal genius, as can be seen from a short examination, particularly as he used for some reason an *ideal* man's navel for his compass point (Figure 26). Le Corbusier again chose an ideal man's navel for his Modulor, with which he then designed houses, blocks of flats, or even cities. Considering the importance of this

Figure 25(a)

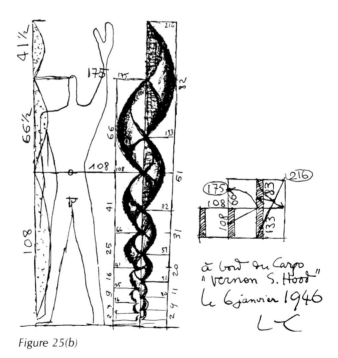

Figure 25(b)

dimensioning system to the large number of people who occupied his buildings, it is worth considering how he arrived at it, although there is no explanation of why both Le Corbusier and da Vinci should consider a man's navel as such an important element in designing a modulor system.

50

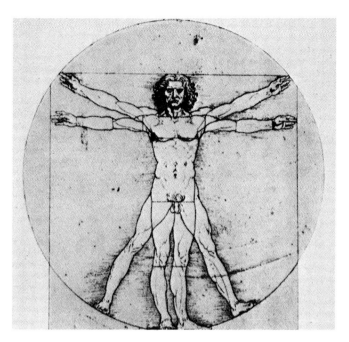

Figure 26

Le Corbusier (1954) describes his development of Le Modulor as follows:

> One day when we were working together absorbed in the search for solutions one of us—Py—said: the values of the 'Modulor' in its present form are determined by the body of a man 1.75 m in height. But isn't that rather a French height? Have you ever noticed that in English detective novels the good looking men such as the policemen are always six feet tall. We tried to apply this standard: six feet $= 6 \times 30.48 = 182.88$ cm. To our delight the graduations of a new Modulor, based on a man six feet tall translated themselves before our eyes into round figures in feet and inches.

It is strange that the roundness of numbers related to an almost non-existent man *exactly* six feet tall should be thought to be valid for the design of a city which included women, children, and all sizes of men. Presumably if the English foot had not worked he would have sought a measurement length from somewhere else which coincided with a whole number! He later developed a more natural language related to nature and the Mandala. With these two languages he brought together the basic symbolism of three thousand years and probably, as much as any architect, symbolized the end of a period of architecture which had started in the early history of man (Figure 27).

Before examining this categoric statement it is necessary to consider

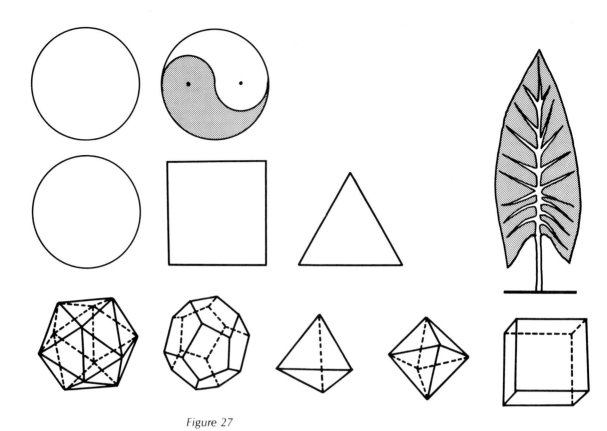

Figure 27

other aspects of architecture and building which happened in the post-war period.

Having already divested themselves of the responsibilities of construction management, structural and environmental design, landscaping, surveying, and measurement, architects were increasingly losing or giving up their responsibility for planning. This was far more dangerous than the loss of the other responsibilities. While the architect was the first activator of the design process he must remain the leader of the building team if for no other reason than that he is the one who initially deals with the client. The obvious threat of the planner becoming the initiator of the activities for many of the larger projects was not recognized until the Reorganization of Local Government in 1974 when there was a sharp increase in their power and status. For many projects today it is the planner, planning consultant, and development analyst and valuer who start the process.

Another problem which many architects did see and tried to correct was the increasing cost and scarcity of building craftsmen. In the 1930s Stillman at West Sussex began to develop prefabricated classrooms and parts of classrooms. In the post-war period these ideas were pursued by Aslin, Gibson, and Swain, and gradually developed into a mathematically based industrialized building system from the needs of, at first, one county, Hertfordshire, and later a group of counties. These were brought together under various consortia which finally embraced most of the authorities in the country. The intention of these early systems was to provide a set of rationalized vertical and horizontal measurements as a basis for the manufacture of standard components. The problem was to balance the flexibility of the design with the needs of production. By arranging for a lot of local authorities to consort together, it was intended that the large guaranteed annual expenditure would form the basis of long production runs. The Government took the matter a stage further by producing a set of dimensional coordination rules based on these consortia dimensions and encouraged (with the help of the change to metric) the construction manufacturing industries to produce components, and architects to design, to these dimensional rules.

In parallel with these developments West Sussex County Council who, from the mid-1960s onwards, were probably the first organization to produce a completely integrated computer-aided design, production, and tender system, as described by Paterson (1977), based their system on these same dimensional coordination rules. Other computer systems were increasingly developed for schools, hospitals, and housing and most of these were also related to these rules.

The problem was that with both computer and building systems the dimensional coordination systems theoretically allowed the potential for substantial flexibility of design but the processes of manufacture and the cost of data handling restricted the number of items that were used. This is common to all industries. But in other industries they overcome the need for a limited range of components by changing them frequently, thereby changing the fashion in their production lines before the public is bored. Architects did not. Not only did the system designers continue with, to the lay eye, the same design for more than fifteen years, but the traditional design architect did the same. The consequence was that, as with all fashion and in all industries, there was a public demand for change which architects did not satisfy. Architects now had to react quickly, but unfortunately building is still usually a slow design and construction process.

Local government reorganization in 1974 meant that the consortia were disrupted and computer developments were set back; both were further aggravated by the collapse of the building boom. This was the moment when the public reacted violently against not only system building but also traditional building, which was often vaguely a derivative of the work of Le Corbusier and van der Rohe and which to the lay eye all looked the same. Just as there had been public reaction against the eighteenth and nineteenth century grid-iron pattern, now the public with much greater power than their forebears virtually brought new building to a halt in any but the most uncontentious low-rise building areas. Architects felt that technology had let them down and retreated into conservation and the nostalgic styles of Languedoc Roussillon.

However, whilst some of the well-stocked countries may be able to continue for a while by refurbishing their old buildings, they cannot ignore the future, and in any case there is still the problem of the world's increasing homeless. It is an inescapable fact that we are now part of and therefore affected by a global community.

Le Corbusier's work was, for a long time, used as a pattern by many avant-garde architects for the solution of present-day problems. But not only was he himself using the social and mathematical concepts of the Renaissance and the Middle Ages to solve the problems of a changing society, which he could barely conceive as an introvert designer, but, in the case of Unité, Marseille, which was used as a pattern for countless thousands of homes, the original small middle class development was built for a very special type of resident. This is not a criticism of Le Corbusier but of those who blindly followed, probably influenced by the photographs alone, without ever visiting the project itself. Unité is still today an excellent example of design for its purpose, with magnificent service management, but it has little to do with the massive problems of housing in Marseille itself, let alone as a pattern for world housing.

Much of the building of post-war housing was pursued with considerable dedication and enthusiasm, but in the case of the architect it was this dedication and enthusiasm which has often been his downfall. To design the total environment of a great house and its grounds for a single enlightened client was the dream (and still is for some) of all architects. It was one artist designing for one patron—and even he, by definition, a sympathetic one, with no financial, property, adjacency, or moral problems. Here was an opportunity for free artistic expression.

With the great social changes of the twentieth century this type of patron disappeared and was imperceptibly replaced by various types of corporate bodies. Small businesses were gradually incorporated into combines and multinationals. Local government which at the beginning of the century was serviced by private practising professionals was increasingly staffed by its own employees. Architects, for example, were largely employed as private professionals before the Second World War, but due to the increasing responsibilities for services being placed on local authorities it became convenient to have these professionals under their own control in the same way as the corporate bodies of industry and commerce. A considerable proportion of the nation's building programmes and therefore the buildings of society were now being designed for a completely different patron. The new patron, sympathetic or otherwise, was unfortunately seen in the traditional form. The place of the individual building owner or patron was now identified with his agent who was often another architect. Together they exalted in the use of the new materials and technologies, but because of the divorce from construction and industry, they did not have the interest, knowledge, or training for their use that should have accompanied such enormous changes. Furthermore, due to changes in education and power, the client and patron was not the corporate body but was *actually the general population*. This had gone completely unnoticed until the eruption of community action groups who began to fight for a say in their environment.

Even now the lesson has still to be learnt in the case of commerce and industry, where trades unions have yet to fully enforce their demands on the design of their work environment.

In the Age of Reason the architect as well as everyone else knew what was right and what was wrong. These as well as all other virtues, as Ruskin believed, were absolute virtues and were in the architect's power to make the environment right. Today only an arrogant fool could believe that he had the environmental solution to the complexities of the present-day social structure. Le Corbusier and a few others like Soleri still had the confidence and the beliefs of the Renaissance to think that one man could create an ideal city for hundreds of thousands of people as a permanent structure, even though that society in the future would be in constant change and each person would be a free individual client. This Unité, this Arcosanti, this Eldorado, this idea of the perfect, permanent total solution is still held in high esteem by many architects. But is it possible, even if it were desirable or moral? Even science can no longer be seen as a stable knowledge base, so how then can such uncertainty be contained by architects in the all-time grand plan?

Before considering this dilemma it is necessary to recapitulate on the changes that have taken place in this century and as a matter of interest compare them with the changes that formed the basis of the revolution that was the Renaissance:

(1) Successive education acts in the nineteenth century led to universal franchise and changes in the distribution of power which in turn created the new patrons of architecture as it had done at the Reformation.

(2) The expansion of knowledge and the attitudes of the mass of people not only through books and education but through films and television have also changed the position of the professions as it did the Guilds. Even fifty years ago it would have been unthinkable for the view of professional men such as doctors, lawyers, scientists, and architects to be challenged by the general public. They would not have dared to challenge what might have been a mystique, but today the power is with the people.

(3) The change in society and architectural education has also created problems within the professional institutions. The Royal Institute of British Architects, for example, not only has a falling membership, but the biggest decline of 11.2 per cent in 1978 was in the category of architects aged under thirty. Only just over half the architects under the age of thirty are now members. The original ethics which formed their constitution are no longer applicable to today's society, no matter how much this may be regretted.

(4) The concept of the ownership of land and property and individual human rights has changed dramatically, as it did in the Renaissance. Not only is there a demand for universal human rights, even among nations that accepted slavery a generation ago, but the world's resources are now increasingly expected to be shared by all. Without an increase in production or technological change, this can only lead

55

to dramatically reduced standards in the industrialized countries, as already instanced by the energy crisis. This is only the first warning of a problem which will not be solved by a retreat into the past and primitivism.

(5) New technology and new management techniques are changing the construction industry itself, even if architects are not always embracing them. Whilst one part of the industry continues to build for architects in a fairly traditional way, another side is becoming increasingly concerned with industrialization and the higher profitability of 'value added' products. The fact that architects have largely dismissed the industrialized building systems (with the exception of course, of such developments as the Building Consortia, the Southern Californian School Development Programme, and a few others), container buildings, caravans, and mobile homes does not obviate the fact that they are becoming more established and are absorbing more and more units of accommodation which might otherwise have been built *and designed* traditionally. Architects, with few exceptions, show no interest in the design of this important and growing industry.

(6) Changes in society have caused changes in the law, and although these were not always directed at the architect imperceptibly his traditional position has been undermined. Apart from the well-known problem of the Limitation Acts where it is now held that the six-year limitation starts from the time when the defect is discovered, not designed—a catastrophe—there are others. The courts, once seeing the architect as an artist, thereby making the contractor responsible for the construction, now increasingly sees him as a specialist and therefore responsible himself. Furthermore, the building or piece of architecture is also increasingly being treated as any other product, even though architecture is not product orientated but process or design orientated.

(7) The role of planning and the other professions is very significant indeed in this period of change, as has already been discussed.

(8) The arts are increasingly affected by young talent from the body of society in every area except architecture. Quant and Rhodes design haute couture clothes with an eye to mass production lines. The specialist design for cars like Hispano Suiza gave way to Farina's and Giugiaro's designs for the mass production of cars. In every field, artists are creating styles for industry which are then offered to the public for their selection. This mass production, so often denigrated, gives such a vast permutation of choice for the individual that it looks like freedom. The denigrators, who may or may not have been fortunate enough to have hand-made personal products in the past, are presumably unaware of the dearth of choice that the masses previously had to suffer or which primitive people still suffer. A few of the wealthy had the choice of elegance and a range of hand-made products, but for the average person it was a standard uniform, a limited range of food, and standard housing. Whilst he can now exercise a choice in other things, the average person is still given

56

buildings in which to live and work without choice. Giedion (1941) said that 'the fact that modern painting bewilders the public is not strange: for a full century the public ignored all the developments which led up to it. It would be very surprising if the public had been able to read at sight an artistic language elaborated whilst its attention was elsewhere, absorbed by the pseudo art of the *salons*'. He could not imagine that the public in general did not even have holidays other than bank holidays, let alone have time to go to the salons. Similar statements are made today. Who is the architecture for, the public or other architects? How much longer can this position hold? Can a progressive art even want to survive unless it can find a way of becoming 'popular' too? No longer can architecture continue to hide its elitism behind the mask of planning committees. It, too, has to become a product-orientated popular art for the new aristocracy— which is everybody.

Some signs of an understanding of the problem emerging can be seen at two extreme ends of the spectrum: at one end, the many participatory design experiments which have evolved from the 'hippy' and 'drop-out' community settlements, and, at the other, such flagrantly 'punk' acts of architecture as the de-architecture of Site (Figure 28a and b) or the anarchistic architecture of Tatsuhiko (Figure 28c). Whilst they may not solve the problems we face, they do at least illustrate the extremes of the traditional position.

(9) Finally, there are the totally new spatial concepts, just as there were in the Renaissance. Instead of their steady, balanced, three-dimensional space, we have Gold (1977) saying 'perhaps three dimensional space is only one of a variety of ways in which our environment can be described. What we really know in our minds is, after all, only an algebraic system, and we note that it has a close correspondence to a particular type of geometry'. Just as in the Renaissance, a new spatial mathematics is emerging.

The absolute certainty of creating a permanent Eldorado has lasted up to the present time, but although the dream has been discredited there is no new sense of direction to fill the void. To add to the confusion caused by these changes, the microprocessor has appeared to speed up the supplementation of the activities of the brain, as the machine has increasingly supplemented the body since the Renaissance.

It is certain that the microprocessor will not solve all the problems which face society, but there will be no escaping its influence, and therefore it is necessary to recognize this changing situation against which its future potential can be evaluated. Too often, as soon as computers are mentioned, architects believe that they will impose disciplines which will constitute a threat to their inborn creativeness, for since the mid-nineteenth century there has been an increasing belief among architects that their art should be free and uninhibitedly creative. Even the client is sometimes seen as an obstacle to this unbridled creativeness. But this is a rejection of the whole history of

Figure 28(a) Indeterminate facade, Houston

Figure 28(b) Peeling project, Richmond

58

Figure 28(c) House in Hokkaido

architecture, which clearly shows that the development of mathematical geometries and spatial concepts have gone hand in hand with architectural development and creativity.

Today, the phenomenally increased complexity of modern expanding societies demand the use of the new tools that are available to us if we are ever going to bring together the individual freedoms demanded by each and every person within the global needs of a world society. To do this, we must try to find out how much we know about man both as a creator and a user.

Chapter 3
THE PURPOSE

Since the time when Vitruvius believed that one saw by rays emanating from the eyes much has been discovered about the working of the mind and the body, but little of this has been used for a better understanding of architecture and our environmental needs whereas the increased knowledge of our body and its mechanisms has inevitably transformed society, whether we like it or not. The invention and production of labour-saving machines has been accelerating, particularly in the last three or four hundred years, whereas the investigation of how the mind works for the purpose of replication by machines, rather than as a philosophical discussion, is comparatively recent. Once having started, however, a new revolution was under way, which is now increasingly seen as being comparable to the Industrial Revolution which preceded it. It is therefore necessary to review some of those aspects of mind and brain about which recent knowledge may not only influence the development of computers but also change ideas about architecture.

In order to do this, it is necessary to go back to the beginnings of evolution when many of the programs of the brain began to evolve, many of which remain with us today, having been handed down through the genetic code. The first thing upon which there is probably general agreement is that once life had started it had the problem of maintaining itself in perpetuity. Any form of life, or any mechanism for that matter, will suffer deterioration and wear of its various parts, which means that repairers would be needed to keep it going, but these repairers would also need repairers, and so on, and so on. A poor solution, because even if that had been possible, it would not be capable of adaptation to environmental change. So life produced the brilliant solution of making itself renewable and at the same time, in the renewal process, capable of adaptation to changing environments. It was also necessary for this life to obtain energy from a power source; this it solved by consuming other life in what is now part of a great symbiotic food chain.

In the beginning, life forms could remain static and wait for food to be swept by or through them in the currents of the oceans. Gradually the need came to move and seek food, which highlighted fundamental characteristics, even of life today.

Experience, in the earlier forms of life, was passed down through the processes of heredity to avoid the constant releasing of the basic essentials of life. Like an automaton, there was a program or programs which could instruct the life form to behave in certain ways under certain stable conditions. These programs and actions can be extremely complex as in sleepwalking and the activities of bees and ants. Somewhere along the path of evolution, probably with the early mammals, the advantage of conscious thought became apparent. In other words, the ability to be able to make individual decisions as opposed to waiting for heredity was clearly of great advantage when, for example, seeking new food sources in a changing environment. But a major change in the working and structure of the brain was necessary. First, a data bank was needed, because conscious decisions depend on the information available. Second, a new type of program(s) is necessary to modify the actions of the hereditary programs. Third, a means of creating 'models' of the world within the brain became of fundamental importance.

A simple way of understanding how such programs developed is to construct imaginary robots. If we imagine a robot which has been given a simple program for the absorption of energy from other living things, it would soon 'die' when either food stopped passing it or it had eaten everything around it. It would have to have a program to make it capable of moving to where other food might be (Figure 29).

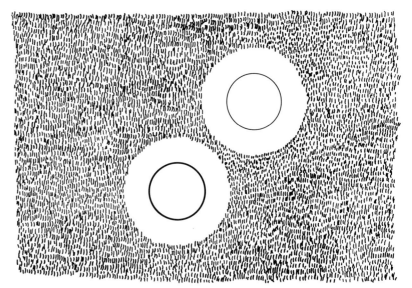

Figure 29

This strangely is the beginning of architecture—not in a structural form but in a conceptual form. From the need for reproduction, already explained, we quickly arrive at a situation where there are two robots, one of which is the reproducing body. Throughout most advanced forms of life it is usual for one body to seek food whilst the other looks after the young. Once the food-seeker leaves the group in search of food, other important programs immediately become necessary:

(1) The robot has to have a means of remembering how to get back to where it started.

62

(2) When it gets back, it has to be able to recognize its own mate or family group, as it cannot afford to spend time feeding strangers.

(3) It needs a strategy program to provide it with a plan of action.

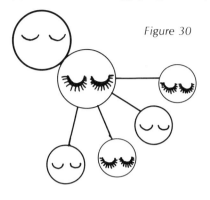

Figure 30

Figure 31(a)

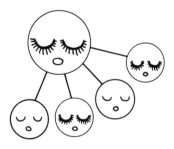

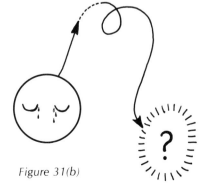

Figure 31(b)

Let us take each in turn.

The food-seeking robot has to have at a very early stage a capacity for 'building a map' or design in its brain. We, too, need the same, for without such a program we could not only not find our way home but also could not build up in our minds the concept of a design without building it item by item to see what happens. The robot would also need a pattern-recognition program so that when it returned to its own 'family' it could identify the infinitely subtle differences which make its mate look different from others of the same species. Without this pattern-recognition program we could not only not recognize our own families but not recognize architectural style or even those varying relationships of symbols such as doors and windows which identify a building. With the third program, the robot now acquires a survival program which also becomes a social program. If the robot is given a simple instruction to move, it might straight away fall over a cliff, which would be a bad survival strategy. If, however, the instruction to move was hedged about with too many precautions, it might die of starvation before it got to the food. Therefore there must be a facility for balancing an outrageously wild, but possibly successful, approach with an overly conservative and timid approach. We now have the radical and the conservative approach which permeates life, and it is the need to balance these two for survival which gives the illusion of balance and 'rightness'. Just as each robot's food gain becomes another one's loss, each is convinced that it is making the 'right' decision for itself, its family, and probably the whole species. Here is the optimization we see today, but, as we now know, life is not the optimization of one set of parameters but the interaction of endless suboptimizations in a continuously changing environment. If we are not quick, by the time we have carried out the suboptimals, the target has changed. When we make our individual or group decision on, say, the compulsory wearing of seat belts, we are making that decision on the basis of some theoretically ideal world which we have created for ourselves, and this world is based on whether we are introvert or extrovert, radical or conservative, etc. Society progresses on these balances, as we shall see later.

Infinite potential for a variety of strategies is now therefore possible, but evolution, and that includes social evolution, would soon turn into chaos unless there was a stabilizing strategy. So life developed a strategy for deciding the 'right road' to take, even though that 'right road' may be a dead end, as the dinosaurs and many other species have found. Once a path is taken, such as giving up wings for legs, there is no opportunity to start again if the environment starts to alter the balance of advantages. To reduce the risk of choosing a route from which there is no escape, mutations are always ready to break out and exploit the changed environment, giving at least some degree of flexibility.

The problem is to choose the most favourable route, and Maynard Smith (1976) has shown how that route might be selected. Life forms have the alternative of either improving the survival chances of the 'individual', or increasing its fertility so that the gene will have a better chance of surviving in the increased number of the progeny. In either situation, the radicals and conservatives begin to exhibit themselves as hawks or doves. It would at first sight seem to be obvious that the hawks quickly eliminate the doves, but, as Maynard Smith shows by simple mathematics, when the hawks have done this a mutant dove could have a great survival advantage whilst the hawks were constantly attacking each other. Gradually the doves would then begin to dominate until the two achieved a stable society; i.e. until changes in the society or environment upset the balance again and started a new search for stability.

Dawkins (1976) uses this same theory to give a mathematical rationale for a balance between what he calls coy and fast females. Again he shows that the balance swings backwards and forwards between the two, finally stabilizing, until some change causes the balancing to start all over again:

> Suppose that the genetic pay-off gained by each parent when a child is reared successfully is +15 units. The cost of rearing one child, the cost of all its food, all the time spent looking after it, and all the risks taken on its behalf, is −20 units. The cost is expressed as negative, because it is 'paid out' by the parents. Also negative is the cost of wasting time in prolonged courtship. Let this cost be −3 units.
>
> Imagine we have a population in which all the females are coy, and all the males are faithful. It is an ideal monogamous society. In each couple, the male and female both get the same average pay-off. They get +15 for each child reared; they share the cost of rearing it (−20) equally between the two of them, an average of −10 each. They both pay the −3 point penalty for wasting time in prolonged courtship. The average pay-off for each is therefore $15 - 10 - 3 = +2$.
>
> Now suppose a single fast female enters the population. She does very well. She does not pay the cost of delay, because she does not indulge in prolonged courtship. Since all the males in the population are faithful, she can reckon on finding a good father for her children whoever she mates with. Her average pay-off per child is $+15 - 10 = +5$. She is 3 units better off than her coy rivals. Therefore fast genes will begin to spread.
>
> If the success of fast females is so great that they come to predominate in the population, things will start to change in the male camp too. So far, faithful males have had a monopoly. But now if a philanderer male arises in the population, he starts to do better than his faithful rivals. In a population where all the females are fast, the pickings for a philanderer male are rich indeed. He gets the 15 points if a child is successfully reared, and he pays neither of the two costs. What this lack of cost mainly means to him is that he is free to go off and mate with new females. Each of his unfortunate wives struggle on alone with the child, paying the entire −20 point cost, although she does not pay anything for wasting time in courting. The net pay-off for the fast female

when she encounters a philanderer male is $+15-20=-5$; the pay-off to the philanderer himself is $+15$. In a population where all the females are fast, the philanderer genes will spread like wildfire.

If the philanderers increase so successfully that they come to dominate the male part of the population, the fast females will be in dire straits. Any coy female would have a strong advantage. If a coy female encounters a philanderer male, no business results. She insists on prolonged courtship; he refuses and goes off in search of another female. Neither partner pays the cost of wasting time. Neither gains anything either, since no child is produced. This gives a net pay-off of zero for a coy female in a population where all the males are philanderers. Zero may not seem much, but it is better than the -5 which is the average score for a fast female. Even if a fast female decided to leave her young after being deserted by a philanderer, she would still have paid the considerable cost of an egg. So, coy genes start to spread through the population again.

To complete the cycle, when coy females increase in numbers so much that they predominate, the philanderer males, who had such an easy time with the fast females, start to feel the pinch. Female after female insists on a long and arduous courtship. The philanderers flit from female to female, and always the story is the same. The net pay-off for a philanderer male when all the females are coy is zero. Now if a single faithful male should turn up, he is the only one with whom the coy females will mate. His net pay-off is $+2$, better than that of the philanderers. So, faithful genes start to increase, and we come full circle. . . .

This perhaps explains why the structure of society does not seem to change greatly over the centuries. Greek personalities are much like those of today, as are Chaucer's people. Furthermore, a strong swing in one direction has always produced an equally strong reaction. Vide Napoleon, Hitler, etc.

For our purposes two important things arise from this work:

(1) Social characteristics can be interpreted and predicted in mathematical terms.
(2) As a development of the example quoted, Dawkins suggests that ideas, or as he calls them memes, can be considered in the same way as genes in the battle for evolutionary survival. This could give a basis for the development of ideas.

We can now bring these two proposals together to form the basis of a new approach to the development of ideas, which can include style or the development of architecture.

If we take a new idea as a successful hawk meme, e.g. modernism, it has to fight hard for survival, and the harder the fight the more its disciples are stimulated to fight. Gradually the modernist meme spreads throughout society until the hawks have only other hawks to oppose them, as the traditionalist dove opponents almost disappear. But the traditionalist doves can now take advantage of the modernist hawk fighting or competing with other modernist hawks, to introduce a conservationist meme which gradually acquires more and more disciples, etc., etc.

If we look at history we can see how this has actually happened as style is replaced by style at ever-reducing intervals. (Perhaps the reducing time periods are the result of the improved speed of communication over the centuries.) In very much rounded-off figures, the architectural cycle seems to be something like:

Roman	800 years
Gothic	400 years
Renaissance	300 years
Revivalism	100 years
Modern	50 years

Within these larger cycles are smaller cycles such as moral attitudes. The open and free style of living in Elizabethan times was followed by a period of Puritanism, again followed by the open style of the Restoration. This was followed by the tight moral code of the Victorians which in turn was followed by today's open moral style. It is obviously certain that we shall now start to enter a period of narrower moral standards.

This constant reaction against an earlier cycle appears to have something to do with generations and may be partly affected by the children of a generation having more sympathy with their grandparent's generation and starting hawk memes to assert their independence from their parents. There must also be an evolutionary need to improve the chances for survival by constantly searching for new social strategies and thereby encouraging the production of new mutations against the time when they are needed. Whatever the reason, each fashion is followed by a period of loathing as the new style takes over. Once the new style is established, the threat of the old is now removed and the old style can now be accepted into the established culture. It would now seem to be possible to develop mathematical models which represent the way our emotions act or react, and also how society adapts to fashion.

But the question now is whether we can understand how we actually select a new fashion or a new idea which will succeed out of the vast number of permutations thrown up. The first thing to establish is that just as the gene is constantly throwing up mutations and holding them in a bank waiting for the moment when the environment changes to its own advantage, so do some mutant ideas such as da Vinci's inventions have to bide their time in a data bank until society is ready.

The fashionable choices made at any one time by connoisseurs or 'men of taste' are proposed as absolutes, but from a relative world. These tastes have been acquired. The taste of the best whisky and the best wine has to be acquired. Scarcity certainly helps this selectivity. For example, oysters which are now such a connoisseur's delight were not so when they were a common everyday food. Herrings and kippers will obviously soon become a connoisseur's delicacy. Replicas of the Parthenon no matter how exact they were could not acquire the same status as the original, and one reason why this is so may be due to what Gregory (1966) calls an 'aha' theory: 'It is little more, perhaps never more than a reshuffling of the pack of one's concepts, to draw a new combination which shows promise. Perhaps the *aha* experience is a gasp of recognition, that the novel draw of concept cards fits surprisingly well with features from the past to improve some aspect of the future.'

Excitement at finding something known only to oneself as well as making a new rationale out of the pack of infinite knowledge must have been in the human mind for a long time. In fact, it must have been a necessity, as the excitement of finding one's own food source, for example, was a necessity for survival. This selection of the special may help the standards of society, but can become snobbishness when it denies the pleasures of many whose taste may lie in other directions. 'Keeping up with the Jones's' is just as much a folly of the intellectual as of anyone else.

The selection of the rare and unique, which may explain the choice of the connoisseur, does not explain the choice of the majority of society for a new style which can be produced in enormous quantities. This is not just a present-day phenomena. The fruits of mass production have been enjoyed by the major part of society since earliest times, for it has always been only a small part of any society which could enjoy the non-standard article. Mass production is still mass production when produced by hand, only usually it is more punitive of human beings actually working as machines. (Mass production by cheap labour does, of course, look more attractive to the quickly passing tourist.)

Therefore it is necessary to seek further if we are to begin to understand the process by which some new ideas are absorbed into society and others rejected, even though the choice may seem to be arbitary or even wrong in the long run. Take, for example, the unfortunate decision to override Brunel's work in the choice of the standard railway gauge. He had a long record of success in decision making and yet unknown committees rejected his view. As we now know, his gauge would have caused less problems today, but, nevertheless, society chose otherwise. Was it just envy or spite, or was it something more?

As individuals and as a society, we try to attain a balance between radicalism and conservatism, hawkishness and doveishness, within a continuously changing environment and with new mutant ideas constantly being developed for selection by society. A lot do not survive. The Library of Congress in 1970, for example, contained more than sixty-one million items. What an incredible amount of knowledge for selection. But how much is actually known or used? In the huge Lenin Library in Moscow, half of the books have never been requested, even by a single reader.

What is the mechanism of selection, then, that gives society its direction? Wynne-Edwards (1962), for example, suggests that starlings rise together in the sky in flocks to perform some sort of population census so that their genes can select the best strategy for survival. If there are many starlings and little food, the best chance for survival is a low birth rate, whereas for a few starlings and a lot of food it is the reverse.

It is presumably a mechanism of this nature that causes high birth rates after wars. But even these strategies, if correct, still leave an unimaginably enormous area of choice. At every microsecond we are confronted with choice, and at each decision with further choice, and so on. It is the same for people in a crowd, for example, who can diverge very quickly if they do not have a strategy, as everyone knows. Two people in a large crowd in Trafalgar Square will, without an agreed strategy, have to choose individually to go left or right of each person they pass. Inevitably, without an overriding objective, they will wander further and further apart. If all the organisms in our bodies were not controlled by the overriding plan of our DNA programs, our bodies would rapidly become chaotic, as some parts with a capacity for fast evolution, even within a single life span, took their own unfettered evolutionary route.

Marais (1937) suggests that the whole society of the white ant in its termitaries acts as a single body, in the same way that all the life forms are integrated in the human body. Just as there have developed different types of ants with specific tasks to make the whole termitary act as a unified social structure, so there are organisms and bacteria carrying out specific tasks within the human body to form what we know as a human being. We could use this same argument to suggest that there is the equivalent of a DNA to unite the activities of life forms in general and human beings in particular into an integrated social plan. In the absence of finding such a DNA which would suggest the denial of free-will, we must for the present assume that the pattern of society is determined by man, even if the social organization of his own body is already predetermined.

The pattern of society might be seen at this stage as a game. The couple in Trafalgar Square, mentioned earlier, have to agree a set of rules if they are ever to meet again. Similarly there have to be rules for games like draughts and chess. If the pieces did not have rules for movement and were not confined to the area of the board, the game could not exist.

Just as the infinity of moves in chess or any other game is constrained by rules, so is society; otherwise everything would quickly become meaningless. But the rules must have flexibility; otherwise ideas and therefore life would quickly become extinct because changes within the total environment had made them redundant. Therefore society seems to act either by a set of rules which are continually moved forward by players bending these rules and the modifications which are gradually absorbed into the game or by the creation of new games. However, rather than moving forward in a straight line, it appears to move in a spiral. Cycles of fashion are recognizable, but the cycle has moved on, and so the pattern begins to look more like a spiral galaxy or the shape of a bedspring (Figure 32).

The hawkish mutations appear on the fringes of each part of the spiral, whilst the majority of people work in some degree of stabilization and coordination upon which evolution has placed a premium. If the

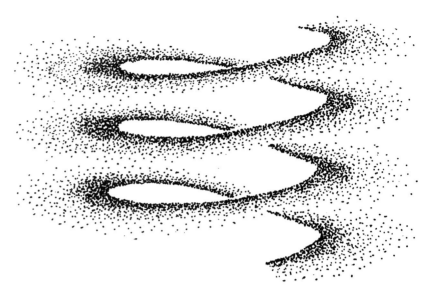

Figure 32

mutations are too far out of the system, we call their authors mad or mentally disturbed. But if a new modification to the set of rules is played with sufficient vigour and gathers disciples, it might then become absorbed by society. Sometimes the mutant is overshadowed on the first cycle, but is gathered up as a later cycle passes. Da Vinci is typical in having to wait for later cycles to be in tune with his ideas, because they were far outside the first and even the second cycles.

Clearly, human beings and human society need both the stability of the core as well as the constant excitement of the exploration for mutations, whether these be in new physical achievements or new mental achievements. Here, then, we might see sport, science, and art as differetnt aspects of the same activity. In fact, they become noticeably similar in philosophies such as those of the Inner Game as proposed by Gallewey.

There is also a need to create competitive hierarchies, as can be seen in our need for ranking everything. There are not only 'Top of the Pops' in records, but there is the same in art, sport, science, and every aspect of society. The human mind insists on trying to rank anything in some merit order, whether they be matchboxes, stamps, or whatever. This must be a product of the need to seek constant optimization for survival. It clearly represents a problem for modern society, for whilst revolutionaries have been fighting for equality—*liberté, egalité, fraternité* is typical of a revolutionary slogan—equality quickly disappears because as a species we constantly seek leaders. The need for social hierarchy and leadership is seen in animals and human beings alike. In open herds, for example, where incoming stock meet for the first time, the rank order tends to be based on physical attributes—agility, strength, and weight. In closed herds, however, seniority is more often the decisive factor. Social hierarchies do not necessarily indicate an overall order of merit but merit in a particular field which is in turn dependent upon strength of interest. A successful artist might count for nothing in a rugger club, and vice versa.

70

No one is at the head of all hierarchies in reality, although in totalitarian societies the head of state might assume to be theoretically so. The strength of democratic societies lies in the growth and death of these hierarchies. Also, the growth *and* death of the idea which causes these hierarchies are equally important to allow any society to grow and change in a direction which no one can predict, but only perhaps suggest.

Equality in property is similarly unobtainable, whether publicly or privately owned. If all the land in the world were equally shared, not only would some people get desert and others mountains but the next child born would in any case upset the balance. So-called global solutions of equality tend to be oversimplistic. Proudhon (1898) is logically correct in saying 'that property is a right against nature and against reason', but nevertheless even the most egalitarian revolutionary cannot deny to himself his own innate sense of property (except when that denial becomes a spiritual discipline). These aspects of society will be discussed later, but now it is necessary to return to the individual as a brain and a mind. The two words are often used synonymously, but in fact they are completely different in every sense. The brain is generally, but not exclusively, split into parts: the left half seems to be predominantly logical and verbal whilst the right controls our creative and intuitive activities. These are neither physically exclusive, for each part can to some extent stand in for the other; nor are they practically exclusive, as we use the interaction of the two throughout our lives. Any new piece of information we receive is located in the appropriate area of the brain with some processing available at the site of information and not as in a large computer system with one large data bank. In order to collect data for processing in the brain, sense organs such as the eye are instructed to search for data which can then be evaluated. This brings out two further important characteristics for our understanding of architecture. We generally believe that the brain sees by means of a picture displayed on the retina of our eyes, in just the same way as a picture is reproduced by the lens on the photographic emulsion. This misunderstanding, which often includes both the architect's and layman's belief that we see and design by means of mental or drawn perspective, is critical to our understanding of the environment.

Seeing is not the passive recording of the visual scene, as suggested by the perspective drawing, but a continual and active search by the eyes for answers to questions posed by the brain. Observation clearly shows that the eyes move in jerks in reading or looking around a room. The movements of the eyes themselves are very fast and occur up to a maximum of about five a second. Even during fixation, small tremors occur. The fact that the eyes are seeking the answers to questions is best illustrated by Yarbus (1967). (See Figure 33.) *Obviously the eyes see different things depending upon the question posed by the brain.* It is easy to recognize this characteristic in ourselves. If we expect monumentality, we shall seek supporting evidence and no doubt find it. If we are expecting a work of art, we shall seek to find the detail which has been described as the hallmark of that art. If we buy a new car, every car we see suddenly seems to be the same make.

71

The amount of evolutionary effort which has gone into the sophistication of the eye in the human species shows how important it is to our survival in general, but the structure and working of the eye is of particular importance to architects, as it is what we see which constitutes a substantial part of architecture.

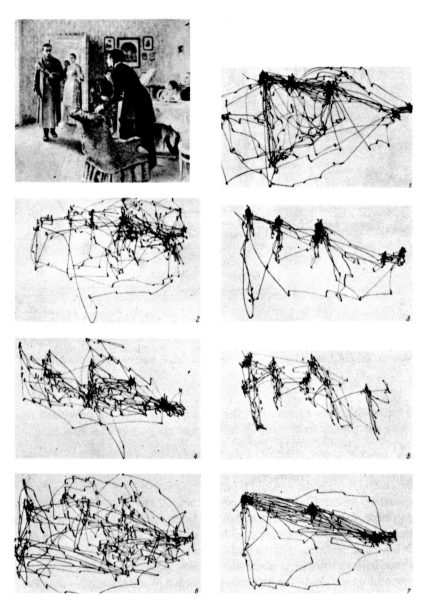

Figure 33 Seven records of eye-movements and fixations during examination of a picture. Each record lasted three minutes. During (1) the subject was allowed free examination. Before the others he was given instructions. (2) Estimate the material circumstances of the family. (3) Give the ages of the people. (4) What were the family doing before the arrival of the 'unexpected visitor'? (5) What clothes were the family wearing? (6) Describe the position of the people and objects in the room. (7) How long had the unexpected visitor been away from the family? The program for eye-movement is adjusted to obtain the required information

72

Each eyeball is equipped with six extrinsic muscles which hold it in position in its orbit and rotate it in order to follow moving objects or to direct its gaze. Both eyes are synchronized. Within each eye there is an annular muscle forming the pupil through which light passes to the lens immediately behind; this muscle varies the aperture according to light and distance. Another muscle controls the focusing of the lens. The eye works efficiently over a range of brightness of about 100,000:1, which makes man's inventive achievements look rather puny. A nerve can transmit impulses of up to slightly under a thousand per second. As the frequency of light is a million million cycles per second, the human brain has developed tricks to overcome the disparity; these tricks are important to our understanding of architecture.

This is not the place to examine the present state of knowledge of optics, but it is necessary to appreciate that there is no such thing as absolute vision and that what we think we can see can be influenced by innumerable factors—shading, lighting intensity, or just plain tricks of the brain. Even such factors as the abolition of shadows by direct high-intensity overall lighting make it difficult for the eye to distance, which makes the constant effort needed to establish depth very tiring for the eye. It is probably similar to the dullness we feel on an overcast day. Do the overall fluorescent lighting ceilings have the same effect? Can we not use the benefits of scientific knowledge in the practise of architecture, rather than relying on intuitive art?

The second aspect of the working of the brain which is important in its relationship to architecture is the routing of information. From an early age, imprinting of pattern is a fundamental to survival. The child must recognize the parent, and vice versa; this happens by continuous eye scanning of significant characteristics. Observation of the baby will show its concentration on the eyes, nose, and mouth of the human face, as these are the most significant identifiers. Again Yarbus (1967) shows the brain is directing the eyes to search (Figure 34).

Figure 34 Eye-movements and fixations during free examination of a photograph for three minutes. Fixations are mainly on points that the brain program suggests are likely to provide interesting information

So fundamental is the search for face patterns that we can find them in things other than faces as well. Figure 35 shows a styrofoam packing, and yet we can read into it not only a face but the emotions of that face. Imagine the deduction the brain would be capable of reading into this simple article if it were found in an ancient tomb. We can even see faces in the elevations of buildings, Figure 36.

Figure 35

Figure 36

74

New information travels along routes to the appropriate information location point, and just as increased traffic creates a need for wider roads, so the routes through the brain need to become larger. Furthermore, looking at a map to find a route from A to B, one is encouraged to keep to the main routes, thereby adding still further to the traffic and encouraging still wider roads, until at some point there is a general search for alternatives because the route has become too busy or one has had a stroke. The major route has now been overexploited. Is this one of the causes of our need to keep changing styles?

In any case, these two factors,

(1) seeing (the search for answers to the brain's questions) and
(2) reinforcement of images,

must be carefully considered if we are to have any understanding at all of the art of architecture and not just rely on prejudice or intuition for making computer programs.

It is now possible to see that in a survival situation the brain is directing the eyes to search for information which might indicate danger or help with survival. Certain characteristics are learnt through imprinting to be dangerous or otherwise—many of which we still have. However, the human brain has developed a two-stage memory and a system of holding data before releasing action, because immediate reaction could be wasteful of energy. An antelope does not run every time it sees a lion, because this would not be energy productive. Whilst information is being collected, adrenalin is being created to give increased muscle power for when action is needed. It therefore seems possible that when the human being no longer needed his brain to be totally occupied with survival, the brain turned the same facility to the decoding of patterns or games for keeping the brain active. If, therefore, the apprehension which builds up before final interpretation of the pattern or game is recognized can be compared with the apprehension build-up as danger signals are interpreted, what happens to the adrenalin?

Koestler (1964) uses the joke for his enquiry into creativity because it is the only activity in which a complex pattern of intellectual stimulation produces an immediate and sharply defined response. Either we laugh at the end of a complex intellectual game or we do not. But in architecture there is no such obvious automatic response. However, there are similarities. The brain is constantly trying to make a rationale for the data it is receiving, sometimes by rationalizing unrelated data, as in Koestler's example of the joke about two women meeting. In this joke, one woman questions why the other has a worried look. She says she is worried because she has taken her son to the psychiatrist who has told her that her son has an Oedipus complex. The other woman replies 'Oedipus, Schmoedipus, who cares as long as he is a good boy and loves his mama.' Another form is the recognition of rhythm, as in the joke by Carroll:

Yet what means all such gaities to me
Whose life is full of indices and surds
$X^2 + 7X + 53 = 11/3$

75

These are only two examples of the brain searching for balance and reason, producing a release in laughter when it is recognized. In architecture the release is seldom in laughter but the build-up of tension can be similar. Just as with humour, music, or any other art, tension and the desire for understanding a pattern is promoted in architecture by the use of invention, alliteration, anagram, epigram, pun, simile, analogue, and so on. Figures 37 and 38 give two simple examples. The first shows

Figure 37

Figure 38

rhythm, polyrhythm, and counterpoint. The second shows repetition, but with the fascinating interest of the discordant notes of the two windows on the right.

The sensation of adrenalin release upon a recognition can become the pleasure of laughter or the understanding of a 'great truth'. Aha! This emotional release can now be interpreted in mathematical models such as the catastrophe theory. A typical example of the relief of understanding

76

after a build-up of apprehension can be seen in architecture where a recent style used glass in a position where we would normally have expected structural support. The greater the intensity of the artist in thinking up a new variation to the game, the greater the appreciation of the observer. Brubeck, the jazz musician, recalls that at an important concert at Carnegie Hall he started playing solo something which could not be recognized by the other musicians. Their fear mounted, as he knew it would, until it was released by a final recognition when he played the theme. He maintains that here they attained their highest level of performance. This confirms the earlier suggestion that the *intensity* of mental activity is one of the most important factors in science, sport, or art.

The degree of subtlety of shape and line which the eye can discern is considerable, and this gives a fantastic potential for ranges of symbols capable of recognition. It has already been seen in Figure 35 that a mood can even be ascribed to a light switch. We can detect very slight differences of mood and attitude from body shapes and facial movement. These are built up into a language of symbols. Just as many species of fish, for example, recognize aggression, submission, sexual state, and so on, from shape and colour, so can the human eye. The subtlety in the difference of shape between a fat woman and a pregnant woman is easily recognized. From this, it might appear to be easy to produce a visual language of symbols, but unfortunately there are many difficulties to be overcome; these involve distortion and illusion. The distortion can apply to the indoctrination or imprinting of ideas as well as their interpretation, which makes it extremely dangerous to be arrogant about what we see. The problem of not having an absolute scale to which we can refer has already been mentioned. Scale is not only relative to the environment in which we have been indoctrinated but is relative to what the eye expects to see.

For example, scale deception is shown in the Ames room. Ames, an American psychologist who started life as a painter, created a room which consisted of oddly shaped planes (Figure 39). The far wall sloped back at one side and did not lie at a normal angle to the observer. The rule of perspective was used to make this odd-shaped room give the same retinal image as a normal rectangular room. The spectator from a rectangular world expects to see a normal room and therefore has to decide whether the room or the people are correct. Something has to be forsaken and generally it is the second person who is turned mentally into a midget. It has been found that wives frequently believe their husband to be the norm and therefore see this room as distorted, which is a comment on the power of belief influencing what we see. Belief and visual image are now confused.

Another example is, of course, the cinema, where the speed of replacing each frame with another is maintained at the point of frequency which deceives the electric impulses to the brain because of the difference in frequencies already mentioned. As a mechanism, the brain and body combine to make the most incredibly sophisticated piece of equipment ever developed, but it is precisely this sophistication which makes it capable of being deceived in so many ways that there can be no

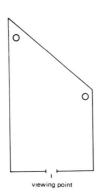

viewing point

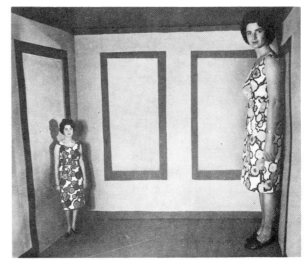

Figure 39(a)   Figure 39(b)

room for absolute truth. This problem is further aggravated by the condition of the brain at the time of observation. The brain is an electrochemical device and, as such, is affected by electrical and chemical stimuli.

Starvation as well as drugs will affect our vision and also our beliefs; as previously mentioned, it is curious that many artists have done much of their best work whilst suffering from one or the other. This again seems to support the theory of mutant ideas, where drugs or starvation allow the rules of conventions to be waived and new mutant rules to be developed. In addition to drugs from peyote to LSD, hormone levels can also affect attitudes and concepts of the brain. Monoamine oxidase inhibitors can drastically reduce the need for sleep and electrical stimuli can change our view of wakefulness.

The gradual understanding of the actions of enkephalins and endorphins as they affect our moods and attitudes increasingly raises issues of morality and the direction and attitudes of our own lives and that of society. It must also affect our views on architecture unless again we try to retreat into the past. Rosenfeld (1972) believes that it is now possible for us to wear self-stimulating electrodes in our brains that will enable us to change our moods by push-button control. Not only this, but already future actions or mental changes have been anticipated by computers. Hanley of the Brain Research Institute of UCLA taught a chimpanzee to play tick tack toe. By planting electrodes in the chimpanzee's brain which were then connected to a computer, it was found to be possible to predict with 99 per cent certainty whether its next winning potential move would be correct or incorrect *at least fifteen seconds before* the move was made.

Another aspect of the working of the brain is one already mentioned—short- and long-term memory. Whilst the mechanism is not fully understood, it is known that data input from the senses is held in a short-term data bank before being transferred into the long-term data

78

bank, if this is thought desirable. Clearly this is a further device of the brain to conserve both energy and long-term data storage. The short-term memory may only hold information for about an hour and then it will either be given up or passed to the long-term data bank. Perhaps consideration of this should be given in the possible difference of design approach to, say, urban and domestic design where the acceptance levels of data are so different.

In order to consider a design approach we must, however, have a concept of space before we can begin. Through the ages this has obviously taken many forms, but even now it is often discussed as a pictorial scene rather than a product of the electrochemical activities of the brain. Plato saw the world as a mathematical model, Aristotle as a biological model, and the Middle Ages saw it as an hierarchical model. More recently Nitsche (1968) described space as follows; 'It has a centre which is perceiving man and it therefore has an excellent system of direction which changes with the movements of the human body: it is limited and in no sense neutral, in other words it is finite, heterogeneous, subjectively defined and perceived: distances and directions are fixed relative to man. . . .'

Norberg-Schulz (1971) disagrees with this theory on the basis that it makes architecture only exist when it is experienced. But what is space if it has no absolute scale, colour, or touch and can be influenced by starvation, drugs, or even hormone levels? Clearly space is a product of a model constructed in the brain. We can feel this model when we are driving a car, for example. We cannot see the rear wheels but we are conscious of their position because we have been able to build up a measured relationship of all four wheels within our brains. For this measurement we need to have a scale of values. A computer operates in a similar manner. It holds spatial information (very often full scale) in a digital form on electromagnetic records for retrieval at any required scale. The problem with the human brain is to agree a scale to which we can become indoctrinated, in the same way as we have accepted a musical scale. But unlike musicians, architects have seldom been able to agree on a scale because in the last hundred years or so they have seen this as a restriction on their creativity. Centuries ago Fibonacci (1175–1230) discovered a ladder of whole numbers which had a remarkable relationship to the Golden Section. Recently, Young (1978) suggested that research indicates a preference for these scales. This may mean no more than that we have already been indoctrinated by the ideas of the past. There does, however, seem to be some reason for believing that an established mathematical structure would help us to interpret space. However, it should not be used in the simplistic ways of the recent past. Wittkower (1978) suggested that the human brain shows a clear preference for the perception of simple mathematical patterns and there is some evidence for this as we shall see later. However, once again, we should be guarded against an oversimplification of the problems involved. Particularly, as has been suggested in Chapter 2, that architectural development often accompanied new mathematical concepts of space. The new knowledge of the brain would now seem to support that theory and may form the basis of future change.

It is as well to remember that one extreme of mental disturbance is an inability to organize patterns, whilst the other is an obsession with the meticulous organizing of shapes and patterns. Even today, students of architecture still exhibit a very considerable interest in a two-(not even three) dimensional Euclidean geometry, as a theoretical expression of the social environment, which has little relationship to real life. Many of these abstractedly planned proposals only begin to become habitable in reality after years of adaptation or modification by the user. One difficulty for architects may therefore be the construction of the brain. The creativity, so necessary for art, is on the opposite half of the brain to the logic, which is so important to the present education of architects, which may form the basis of the problem of whether they can achieve the best of both characteristics in today's world, using traditional processes.

Where does the purity of the art of architecture stand in all this, when all is illusion anyway? We can only consider the problem of the mind, as opposed to the body and the brain, to see if this gives any clue. The mind can best be described as the concepts which are created through a system of operations of the programs of the brain during consciousness. For this we can only return to the game strategies which we set up, and against which we enjoy playing. As the games become more developed in one area, other areas are lost. For example, an urban man may have a great ability to recognize complex urban situations and yet be unable to even observe the signs of the countryside which are obvious to the countryman. Part of the countryman's appreciation can be based on especially selected sets of smells which together with the sound constitute a major part of his environment; even so, the countryman is still using fashion and tradition as much as anyone else. His brain searches for information on the basis of previous indoctrination and fashionable trends.

Even the choice of such a basic factor as the most sexually attractive physical characteristics of the opposite sex seems to be confused in developed civilizations. A recent National Opinion Poll found surprisingly little consensus on this issue so fundamental to the survival of the species. Yet another survey found that a majority of men considered that girls named Susan were likely to be more sexy, which seems to suggest that the propagation of an idea can be more powerful than even a fundamental of 'nature'.

As the need for continual physical occupation recedes in the developed world, life as well as architecture increasingly becomes a game. That game becomes a more and more complex one. *It is much more complex than the positioning of the navel of a theoretically standard man or the choosing of a new style or even a simple computer program.* Our brains are operated by a network of electrochemical switches connected to 50,000,000,000 nerve cells which capture the impressions received from the senses and store them as a memory bank for our thoughts. To get some idea of the problems of retrieving information from so many cells and the scale of the problems to be solved, we may consider chess playing as an example. As any chess player will know, white has twenty possible opening moves to which black has twenty possible replies. This gives 400 different first-move combinations. Then there are more than 100,000 possible two-move sequences; this quickly expands into millions and billions in the third and fourth moves. And yet grand masters can 'see' five, six, or seven moves ahead where the possible moves are astronomical. Perhaps even more remarkable is the fact that computer chess-playing games have been developed up to this level of play.

Each one of us, then, not only starts with a different mechanism, collects different impressions, and has the mechanism varied by interference, medical health, starvation, or drugs, but also seeks different information from this 'world'. This makes every individual very individual, with only the 'games' of society to give coherence. The Cubist emphasis on the patterns made by the spaces rather than the pattern of the objects themselves is a typical example of this selectivity and game playing. This raises the question about both the structure of the data in the brain and the language of communication within it. These are now causing considerable interest as a possible means of finding out out how we structure our world. Popper (1972) and some other philosophers have, in the past, supported the view that there is a sharp distinction between the intellectual, emotional, and other aspects of the brain's working, but research shows that there is a close integration of the data-handling characteristics of the brain that cannot be replicated in hierarchical form alone. Yet our manual and computing coding and other systems are traditionally put into hierarchical structures. Perhaps this is because historically we have represented our views in two dimensions on paper or papyrus and this has influenced our thinking. Perhaps we should learn from the mathematicians and astronomers and begin to think of multidimensional models for the structure of our ideas, particularly, as Chapter 2 suggests, the idea that architectural development throughout history has been related to mathematical concepts of space.

The hope for a language of communication is different. Whilst artists, architects, and sociologists have begun to show an interest in linguistics and semiotics, some scientists are a little fearful that some of this work might be used as a last-ditch support for the old order in which artists can escape the rigours of scientific discipline. There is not sufficient progress so far to be able to judge the validity of such fears. Whatever we believe, it is clearly important to us to be able to understand the language with which we not only communicate with each other but also within ourselves. Language is probably less than 10,000 years old, but nevertheless has for a long time been a source of fascination for people trying to find the origin of language, and presumably the universal lexicon. Psammetichus, an Egyptian King of the seventh century BC, and James IV of Scotland are only two of a long list of people who have tried to find the basis of language. We do seem to be getting nearer today, however slowly.

Chomsky (1976) is only one of several philosophers now working in linguistics, as de Saussure did in semiotics, trying to establish whether there are deep structures or fundamental rules controlling our use of language. Linguists have been able to identify a number of universal characteristics across all languages—in phonetics, in syntax, and in semantics. All languages are based on words as primary units with phonemes as lesser units. Whilst the phonemes have no meaning in themselves, they are grouped together to make words which are meaningful. As we shall see later, we are now able to replicate this sort of activity very cheaply on computers.

Having created the words, we can then combine them together into a variety of ways to form a surface structure for communication. 'John ate the apple' and 'the apple eaten by John' have the same deep structure but different surface structures. When these words or symbols are combined together in a way which creates a tension or an 'aha', they may then be described, as suggested by Bernstein, as a super-surface structure. He uses as an example a quotation from Shakespeare—'Juliet is the Sun'. This poetic statement is in actuality a teasing of the brain, for how can Juliet be the Sun? But Juliet is radiant and the Sun is radiant, and therefore both have a common quality. If that common quality is removed it leaves the anticipatory statement—Juliet is the Sun—and, as with a joke, a relief when one understands the riddle. It may be abhorrent to the intellectual, but there does seem to be a great link between the work of the poet and the comedian, as we may yet find with the artist and the architect and the sportsman.

There is, in fact, good reason for believing that we can now look at architecture in the same way. The fashion of the 1930s, already mentioned, in which windows appeared at the corners of buildings where traditionally everyone had expected supporting structures had the same effect as 'Juliet is the Sun'. The first shock was relieved by the discovery of the use of cantilevered support. In architecture we replace the words with symbols and the phonemes with the lesser components. It is possible that as with zoosemiotics, which examines the language of signs in animal signalling systems, the language is less complex.

To give an example of the problem, which will be considered later in more detail, we can travel from country to country and have difficulty in finding the word for door or window in the local language. But no one is ever confused visually as to which is a window, wall, or door. From this simple recognition, we can examine in the next chapter the setting up of understandable rules and for this our understanding of the importance of intervals in language and music may help us to understand their importance in vision. However, it is worth remembering that whilst the idea of *tabula rasa* is increasingly replaced by evidence that we are born with a considerable amount of hereditary information, that information is still very individual. There seems little evidence for the beliefs in the past of absolute standards of beauty. Rules are only set up to be broken; take, for example, the rules set up for colour adjacency in the middle of this century, which have been deliberately smashed. Once a new hawk mutation begins to succeed because of its favourable environment, indoctrination begins to take over and the brain is then exposed from childhood to the paintings, photographs, and buildings of its culture.

Surprisingly, the outrageous suggestion made in Chapter 1 on the methods of selection for works of art now seems less absurd. Snobbishness, uniqueness, indoctrination, fashion, etc., all play their part in the grand aesthetic experience. We can also see that one man's vision is as valid for him as any other's, but for social reasons we limit ourselves to acceptable game rules. One of the unanswered question is, of course, who is to make the game and the rules? But whoever makes them and whatever they may be, there is no question that the complexities of an expanding global society will not be solved by the simple methods of the past. Hopefully we shall also be a little more humble in developing theories and models for a society which finds difficulty in distinguishing between a so-called material world and an absolute or spiritual world. Are radio waves part of a material world when we have not seen them? Are they different from our concepts of numbers? Where does the material world end and the spiritual world begin in the electrochemical systems of the brain?

Before moving on to the next chapter to examine how far we have gone to produce methodologies for the theories produced so far, it may be as well to consider the human being as a factory with a computer management system, as Young (1978) suggested. The brain and the computer are similar in the way that they convey information by electrical impulse. They both need clocks and diaries to ensure supplies of raw materials and energy at the right time, a method of estimating demand, both short term and long term, and construction systems for the maintenance and renewal of the factory. They require a method for storing, searching for, and retrieving data, and a language for transmitting the data within the system—in other words, a program language.

How far has man gone in replicating some of these activities? In some areas we have gone a long way but in others we have only succeeded in recognizing the enormity of the problem. In either case, our understanding of man both as a creator and spectator or user is now far beyond that which has influenced architects of the past. Where lie truth and integrity now? On what can we base a morality? The only answer now seems to be not a new messianic approach based on one man's fixed ideas but one based on the knowledge of the methods and tools available and the flexibility of mind to use them in a fast-changing world. After all, that is how the human species has pragmatically survived and developed until the present time.

Chapter 4
THE METHODS

Even our present knowledge of how the brain works makes the so-called philistine views of architecture given in Chapter 1 rather less ridiculous, and, whilst this still leaves a lot to be explained, it is worth considering how far we have come or are likely to go in translating our mental activities into manual or computer methods.

First, we know that the human brain uses indoctrination or reinforcement of images from childbirth and continues to use such mechanisms for building up long-term memory banks. Just as a mother's or father's face is gradually imprinted in a child's brain, so will architectural images be reinforced by drawings, photographs, or familiarity.

Second, the brain tends to use 'main roads' or well-developed neural paths wherever possible in the processes of thought, even though alternative routes are always available. This may explain the preference of the main body of society to conform to accepted standards because, as with driving, it needs effort to constantly pursue new routes through the side roads. We see ourselves doing this in many things, like going to work, making a cup of tea, and so on, which are done automatically and without detailed thought. Similarly, many of the processes of creative design are accepted automatically. Fashions, materials, constructions, and processes are often clearly taken as established information without being given new detailed consideration on each new project.

Third, in spite of a desire to conserve mental energy resources by using automatic routines, the brain nevertheless leavens the loaf of repetition by seeking stimulation from trying to make sense out of the visual and other sensory data it receives. This stimulation at its most creative level is like, and appears to be related to, sexual stimulation, often completely taking over our being in a way that only orgasm and laughter can otherwise do. In these three situations all other sensual inputs are temporarily suspended. The most sublime form and the most totally absorptive are those in which an extremely complex task or game is matched by an equal determination to find a solution. Chess is obviously one example.

The creative act of architecture has this same need to rationalize that part of the data which has been selected for the game. We may think that we are selecting all of the data or starting with a clean slate or piece of paper, but this is clearly not true. To believe this is to delude ourselves.

Some architects accept preconceived ideas at higher levels and others at lower levels, but all nevertheless do at some level. For example, a style or design approach is taken for granted. A method of planning such as grid or geometric shape is assumed. Components and materials are selected from a familiar range and only very occasionally, if ever, is the full range examined.

The observer or the user, on the other hand, will also expect certain rules to be played, and is stimulated when a small rule change is discovered—as with a joke. Now it is possible that these two aspects of the same thing are not always compatible. For example, the architect would get the greatest stimulation from constantly making more and more variables on the game, as would, say, a composer. On the other hand, the observer might enjoy this when, say, leisurely appreciating a Renaissance palace, but may find it overstimulating and tiring in a work situation. It is easy, for example, to work and talk with a 'muzak' background of noise but not easy with a similar sound level of Bach or Beethoven.

Therefore it would seem that because of the infinity of data which is available to us, we make or accept games of differing levels of complexity according to our situation; that is with the exception of architecture where architects are often trained as though they will all be artists and everything they design is to be at the same level of artistic creation. But the levels of complexities and concentration which vary from tic tac toe to chess also apply to our environment. The games which attain the classification of art are those which are subtly complex and offer a great potential for exploration, and which are also played with intensity. It must be reemphasized that these games can be played solo with the same effect. Just as there can be complete absorption in solitaire, so can the architect become absorbed with his own internal game to the point where the user and/or client is completely forgotten. Farnsworth House, designed by van der Rohe, could be such an example. Very often, it is just the fascination with the shapes on the paper which the initiated alone can enjoy. Here the user can even be a nuisance.

In painting, music, poetry, etc., the games are a personal interaction with the chosen media and the observer can be, and usually is, irrelevant. In fact, it is almost essential that these forms of art should be personal explorations. But the user and observer can never be irrelevant in architecture unless perhaps it is some remote folly. The architect must interact with society. Society is constantly seeking leaders, and the leaders are those with extreme intensity of thought, for whatever the cause, who create the mutations. However, in their intensity they can, in the case of architecture, ignore the accepted fundamental aspects of society in their designs. This aspect was not important in less democratic societies, but now the problem is very different.

Fourth, we need to find objects to fit into a hierarchy, irrespective of how well the game is played. Just as with herd cattle, we can be impressed with size, power, and so on. The existence and popularity of the Guinness Book of Records is a testimony to this.

The first and the fourth can come together in buildings such as the White House, Washington, the Houses of Parliament, London, the

Kremlin, Moscow, etc., where size, importance, and constant imprinting come together in such a way that any building, however it was designed, would become a symbol with status.

It might now seem to be less irreverent for those architects who see themselves as artists to examine some of the methods which might help us as tools in the creation and production of architecture. We may examine these methods under four headings:

(1) Tools
(2) Simple routines and repetitive systems
(3) Analytical systems
(4) Creative systems

The tools we use are clearly a very important factor in the methods we develop and use. The invention of papyrus, the tee-square and set-square, typewriters, printers, telephones, and so on, have had a considerable effect on both our methods and our concepts. There is, for example, a considerable difference between the design that emerges from a 2H pencil on a hard surface and that of a 2B pencil on a soft surface. The media and the tool is important to the process.

A recent example of the effect of a tool on architectural methods is printing. Before the Second World War printing was slow, difficult, and expensive, and therefore kept to a minimum. Some small architectural practices, even post-war, used sensitized paper on which was placed the negative in a frame to be then put into the sun for developing. No sun—no print. Even in larger organizations the architect himself made his own prints on a simple machine. Because of the cost and difficulty of the process, many different labours were shown on a single print by a recognized language of colouring. The invention of more sophisticated printers together with the increased complexity of the processes in the industry meant that the demand for prints increased whilst the price of printing dropped. As it was a labour-intensive operation and therefore costly, colouring gave way to a system of indicating trades and materials by signs and symbols which would be intelligible even on black and white prints.

Just as the tee-square and set-square set limits on creativity, so even support tools have influenced methods and sometimes even concepts. Seldom does the architect involve himself in the creation of the tool which may later, albeit surreptitiously, create the rules of a new game which can have an effect on his creativity. The microprocessor in its multitide of roles will undoubtedly create new rules. It will be up to the architect to decide how far he influences their use and development. If he ignores them, eventually he will be provided with a ready-made tool over which he has had no influence. Over the coming decades, the effect of the microprocessors will be as great or greater than were the effects of the Industrial Revolution, and those were dramatic enough. As the tool itself is so important in this case, it will be dealt with in detail in the next chapter. Meanwhile there has to be a bridge between the knowledge of what we are trying to do and a methodology of how we achieve the various types of goal. Therefore it is now necessary to start with the methods for simple and routine tasks. In this case we have as an example a simple linear strategy (Figure 40).

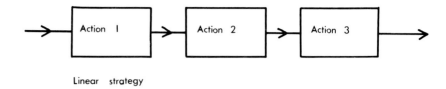

Linear strategy

Figure 40

Here we have a pre-planned strategy rigidly fixed in advance and put into automatic sequence by a starting signal. Just as the brain automatically puts into action a complex sequence of actions to close an eyelid as a fist approaches, so we can make machines carry out a sequence of small actions from a single initiator once we have worked out the methodology of the action. To do this the machine needs not only a clear specification and understanding of the actions but also a knowledge of the data necessary for the actions. These routine tasks have varying degrees of apparent complexity, even though the underlying principles are simple.

A washing machine, for example, goes through, without instruction (beyond the initial one), a series of operations which replicate those of the human being. The action of washing, rinsing, and drying clothes has been analysed and reduced to a simple chain of related events, in which electrical impulses form the means of instruction. This is very similar to the actions of the human brain both in the method of instruction—electrical impulses activating muscles in an interactive manner—and in the rationalization of the actions and data to conserve mental effort and therefore energy.

The human brain carries out many operations in a similar way and eventually these groups of actions become units of thought or blobs of information. There are many examples of this type of automotive blob. Can we remember treading each step after arriving at the top or bottom of a flight of steps? What colour were the traffic signals that were passed on a routine journey? Once we have set out on a routine a few times, the mind parcels the actions into a package and files it as a ready-made subroutine for future use, as and when required, and the whole operation is set in motion with one key code rather than having to re-program from the beginning each time. This is an economy of effort and storage.

We are now becoming adept at sorting out this type of mental activity for applications to machines and computers. Systems analysts analyse these simple repetitive actions, which are usually boring and uneconomic, and then program them for computers. At this level we have activities such as addition, subtraction, multiplication, and division, or simple logic, as well as simple human activities, thereby making it simple to produce any system which involves numbers and/or which also have limited and known variations. These types of simple strategy do not permit changes of mind; nor do they deal with unanticipated alternatives.

A simple routine would be one which enabled us to climb stairs but did not allow us to return from half-way up if we had forgotten something. We therefore sometimes need programs which allow for alternative actions. We might allow for adaptation by containing the strategy shown in Figure 41' within action statements, making sure that each one is completed satisfactorily before moving on to the next. It is possible with

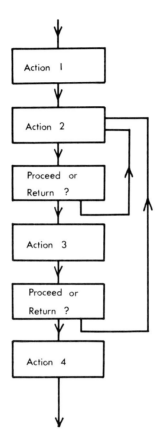

Figure 41

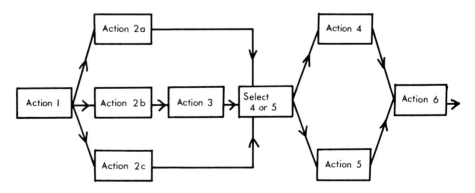

Figure 42

89

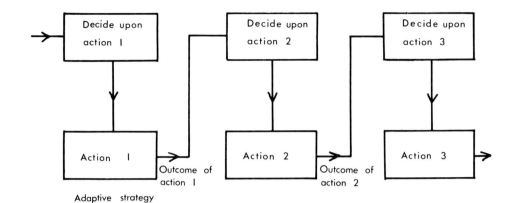

Adaptive strategy

Figure 43

these apparently simple strategies to produce quite complex operations (Figures 42 and 43), but in order to do this we need to have data.

When a fist or fly approaches the eye, the brain puts into operation a package of actions which has been held in one instruction and we can see this same operation in very much more sophisticated, or so we think, aspects of our thoughts. If we are asked suddenly for our views on

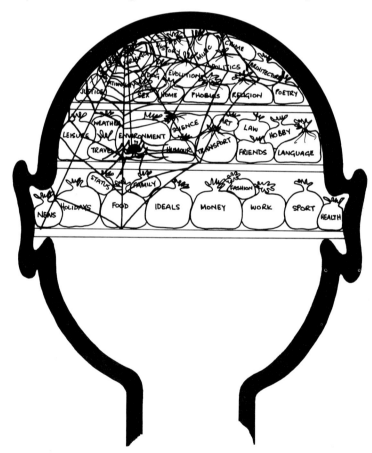

Figure 44

90

politics, religion, art, and so on, we will in many instances bring out a package of thoughts which may well be out of date with our current views. It is as though we store packages of ideas on shelves in our brain and only occasionally bring them down for examination. Sometimes the packages are small and sometimes large (Figure 44).

It would clearly be very energy intensive for the brain to keep questioning everything all the time. Am I still a Christian? Do I still love my family? Have I changed my politics? and so on. Even, how do I get to my own home or pick up my pencil? To conserve energy which is important to the brain, it will try to keep these data at the highest re-usable level. Theoretically, then, creativity reopens these parcels on the shelf and reshuffles some of the contents. Before examining these more complex problems there are many more ways in which we can use these standard routines in architecture than we may think, particularly if we have the assistance of the infallible memory of the computer.

We know that we can hold files of numbers. Once we have a program for addition or multiplication, etc., we can go on for ever, as with a pocket calculator. We can now use other contents of files to get other information. Under A we can put the name and cost of staff per hour and under B the number of hours to carry out certain activities. Plug in the multiplicator program and we have the cost of labour resources.

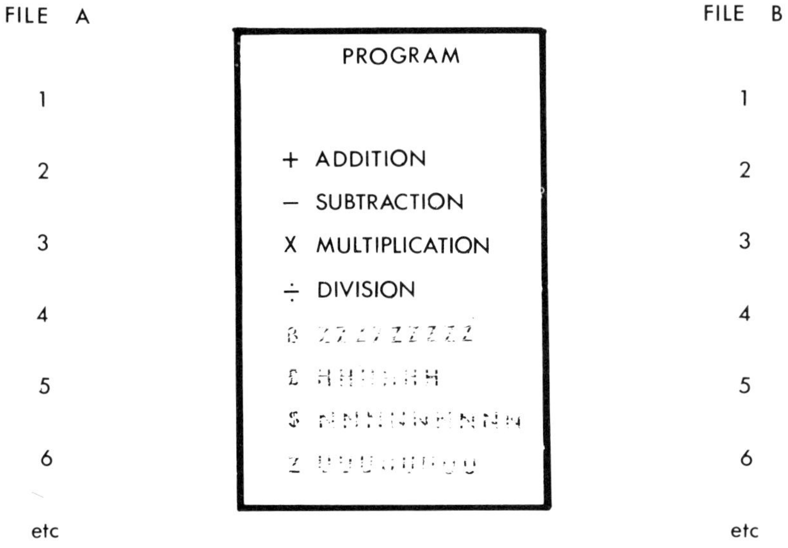

Figure 45

It is not difficult to see that many operations can be defined in such a routine manner, and it is this very fact which lies at the root of automation. By carefully examining such tasks, industry and commerce have reduced the number of repetitive actions and thereby the boredom of the task for the person carrying out the work. This has been criticized but when people yearn for craft manufacture, it is as well to remember the slavery there would have to be to create, for example, just the cups and saucers of this vast growing society. Machine work might still be boring, but is nothing like the slavery that all would have to accept without the machine. Nevertheless, it is now a commonly accepted fact that such tasks as those carried out by Chaplin in *Modern Times* are still an affront to human dignity, and every effort is being made to eliminate these 'blue collar' jobs. Strangely, many of these 'blue collar' jobs have just been replaced with 'white collar' jobs of equally boring repetitiveness, and this is where the computer can be both foe and ally.

Whilst industry and commerce are making large inroads into these problems, mainly to remain competitive, the professions have seen the whole of their work as creative and therefore not susceptible to such techniques. A secretary, clerk, or technician does not suddenly become something different when working for an architect. If their work can be rationalized elsewhere, why is it thought that it cannot be so in a professional office? Some doubts about this might have occurred, one would have thought, when architects found their profits dropping, even though their fee was a percentage related to a high-cost product such as building. Surely it must be the process which is becoming uncompetitive by present-day standards.

Even the simplest time- and labour-saving equipment has tended to be ignored. The reasons for this are probably as follows:

(1) Professionals have, by tradition, never needed more capital than was required to buy a drawing board and stool for himself and his employees. He has no background or training in capital expenditure for himself.
(2) As he is trained as an artist, he sees himself, his work, and that of his staff as artistic.
(3) Apart from the large interdisciplinary practices, there is, in any case, little capital available, which is a product of the separation of design from construction.

But there is nothing artistic or creative in searching for appropriate building regulations, or properties of materials, or even evaluating a brief. After all, this is a simple question and answer approach. Possible applications at this level of strategy will be discussed later in their relationship to organizations, but it is as well to consider a point of warning before embarking on such exercises when they involve the computer.

Throughout history, these repetitive aspects of human activity have been embedded either in canonic concepts or machines. In the case of the machines, they are superseded by new machines for new tasks, old ones being thrown away when they outlive their usefulness. If the old ones are still used beyond their design life span, it is well known and obvious that the organization will probably go bankrupt. But in the case of canonic concepts this is not necessarily recognized at all. Routine operations to save time and/or energy are incorporated into our brains, and in our organizations and institutions. In human beings, people become Colonel Blimps and Institutions incapable of changing long-held traditions, even though the whole social environment has changed since the inception of their original ideas and traditions.

The use of a traditional methodology is often held to be an asset, whilst to use a horse and carriage and wear a frock coat would be considered, at the least, to be eccentric. Whilst material things can be seen to be out of date, organizational methods are not so obviously recognized; the larger the organization, the easier it is for each individual to think that his useless task must have some use somewhere in the process.

When we start to build computer systems this problem can be further aggravated for a number of reasons:

(1) The enthusiasts who have set up the system may have either lost interest or left, and no one else dares or wishes to meddle.
(2) The cost of programming is expensive and therefore there is a great reluctance to spend money on rewriting programs.
(3) The process is less noticeable than ever, particularly if it is a system within a system.

The danger here is obvious. Organizations and animals both seem to have a tendency to increase in size as a product of making the best use of resources, until the control system becomes too inflexible to adapt to a changing environment. New mutations then tend to become stifled in such a fossilized system. Therefore, oversimplistic method systems not only need to be monitored but programmed to be monitored, if this is to be avoided in computer systems in which such ideas are embedded. Nevertheless, the process of examining simple activities will continue in the future, and they will continue to be organized into systems whether they be Kalamazoo or computer systems.

At the next level there are the analytical methods, which are useful as an aid in more complex searches. The most obvious of these is by the use of a matrix. In this we can structure information according to the functions to be fulfilled and the ability of items of data to fulfil these functions. For example, if we were to go the Motor Show to buy a car in a hurry, we would not start at one end of the exhibition and go through each and every car in turn. We would almost certainly start off with a set of criteria such as maximum cost, mileage per gallon, number of seats, and class of car. The more factors that are stipulated, the more the selection of possible cars is reduced. This process can be replicated in a method and can be illustrated in a simple form. There are at the present time more than six hundred different makes and types of motorcar available on the British market alone. A card for each type can be completed stating its ability to fulfil basic criteria. These criteria would be such things as number of seats, petrol consumption under certain conditions, cruising speed, cost range, etc.—in other words, the normal factors included in any road test report. This makes the input of data very simple. The selector or user now specifies his need: i.e. four seater, petrol consumption not less than 30 m.p.g., cost range, etc. All that is now needed is a means of making a match, and this can be done in a number of ways (Figure 46).

One way is to use edge punch cards. In this system a card with a set of holes is used to hold the data which is sited around the edge (Figure 47). A simple tool converts the hole to a slot where the item being recorded is compatible with the criteria listed around the edge (Figure 48). If needles

max speed·in miles per hour
cost in use·in pence per mile
carrying load·in kilograms
mode·land, sea, air
UUUUU
WW
UUUUU
ZZZZZZZ
KLLLLLL
JJJKKKKK
UUUUU
FFFFFFGGGG
ZZZZ

scales of values		0	1	2	3	4	5	6	7	8	9	
speed	A			X								mph
cost	B								X			ppmile
load	C					X						kg
mode	D				X							
UUUUU	E		X									&
WWWW	F						X					££
UUU	G										X	$
ZZZ	H									X		฿
KLLLL	I	X										
JKLKK	J											
UUUUU	K											
FFFGGG	L											
ZZZ	M											

IMPLIED CODE: A3, B7, C5, D4, E2, F6, ETC.

Figure 46

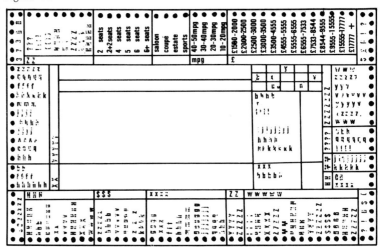

Figure 47

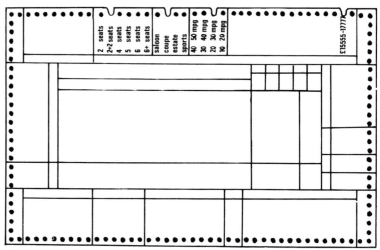

Figure 48

94

are put into the pack at those points which indicate the user's requirements, those which satisfy the needs drop out. This system can be used for a wide variety of search tasks such as estate agents for house selection and for marriage bureaux and even material or component selection. It can also be used in computer form, as witnessed by computer dating.

A system such as the one described was demonstrated at the RIBA in 1968. This type of system can be used not only for the retrieval of data but also for the stimulation of ideas. Solutions often drop from the pack or the computer which would not otherwise have been considered. The matrix can also be used in the form of a morphological chart.

Jones (1970) explains the use of such a system in finding a solution to a space heating problem. Choose functions which are reasonably independent of each other and make sure that no essential functions are omitted. Set these down on the left-hand side of the chart:

(1) Air temperature to give body satisfaction
(2) Radiant temperature to avoid cold sensations from windows, etc.
(3) Air movement to provide necessary ventilation without draughts
(4) Humidity control to avoid condensation or dry throats
(5) Temperature gradient control to avoid hot heads and cold feet

In the other direction subsolutions are listed against these functions. These alternative ways of satisfying the problems should be as all embracing as possible (see Figure 49). A route may be chosen through the alternative provisions and a new solution possibly selected.

Morphological charts are intended to force divergent thinking and to safeguard against the possibility of overlooking alternative solutions to a design problem. Clearly, in using this approach manually, the matrix must be kept quite small because even a 10 by 10 matrix produces, 10,000,000,000 sets, whereas with the use of a computer, together with some additional techniques, the problem of size need not be so acute, as we shall see later. Also, it will be seen that three-dimensional and multiple matrices are also possible.

In both types of example, the very great danger, in both human and mechanical methods, lies in the fact that each criteria not only exists but also has its own weighting and may be overlooked. It is not sufficient to have a list of needs to be satisfied alone, because we give different values to these needs. One method of weighting which may be used is the possibility of putting loading factors on to certain parts of the search. For example, our total list of requirements for a new car do not always hold equal value. A designer also sometimes finds that he has been struggling with a client's requirement which he later finds to be of low importance, whereas it was given to him on an equal level of priority as other criteria. Another method is to organize the order of search. A third is to use the mathematical technique of fuzzy sets which is a mathematical means of handling imprecisely defined boundaries of information.

These aspects of loading or preferences in making searches contain an important philosophical and social problem. It is easy for an architect to forsake, for example, maintenance costs in the search for low capital cost or energy considerations in the search for visual stimulus, but at least that particular danger is confined to one architect at one time. If such a bias is

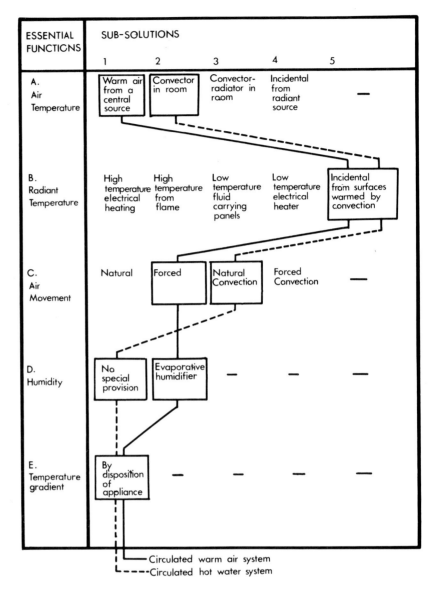

ESSENTIAL FUNCTIONS	SUB-SOLUTIONS				
	1	2	3	4	5
A. Air Temperature	Warm air from a central source	Convector in room	Convector-radiator in room	Incidental from radiant source	—
B. Radiant Temperature	High temperature electrical heating	High temperature from flame	Low temperature fluid carrying panels	Low temperature electrical heater	Incidental from surfaces warmed by convection
C. Air Movement	Natural	Forced	Natural Convection	Forced Convection	—
D. Humidity	No special provision	Evaporative humidifier	—	—	—
E. Temperature gradient	By disposition of appliance	—	—	—	—

———— Circulated warm air system
- - - - Circulated hot water system

Figure 49

built into a computer or any other system, it may last for a long time. *It is therefore essential that we learn about and take notice of the mechanisms of choice.* As individuals, we hold our own prejudices, but *architects and computer programmers can impose their own prejudices on others for a long time to come.* It is therefore surprising how little interest is taken in the systems which are increasingly being used or even imposed upon society.

Computer systems are being developed for the search for cars, houses, wives, companions, holidays, and so on, and increasingly these have become commonly accepted tools—except, of course, in the construction industry. The construction industry in general, and architects in particular, rather than using matrix searches tend to be committed to using hierarchical search structures. But apart from being complex in operation for both the user and the information handler, they also tend to require a knowledge of what one is looking for before one begins, when the search in design is often a search for the unknown. In the matrix search, any item can be considered a high priority in the search. In a hierarchical search the path is already predetermined.

The brain seems to have both of these capabilities, plus a third:

(1) Hierarchical layout of the brain
(2) Matrix-type search capability
(3) Long- and short-term memory

We can actually feel these characteristics in ourselves. We could mentally follow in our minds the hierarchical structure of the Royal Family, or our own family, as progeny develop from progeny. We can also feel within ourselves the capacity to search crosswise through our data banks. For example, we find

Italy under politics via Garibaldi
Italy under holidays via Portofino
Italy under geography via Mediterranean
and so on

We can in fact enter into our brain a search pattern similar to that described for the car earlier.

Example: Where shall we go for a holiday?

(a) Somewhere cheap
(b) Somewhere sunny
(c) Somewhere to get to by air
(d) Somewhere where they speak Fnglish

Solution: Malta or Gibraltar

This same method is used for much of what we call creativity. The third factor we know about our brain is its ability to hold information for a short period before deciding whether to put it into the long-term memory bank. We can also feel this, but in any case it is proved beyond doubt by scientific research. People who have been concussed, for example, can remember what happened immediately after an accident but can remember nothing half an hour later. Obviously this is an energy-conserving device to reduce storage in the brain. It would therefore seem desirable to try to obtain the best method of using all these devices and for this it might be worth making some comparisons with language, which is the medium for transmitting, and probably conceiving, these qualities.

For this we need to understand at least some of the linguist's terminologies. (The philosophical problems of using words to explain the brain's use of words should be noted but cannot be discussed here.) Language consists of a set of components (dictionary of words) and a set of rules (syntax). Meaning is then conveyed by

| *Icon* | a signifier which resembles the signified |
| *Index* | establishes a causal relationship between the signifier and the signified |

Sign	the relationship between the signifier and the signified
Syntagmatic plane	relationship defined by adjacency
Paradigmatic plane	relationship founded on substitution
Denotation	verbal equivalent for the sign
Connotation	meaning of the sign within the observer's ideology

Vitrivius was also aware of many of these characteristics in a visual sense. Dunster (1976) also uses town planning, architecture, and tourism for an illustration (Figure 50).

TOWN PLANNING

		PARADIGM	CATEGORIES OF SIGN
SYNTAGM	LONDON	PARIS	CAPITAL CITY
	MALL	CHAMPS ELYSEES	LONG AXIS
	ST. JAMES' PARK		LANDSCAPE
	BUCKINGHAM PALACE	LOUVRE	AXIAL NEO-CLASSICAL BUILDING
	VICTORIA MONUMENT	ARC DE TRIOMPHE	FOCUS OF AXIS

TABLE I: syntagms and paradigms

SIGNS	DENOTATION		CONNOTATION
CAPITAL CITY	CENTRE OF COUNTRY	REPRESENTATION OF STATE IDEOLOGY	CONTAINMENT
LONG AXIS	STRAIGHT ROAD		STABILITY
LANDSCAPE	ORDERED NATURE		ORDER
AXIAL NEO-CLASSIC BUILDING	ORDERED BUILDING		ORDER
FOCUS OF AXIS	START/FINISH		CERTAINTY

TABLE II: denotation and connotation

ARCHITECTURE

		PARADIGM	CATEGORIES OF SIGN
SYNTAGM	MALL	REGENT'S PARK	PLACE
	CARLTON TERRACE	HANOVER TERRACE	NEO-CLASSICAL TERRACE OPPOSITE PARK
	ADMIRALTY ARCH	MEWS ENTRANCE ARCH	ARCH AS CLOSER
	X	X	WHITE STUCCO

TABLE III: syntagms and paradigms

SIGNS	DENOTATION		CONNOTATION
NEO-CLASSICAL TERRACE	ARCHITECTURE	ARCHITECTURE IDEOLOGY	HISTORICAL STYLE / CIVILISED LIVING
PARK	NATURE		TOWN + COUNTRY (RUS IN URBE)
ARCHES	ROMAN TRIUMPHAL ARCHES		PAST VICTORIES (HISTORY)
STUCCO	STONE		EXPENSIVE BUILDING (STABILITY)

TABLE IV: denotation and connotation

TOURISM

		PARADIGM	CATEGORIES OF SIGN
SYNTAGM	LONDON	PARIS	CITY SIGHTS
	ST PAUL'S	NOTRE DAME	CHURCH
	BUCKINGHAM PALACE	VERSAILLES	PALACE
	HOUSES OF PARLIAMENT	PALACE DE BASTILLE	HISTORY
	NATIONAL GALLERY	LOUVRE	CULTURE
	CHANGING OF THE GUARD	EIFFEL TOWER	NATIONAL CHARACTERISTIC

TABLE V: syntagms and paradigms

SIGNS	DENOTATION		CONNOTATION
CITY SIGHTS	REPRESENTATION OF THE CITY	NATIONAL ESSENCE IDEOLOGY	KNOW THE CITY
CHURCH	TOMBS OF GREAT MEN		HISTORY IS MADE BY GREAT MEN
PALACE	HEAD OF STATE		SEEING PALACE = SEEING HEAD OF STATE
HISTORY	THE PAST		THE PRESENT IS THE RESULT OF THE PAST
CULTURE	ART		CIVILISATION
NATIONAL CHARACTERISTIC	ENGLISHNESS OR FRENCHNESS		FOREIGNESS

TABLE VI: denotation and connotation

Figure 50

This now begins to suggest a structure for both a hierarchical and also a matrix system, and if we move from linguistics to the less complex zoosemiotics, it might be possible to create a very simplistic but recognizable architectural language of function. Style, being more complex, will be left until later.

At a functional level, the build-up of the *equivalent* of a simple sentence or a story in building from a set of words or components is comparatively simple. We desire shelter from the elements and therefore make an envelope of protection: Stage I (Figure 51). Having done that, we cannot get in or out, and so we must have an entrance/exit and, to preserve the envelope, a door: Stage 2. Now we have neither light nor ventilation with the door closed, and so a window is necessary: Stage 3.

Figure 51

The size and number of the window(s) and the door(s) can be varied, thereby varying the quantity of solid between. The holes (doors and windows) can be increased so that the walls almost disappear and become columns or piers. From here it becomes a problem of style, which in turn is a problem of all those things previously mentioned—rhythm, polyrhythm, repetition, discord, anagram, etc. Gradually a simple language of function builds up to a complexity of style because of the brain's need and desire to make games of visual data once the functional requirements for survival are satisfied. Style is the game we propose to play for and against.

This language of symbols can also be applied to spaces, as shown by work at present being developed by Musgrove, Hillier, and others. They suggest that spatial and social organizations are complementary, rather than the former being a reflection of the latter.

Hillier, Leaman, Stansall, and Bedford (1976) propose a language of symbols with which to analyse these interactions. They take a disk and a ring (Figure 52). If we consider each as an independent form, then it can be seen that not only is the ring an emergent structure of the disk but also that the disk is an emergent structure of the ring. Furthermore, if *d* is substituted for *c* in the case of the ring (i.e. if the ring is a *d*-object), then the object is a closed boundary, or enclosure (Figure 53(a)); which then

Figure 52

99

develops as shown in Figure 53(b). Although it is not proposed to develop here this particularly interesting piece of research, it does illustrate the possibility of also building up a language of socio/spatial patterns which have a relationship to both the social structure and its attitude to property, as portrayed in the following extract from Park (1974):

> An apparent general property of domain processes concerns all of these: *the larger a compact spatial aggregate becomes, the stronger must be the social structure which relates it to comparable aggregates across the carrier space.* The converse of this is a general proposition, argued by Sahlins (1974), that spatial fission occurs in the 'state of nature' to avoid the construction of an overstrong social structure.
>
> To illustrate the proposition itself, we may refer to recent work by Bradfield (1973). Among the Tallensi, the compact aggregates are small, familial compounds which never grow above a certain size. In such a case, a relatively weak social structure is adequate at the combination level, consisting more of symbolic and ritualistic arrangements than explicit sanctions. The villages of the Mende, on the other hand, where the compact aggregate is much larger, have much stronger secret societies (which Bradfield suspects may have to do with the emergence of social classes) which operate largely at the level of relations between villages. When considering towns, this development reaches a new level. The exigencies of relationships between settlements are such as to

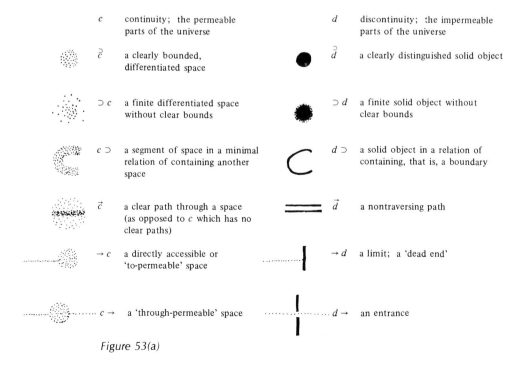

c	continuity; the permeable parts of the universe	
$\overset{\supset}{c}$	a clearly bounded, differentiated space	
$\supset c$	a finite differentiated space without clear bounds	
$c \supset$	a segment of space in a minimal relation of containing another space	
$\vec{c}$	a clear path through a space (as opposed to c which has no clear paths)	
$\rightarrow c$	a directly accessible or 'to-permeable' space	
$c \rightarrow$	a 'through-permeable' space	

d	discontinuity; the impermeable parts of the universe	
$\overset{\supset}{d}$	a clearly distinguished solid object	
$\supset d$	a finite solid object without clear bounds	
$d \supset$	a solid object in a relation of containing, that is, a boundary	
$\vec{d}$	a nontraversing path	
$\rightarrow d$	a limit; a 'dead end'	
$d \rightarrow$	an entrance	

Figure 53(a)

100

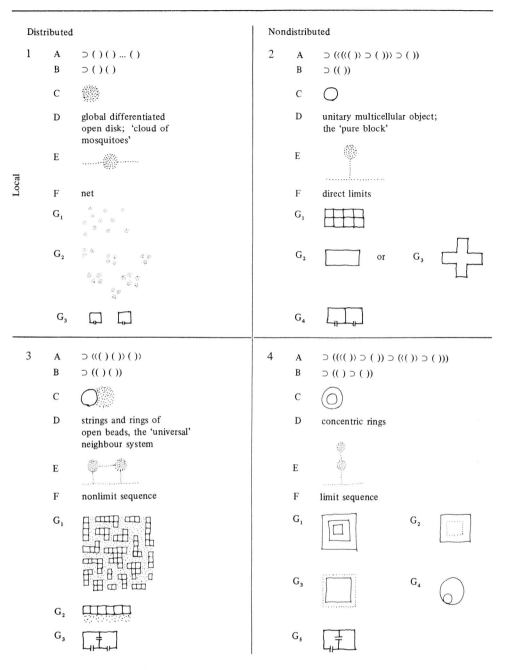

Distributed

1 A ⊃ ( ) ( ) ... ( )
   B ⊃ ( ) ( )
   C
   D global differentiated
      open disk; 'cloud of
      mosquitoes'
   E
   F net
   G₁
   G₂
   G₃

Nondistributed

2 A ⊃ (((( )) ⊃ ( )) ⊃ ( ))
   B ⊃ (( ))
   C
   D unitary multicellular object;
      the 'pure block'
   E
   F direct limits
   G₁
   G₂   or   G₃
   G₄

3 A ⊃ (( ) ( )) ( ))
   B ⊃ (( ) ( ))
   C
   D strings and rings of
      open beads, the 'universal'
      neighbour system
   E
   F nonlimit sequence
   G₁
   G₂
   G₃

4 A ⊃ (((( )) ⊃ ( )) ⊃ (( )) ⊃ ( )))
   B ⊃ (( ) ⊃ ( ))
   C
   D concentric rings
   E
   F limit sequence
   G₁   G₂
   G₃   G₄
   G₅

Local

Figure 53(b) Part 1

transform the within-settlement social structure into the embryonic form of a class structure. . . . Urban societies are essentially based on the primacy of man-to-nature relations, the division of labour, the compacting of space, and the consequent increase in the strength of a sanctions-based social order.

101

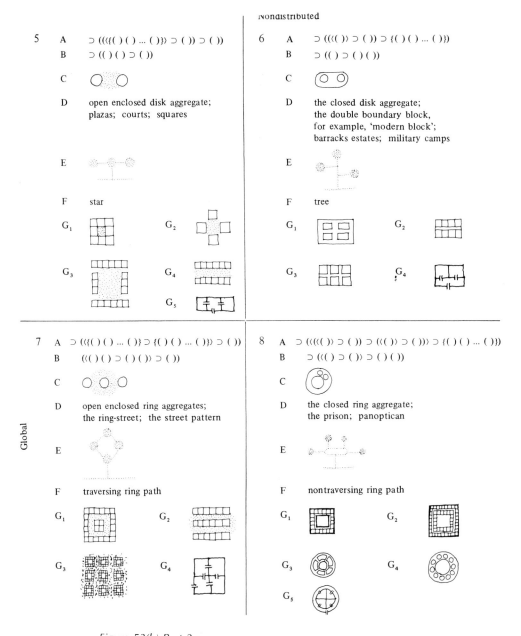

Figure 53(b) Part 2

Another aspect of visual language which is being developed is shape grammar. This provides a means for the recursive specification of shapes. They are similar to the phrase structure grammars developed by Chomsky for language, but developed over an alphabet of shapes to generate a language of shapes, instead of an alphabet of symbols to generate a language of sequences of symbols. It is dangerous to read too much into a limited series of tests, but it may be worth noting at this point the tests made by Birkhoff (1933) and Eysenck (1968) to see whether there were greater preferences for some shapes than others (Figure 54).

Figure 54 Polygons used to test preferences by Birkhoff (1933) and Eysenck (1968). The best-liked ones are included in the group on the left, and the least-liked ones in the group on the right. In each case those on the left of the rows were the most preferred. The disliked figures are simple and familiar and have few non-parallel sides. The liked figures are unfamiliar, have non-right angles and many non-parallel sides

One of the problems that becomes increasingly critical as a society grows and becomes more complex is the need for obtaining a consensus as a basis for making decisions. In recent years there have been developed a number of techniques and methodologies to assist this problem, one of these is the Delphi method. There are many different interpretations of the system but the one chosen here is now described. Some of the weaknesses of committees have already been mentioned, but another is the problem of dominance by an individual because of status, personality, etc. The effect of these characteristics in people can influence the direction, character, and validity of a discussion in a committee-type situation. Not only can deliberate strategies be employed, such as a planned diversion of a discussion into a particular direction, but similar imbalances can be caused, even with the best of intentions. Therefore the Delphi technique in its various forms allows each 'expert' to give his opinion or view on a particular problem anonymously and in isolation. Each 'expert's' answer is passed to all the others so that each expert can modify his viewpoint in the light of the new information provided (without personality pressure), and the process is then repeated over and over again. One such exercise in Japan for a prediction for a ten-year period involved 4,000 experts for six months.

The process can be a long drawn out one with traditional methods, but with a computer and an appropriate number of terminals, the problems can be interactively discussed at great speed, subject of course to an adequate program.

There are other models, computer based or otherwise, which can be used for consensus, forecasting, and monitoring. A few are listed below, some of which will be referred to later in applications:

(1) Abt model: computer-assisted scenarios
(2) Braille (Balanced Resource Allocation Information for Logical Evaluation)
(3) Cross impact matrix: interactions between pairs of alternatives examined in turn to produce synthesis

(4) Decision trees: network indicating the interrelationship of action choices and giving results of alternative actions
(5) Functional array: structural device for organizing factors such as environment and technologies into graphical presentation
(6) Fusfeld model: correlates technological progress with cumulative production quantities
(7) Gompertz law: analogy to economic growth; forecast by analogy
(8) Hartman model: assumes information gain is proportional to information available
(9) Leontief model: analysis and measurement of connections between the producing and consuming sectors of the national economy
(10) Lenz learning model: dynamic simulation relating developments to facilities and restraints
(11) Macro (Methodology for Allocating Corporate Resources to Objectives)
(12) Morphological analysis: structuring device for systematic cataloguing of possible opportunities (see above)
(13) Pattern (Planning Assistance Through Technical Evaluation of Relevance Numbers)
(14) Probe: modified Delphi system to map technical future
(15) Quest (Quantitative Utility Estimates for Science and Technology)
(16) Scenarios: a projection of the future
(17) Seamans' model: predicts technological progress as a function of the number of competitors
(18) Technology scanning: grid on which systems goals are arrayed against solutions
(19) Torque (Technology Or Research Quantitative Evaluation)
(20) Trend extrapolation: forecast based on development of historic time and series

There are other types of models such as the catastrophe theory already mentioned which give a geometrical topology and which may be used even for the projection of emotions (Figure 55).

Another form of mathematical model is dimensional coordination. This is usually dismissed as an oversimplistic and unnecessary discipline, even though it has a long architectural heritage. This disinterest is particularly unfortunate at a time when the best creative brains are needed for its architectural development. It is one of the most complex of mathematical problems and has been the basis of all architecture since the beginning of time.

It is surprisingly difficult to design a building which is not dimensionally coordinated, but yet most architects feel that they need not or should not use such a system. At one time architects used mathematical frameworks as a stimulus and structure for their design, but, as suggested in Chapter 2, there are recent historical reasons why architects often feel today that the use of such valuable tools is inartistic. At the same time, however, they are constrained by physical dimensions of standard components and building or other regulations, as well as structural necessity. This often means that even when a national discipline is rejected, an office or personal discipline is used as a structure for the

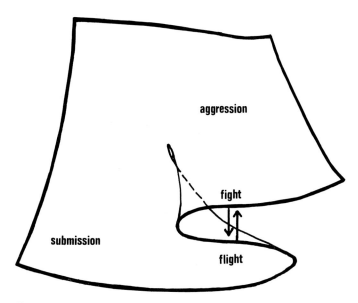

aggression

fight

submission

flight

Figure 55

design process. At the earliest sketch scheme stage, the grid basis is not only present in the subconscious but gradually intrudes more and more until it provides the basis for the integration of the spaces and the theoretical framework for the structure and components. As every student knows, at the production drawing stage the lines acquire thickness, and this is where the problems start (Figure 56). If components had no thickness, junctions and intersections would not constitute a problem for anyone. Even when the thickness of walls, for example, is accepted, there is still the problem of their relationship to the grid (Figure 57).

This building and design problem is also relevant to data-storage

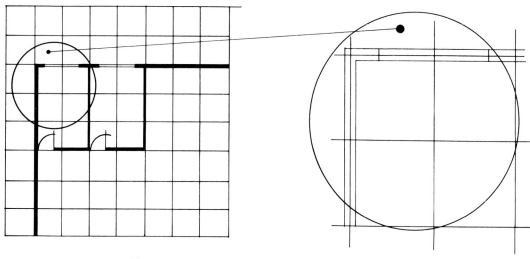

Figure 56

105

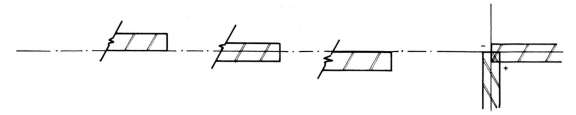

Figure 57

methodologies because data need to be held in discrete packages. If the information packages sometimes overlap and sometimes they do not touch, it is not even possible, as in building, to saw a piece off or fill up the gap with mastic. Just as the High Street bank computer holds everyone's account as a discrete entity for computational manipulation, so must a building methodological system hold information in discrete forms. Unfortunately, a long period of indiscipline in which functions and components were dealt with on an *ad hoc* basis has left a heritage which creates great difficulties for both data-handling systems and the industrialization of components. There are a number of different ways of looking at the problem in both cases:

(1) To use an infinitely small unit of measure, so small that the gaps and overlaps can be ignored. Sand and cement might be used as an example, but bricks or even shuttering for concrete may not. It is therefore an impracticable system in building and beyond consideration in terms of cost for data.
(2) To use larger components and thereafter create a method for dealing with the junctions. (The scale of this problem should not be underestimated.)
(3) To use a closed system of building and data components which must always fit together however they are used.

As most architecture is orthogonal in drawn, if not visual, form, there is little need for type (1), except for the work of architects like Goff and Utzon, etc. Type (2) is the most commonly used in various traditional ways and (3) has been to an increasing degree because of the cost advantages in the prefabrication of factory-made components.

In order to try and find a solution to the problem, a number of recommendations for the coordination of dimensions in buildings have been produced. These have usually recommended zones within which components should be contained (Figure 58). From these preferred dimensions shapes can be made which can become a language of symbols (Figure 59). These may or may not be identified with the component, but they do provide a framework for data manipulation enabling a dimensionally coordinated building to be theoretically designed as a spatial concept if the symbols are given height. This spatial concept can now have components and materials inserted as required, and as the library of data for these items can contain, on a comparative basis, data on cost and performance, etc., a variety of alternatives can be tried out. As we shall see in the next chapter, a computer makes the task

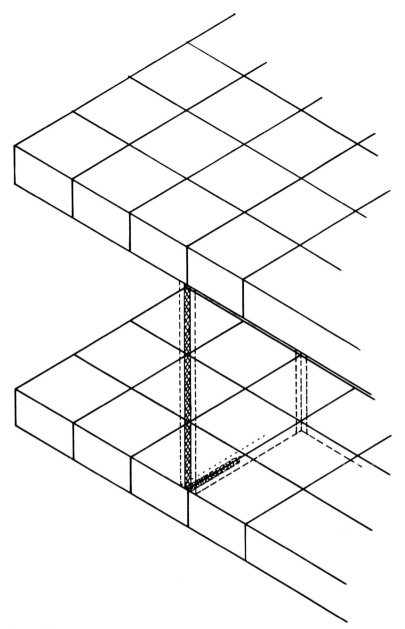

Figure 58

easier. If we want to incorporate shape, such as a pitched roof, clearly the model becomes more complex, but fundamentally these principles must apply, no matter how sophisticated they become, if data are to be economically handled.

The problems of data handling and component production are remarkably similar. The problems of free shapes are applicable to both, i.e. increased cost and time penalties which result in the need to balance the advantages and disadvantages of discipline and indiscipline. In almost all products in the industrialized countries of the world, the problem has

107

Figure 59

been resolved by having leaders of fashion who operate completely outside the discipline of industry but within strong personal limits—in other words, 'playing hard against the game they have set up for themselves'. An example of this is the haute couture clothes designer, specialist car designer, food and drink connoisseur, etc.

These specialists either tease out the fashion to which society is sensing its way or, if they fail, disappear into oblivion. The successful ideas are reinforced in the brain by the methods already suggested and are then converted by industry into standard methodologies for mass production. The end-product is in fact a potential for choice by permutation which is quite unknown in a primitive society. Even a cursory look at an industrialized society shows the extraordinary variety of personal expression in clothes, food, and so on. This is because of the availability of a wide variety of cheap components which are themselves products of long production lines of limited variety. On the other hand, less privileged societies also have less freedom of choice (except perhaps for the very rich) because short production runs which are also labour intensive only produce a small range of fairly standard products.

Architecture and building is one of the few products, if not the only one, which has not followed the course of mass production with enthusiasm. In fact building is not seen as a product at all, and this may yet be seen to be a problem to be resolved. A mobile home comes from a product-orientated industry and therefore has certain tools available to it which will be described in the succeeding chapters, whilst architecture generally is a design-orientated industry with very often different tools. Modern architecture assumes that the architect for each project sets his own style and has a large proportion of the component range especially designed for that building whilst using its own dimensional standards, even though the reality is quite different.

If all the other industries have found such couturier designing and craft manufactures too expensive for general consumption, why is it that system building and traditional building often appear to be comparable in cost? There appear to be a number of reasons for this.

(1) Because at least half of the work of the industry comes from the one-off market, manufacturers subsidize their one-off components with the profits of the standard components. It is necessary for them to tempt the one-off market whilst the standard market has little choice. However, if the balance tipped towards industrialized or rationalized systems, the change in costing would probably be dramatic.

(2) Because the industry has been used to their standards being modified and altered by the architect whose training as a creative person makes him want to change and create new items, they accept modifications without demur, and staff and cost their organizations on the basis of interrupted production lines. This largely puts them into the same position as a one-off contractor, and sometimes worse.

It is like throwing specials into any mass-production line—chaos and a return to semi-traditional ways quickly emerges.

(3) All architect-designed buildings are classified as architecture, whether they be the Beaubourg centre or a suburban house, a hospital or an infill housing scheme in a conservation area. But this is as absurd as putting one-off cars into the Fiat production car system as well as servicing and repair work on the same flow lines. Furthermore, to combine the education and training of all three together seems to court disaster.

(4) The industry as a whole has very little experience of the investment of capital and its return on production, as it is an essentially low capital industry which has been encouraged by government interference with building expenditure.

By its very nature, some aspects of building are different from those of other industries but, nevertheless, there are also many comparisons. First, there are leaders of architectural fashion carrying out designs which not only suggest new trends but act as symbols. Second, there are 'clear site'-type projects for housing, education, health, and so on, for which there is little reason why they should not be more economically and efficiently produced by industrialized means, provided that they are designed to adequate standards and either keep abreast of or ahead of fashion. Unfortunately architects have largely ignored the design and manufacturing processes of industrialized building because it appears to lack creativity, whilst the industrialized building manufacturers themselves have usually felt it desirable to economize on their design staff. Third, there is the category of buildings which includes infill conservation and complex building projects which should be design orientated, and for which different educational standards and different production standards are needed.

All three categories need good designers to create the game and they also need enthusiastic players with appropriate expertise but not necessarily the same training. This means specialization in architectural and building education. All three categories will also have to learn to use some of the new methods described, as well as further new tools as they become available. All need some common language, but a more complex language than we have ever used before or have even been able to use before. Also, there will be a need to give up the simple geometrical models of Euclid and others, and start to use the new mathematical models which are emerging. The increasing complexity and expansion of society will inevitably need the use of these models and tools, and for this it is necessary to consider what is available or likely to be available.

Chapter 5
THE TOOLS

From earliest times, man has developed tools to supplement his body muscles. This development was stimulated by the concepts of the Renaissance in which the Universe was expressed as a giant mechanism. This then led to the crescendo of the Industrial Revolution, based not only on this belief but also on the work of the anatomists. Also from earliest times, there is evidence that man supplemented his mental abilities with tools, from pebbles in sand trays, knots in ropes, marks on pottery, and eventually devices such as Napier's rods and various mechanical machines from Pascal (1623–1662) to Babbage (1792–1871). But in spite of this concept that the physical world was like a machine, art, together with the spiritual world, was thought of as something else, and therefore the few tools that there were for assisting the mind were still directed towards simple arithmetical problems. It was not until 1950 when Eckert and Mauchly produced a machine known as UNIVAC I, which was the first commercially produced electronically operated stored program computer, that a totally new concept began to emerge. Just as the early anatomists, in dissecting the body, had influenced the emerging designers of machines, an influence which continues to this day, so did the psychologists, brain researchers, and philosophers begin to influence the emerging computer industry. The translation of the brain's activity into computer programs has only started in earnest comparatively recently, several hundred years after the translation of the body's physical properties to machines began in earnest; however, the speed of development has been much greater. The electronic computer in its many forms is therefore moving quickly beyond the realms of arithmetical calculations and developing towards the world of artificial intelligence. But first it is necessary to look at some of the activities which have led to the present situation.

As already mentioned, new concepts of space in the Renaissance required a new mathematics to cope with the increased scope and speed of calculations. Roman numerals had to give way to Arabic numerals for the obvious reason that Roman numerals are extremely difficult to handle in large quantities and at speed. Similarly, and for the same reason, Arabic numerals are now giving way to binary, even though some new developments in computing allow the use of Arabic numerals. Although binary was known to have been used in the sixteenth century, it is its use with the electronic digital computer which has helped to create a new revolution. Its use with computers for communication purposes can perhaps be thought of as an incredibly fast form of Indian smoke signal.

The electronic computer itself has also been going through some dramatic changes in its short life. The first important step was the change from the brilliant but mechanical computers of Babbage and others, through electrically driven mechanical computers, to electronic computers using electrical impulses as the basis of calculation. At first radio valves were used, later to be replaced by planar silicon transistors. Then printed circuits replaced unreliable copper wiring which were in turn developed to monolithic integrated semi-conductors and solid-state electronics.

Whilst these technicalities are of no more interest to the architect and layman than knowledge of how the telephone or the television works, the important thing was that these developments had the effect of

(1) reducing the cost,
(2) reducing the need for special computer environment,
(3) reducing size,
(4) increasing power, and
(5) increasing reliability.

During this period of change, an understanding of the real problems to be solved in society generally began to emerge.

At first in the 1950s there was the oversell of the 'electronic brain' in which the media gave the impression that the new world had already arrived. This was immediately followed by public disllusionment due to the unreliability of the machines, inexperience in programming, and general fear of the computer taking them over as a 'big brother'. Whilst a lot of this still remains, the computer has relentlessly crept into every aspect of our lives, to such an extent that if they all stopped working at once, there would for most people be no pay, no transport, no entertainment, and so on. Increasingly, and with little fuss, industry and commerce have developed complex and sophisticated computer systems, and even the general public have bought them for their homes, children, and small businesses (over 30,000 costing less than £1,000 were bought in 1978 alone in the United Kingdom). At the same time, the professions have been hardly influenced at all, in spite of great efforts to promote interest by governments. Whilst it is true that programs developed by local authorities such as West Sussex County Council (Ray-Jones, 1968), hospital boards (e.g. OXSYS), and government departments (CEDAR) and others described by Cross (1977) were in general use for a long time, not only has the work tended to be developed in small pockets but a number have also largely disappeared. Unlike Brunulleschi and Alberti who had been so excited by the new mathematics that it stimulated them into totally new spatial concepts, the architect today has often seen the computer as a threat to his art, even though that art could not be defined and even though a lot of his work is not in this category. Even amongst the enthusiasts of what is often and unfortunately called computer-aided architecture, the question was seldom asked as to what was architecture anyway. What was it that was being aided? The inherited view of art-architecture was taken for granted and systems were developed to try to simulate the traditional methods. Even allied professions without the problems of art, such as quantity surveyors, became disillusioned with computer solutions because in trying to replicate manual methods they were usually uneconomic, as one might have anticipated. Then, as previously explained in Chapter 2, in the early 1970s many different factors came together to disrupt even the small progress which had been made. By 1977 few of the original systems had survived unscathed and those that had were fighting against fairly heavy odds. Apart from desultory correspondence in the architectural press, the computer was hardly mentioned by the architectural profession in 1978, at a time when the microprocessor was expected to change everyone's lives. Will the development of the microprocessor make things any different? In order to answer this question and to appreciate the possibility of its potential impact, it is necessary to understand a few very simple computing principles.

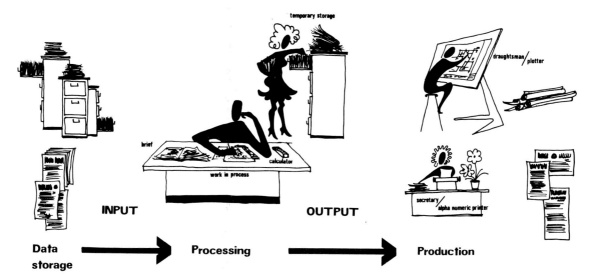

Figure 60

Imagine a person sitting at a desk on which there is a calculator, his brief or instructions, writing paper, and a filing tray. In a computer this compares with the processor. The calculator constituting the arithmetic, the brief or instructions, the logic, and the filing tray compares with the temporary short-term storage. He and the processor now both need an input of data, which in the case of the man is stored in filing cabinets. He also needs output, which can be a typist with her typewriter or an electronic printer. If he has not organized his data input he will have to spend a long time sorting through his files and papers. The calculator will speed up his calculations providing that his instructions are clear and logical. If not, it may speed up chaos. He uses his logic to process the data and puts the processed data into his filing tray as a temporary storage which his secretary collects and turns into a respectable output format.

113

There have been great developments over the last twenty years in both the input and output devices, but it is the processor which is the subject of the big revolution at present, and probably will be for some time. In the early 1970s this processor, which had already been reduced in size and cost over the twenty-year period, began to be produced on a chip of silicon about 5 mm square and about 0.1 mm thick. In 1971 the first standard commercially produced microcomputer was produced which incorporated both this microprocessor and a small amount of peripheral circuitry—the Intel 4004. But the computer industry which had been used to working on large mainframe and minicomputer installations only saw these new cheap microcomputers as toys, and even as late as the mid 1970s they were left to the do-it-yourself enthusiast market as they believed they constituted no threat.

Incredibly, the bomb was ticking but was ignored. Already the computer establishment had become resistant to change. This included many researchers who were reluctant to give up their hard-won mainframe and minicomputer programs. The belief seemed to be that something as cheap as the price of a very low-priced car and yet which claimed to be as powerful as quite large computers costing many times as much could not be good. There were, however, a number of factors which only slowly began to dawn on even the computer specialists.

The microprocessor, far from being a toy for laymen and children *had* to become big business. The silicon-chip technology which had formed the basis of the pocket calculator industry and which turned to digital watches when that market was saturated now turned its attention to the computer industry. By 1976 there were approximately fifty-six different types of microcomputers on the market and yet there was hardly a single business application written for them. Not only was the establishment uninterested in the new product, but the public was a little chary of the new microprocessor age that the media was presenting, having been bitten once by the 'electronic brain' campaign.

But the size and power of the silicon-chip industry was too great to be held back by prejudices. The existing installed computer base was much too trivial to sustain the high-volume production lines required by the industry. Therefore the microprocessor must be seen not just in its application to the existing mainframe and minicomputer market but as a development which must create, by its nature, new markets in the creative, administrative, and processing aspects of architecture, and the manufacture of components with which it is constructed.

The cost of computer hardware may well be reduced by 50 per cent every five years for some time. However, software costs may well increase, giving a slower decrease overall. The software will cover vastly superior services, e.g. advanced interactive facilities between microprocessors and mainframes. In the case of data-storage devices such as disks, the introduction of floppy disks has offered a better price-per-byte raio and a lower original capital cost.

The situation is very fluid and the edges between mainframe, minicomputer, and microcomputer types becomes blurred as all now use the same type of component (silicon chip). The concept of a 370/168 processor on a chip was at one time considered to be a joke. Now the

114

hardware logic of an early 370/168 is now available on a few chips. Therefore, for some time, the cost of a computer installation is likely to be dominated by the cost of its peripherals. The other factor is the software.

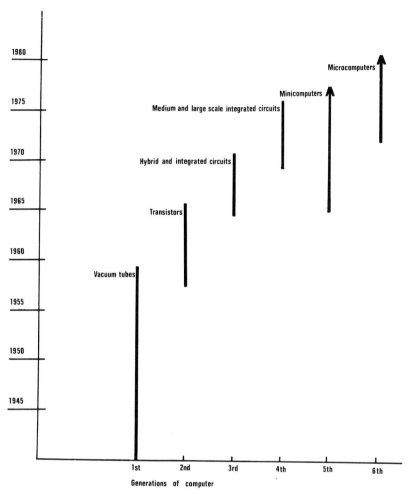

Figure 61

Since the existing computer market only represents one month's microprocessor production capacity, there is unlikely to be adequate software support for some time. This means that there will be various approaches to the problem of software:

(1) A need for low-cost high-volume programs which will be produced by the large manufacturers of all types of computers
(2) The continued and expanded role of the software houses in preparing programs for particular applications as well as basic software
(3) An increased quantity of personal programming which at first will be comparatively expensive, but may later reduce and become simpler with the introduction of cheaper and improved fault-finding and debugging devices

At the cheapest end of the market will be the microprocessor-based

115

Figure 62 Experimental Micro-computer 1976, University of Reading

microcomputers such as that created at the Department of Construction Management, University of Reading. Whilst these are slower than their traditional counterparts, in this sense speed is comparative. Whilst a mainframe may actually carry out operations at a phenomenal speed, it is of little value if you cannot get access to it. In any case, for many processes it is rather like a motorway speeding you along to the next hold-up. Even the slower microcomputers are usually fast enough for most architectural processes. However, it is the advantages which are important:

(1) Cheapness—within the price capability of the smallest office
(2) No special environment needed
(3) Can even run on car batteries
(4) Simple programming can be used which can be learned in a day
(5) Program packages for sale at a price comparable with radio cassette recordings

For a few pounds we can already purchase network programs, diary programs, linear regressions programs, personal cash-flow programs, etc. At a higher price, more complex programs such as the heat-loss analysis of buildings are increasingly becoming available. The RIBA is probably one of the first Institutes to start selling such packages, including desk-top computers, and these will undoubtedly multiply.

The RIBA package is based on a Texas T1/59 programmable calculator with a PC100B print cradle. The program calculations have been developed for the following outputs in the first instance:

'G' value—design heat loss and average heat loss
Gross space-heating energy consumption—empirical method
Gross space heating energy consumption—degree day method
'U' values for wall, floor, and roof up to eight layers
Condensation risk

Both energy-consumption calculations allow for solar and internal gains, but do not provide for air-conditioned buildings. The package has been criticized for not being precise enough in its evaluation, but we need to question the level of accuracy required for any given problem. The manuals are very competent and comprehensive.

The market for this type of work will dramatically increase to provide facilities which a few years ago were thought to be near impossible, and not only as programs but as microchips embedded in the systems. A microprocessor chip for speech input, for example, now only costs a few pounds and yet the money spent on computer speech research in the past has been astronomic.

The construction industry at the present time is largely made up of small professional and contracting units which in the past had little capital available for hardware, let alone programming back-up. This low capital investment and payment as work proceeds permits low profit levels. With the high cost of computing as it has been in the past, it has meant that a great deal of faith was needed for a big commitment to an idea. Now, it is possible to start with a very small commitment and see how it develops. Even for the larger organizations in the industry there is great advantage in

(1) reducing the need to concentrate power in one place—the computer section—and
(2) reducing the 'us' and 'them' syndrome.

As mentioned in Chapter 2, organizations have steadily grown larger and larger as they centralized their resources to improve communication. In fact, organizations are often still using this argument to support the construction of enormous monolithic halls of bureaucracy at a time when the need for the concentration of people is no longer necessary because of the improved capability for cheap communication.

Not only have there been changes in the hardware but there have also been changes in the software. Just as it has been seen that the brain needs an internal language of communication between its internal processes, so does the computer need a language for the same purpose. In the mid 1960s a computer language called BASIC (Beginners All-purpose Symbolic Instruction Code) was developed by Kemeny and Kurtz. This has come to be one of the most widely used programming languages of the many available. Its popularity is undoubtedly due to the ease with which the average person can learn enough of its rules to be able to use a computer effectively. Over the years, the language has been improved so that today the average person can learn it in a day. It is true that it is not a powerful enough language for large complex problems such as commercial processing, where COBOL (Common Business Orientated Language) might be used, or scientific and technical work, where FORTRAN 'FORmula TRANslator) might be used, or even PL/M as a high-level language for microcomputers. But nevertheless, the area that it will cover is substantial. Furthermore, most children in industrialized countries now leave school with an education in binary and BASIC, and will therefore be able to develop programs of their own. There have been other changes as well. Whereas the inputs and outputs of data and instructions to the processors of mainframe and minicomputers were often held on vulnerable tape or expensive disk, the new microcomputers can use either ordinary music cassettes or floppy disks which are very cheap. The floppy disks are similar to the gift records which can be sent through the post. Both the cassettes and floppy disks are not only cheap in terms of capital outlay but, more importantly, are easily posted or transported.

As well as programs being sold on these disks or cassettes, there are firms now selling the complete microcomputer built into a desk with programs, operating instructions, and forms. In other words, a 'black box' approach—an approach which will probably increase exponentially. Undoubtedly, although the architect spends the majority of his time on non-drawing activities for which these types of equipment can be a useful aid, he feels that until he can use it for drawing it will not really be of much use to him. Therefore it is necessary to consider the different forms of input to the computer.

As human beings we communicate by

(1) writing—alphanumerics—letters and numbers,
(2) drawing—graphics, and
(3) speech—aural symbols.

The first is the one which is most easily adopted by users as the input and output to a computer in alphanumeric form, as it is seldom dissimilar from an ordinary typewriter. In fact, when a typewriter incorporates a microprocessor it can become a word-processor or simple computer. The word-processor is bound to have a revolutionary effect on both practice and society because it can carry out, automatically, many of the operations for which secretarial and typing staff were employed. Not only can they produce endless standard letters, with or without variations and without supervision, but also produce a suite of coordinated documentation from one single command. Here, the needs of the best modern management techniques and, of course, the type of systematic methods described in the last chapter are desirable for the greatest success. For these, the simple methods of analysis described are usually sufficient, but for more complex operations than word-processing, more complex computers and more complex methods are needed. The limitations then become those of our own logic and language. Not only must we be able to analyse every detailed operation in a system and set it down as we would a theorem, but the language must have a known value.

The same applies to the second category—graphics. Many cheap microcomputers either have their own screen or can be plugged into a black and white or colour television screen. Drawing on these screens is done either by means of a four-button control or a joystick control, which sends a cursor up, or down, or left, or right. In either case, the cursor leaves a symbol trace when the control is used in conjunction with an instruction at the alphanumeric keyboard. In other words, it will leave a trace of letters or other symbols. It is an easy matter, either by buying or writing a simple program, to draw any two-dimensional shape or two-dimensional drawing of a three-dimensional shape.

There is a problem which is so simple that it often goes unrecognized. An architect can draw a building shape in a completely free form; e.g. Bruce Goff's design for the Bavinger house in Norman, Oklahoma. But the line only contains a message regarding shape; as any surveyor knows, unless the line is related to some dimensioning system, it cannot be communicated, measured, or set out. A line such as that shown in Figure 63 would have to be set out on site from a grid, and, furthermore, the line would not contain any further information such as type of material, cost, thermal values, and so on.

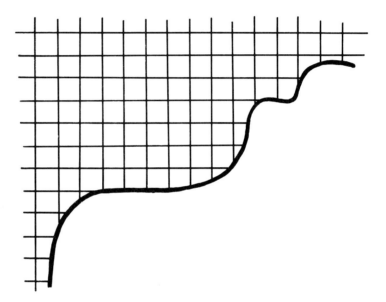

Figure 63

The type and quantity of materials have to be specified in alphanumeric form separately, and the costs, thermal values, etc., are obtained by specific measurements in separate operations—usually by other professions. The accuracy of such non-straight lines depends upon the number of measurements made. A circle, for example, consists of an infinite number of points, but to describe a circle by giving the position of each point would be impossible. And so either an algorithm, or descriptive formula, or the minimum number of straight lines is used to simulate the curve or circle when using a computer. This usually explains the odd-shaped '0's' used on electronic scoreboards, watches, and computer printouts. Storage of information costs money, on the one hand, whilst information about line is only as accurate as the measuring increments allow. This even applies to straight lines.

It is therefore obvious that if a grid of a known measure is assumed, it

119

would be possible both to describe the shape of the line as coordinates of the grid and also to use this pre-dimensional grid as a measure. It is also obvious that the larger the grid and the more the shapes are orthogonal to fit that grid, the easier it will be. The only inhibition against using non-orthogonal shapes is not any restriction caused by the system but in the cost of description. The processes of the manufacturer also impose cost penalties for similar reasons, which means that for reasons of economy of production and description, we live in a square world.

Therefore, if the screen is given an actual or theoretical grid, e.g. one cursor space, and a scale of values is applied to the grid, then a shape can be described by its relationships to that grid. If a language of symbols is then developed, the values and measurements can be applied to the symbols so that when they are applied to the grid they themselves can in turn be measured (e.g. see Figure 64). The position and direction of

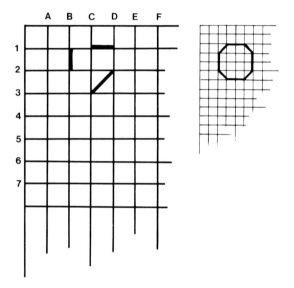

Figure 64

shapes can be described by numbers and letters on the grid in Figure 64 or as the distance from each axis. A circle or curved shape would be approximated according to the fineness of the grid. Each of the symbols in Figure 65 can now be programmed and produced on the screen and then manipulated as in a television game.

The manhole or unit-type symbols can be counted and located, and the lengths of linear symbols measured by the computer with reference to the

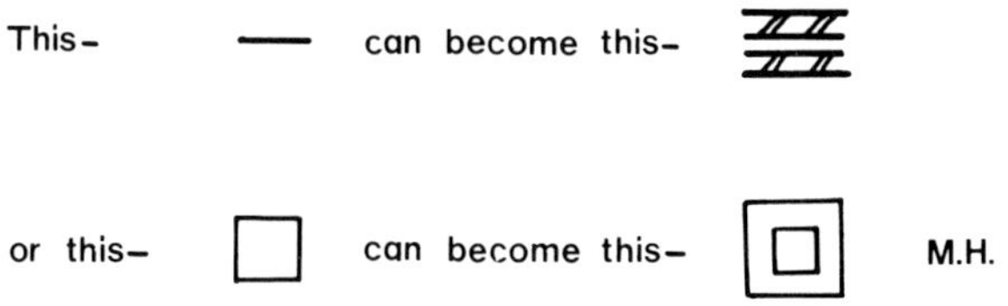

This– ——— can become this–

or this– ☐ can become this– ▣ M.H.

Figure 65

120

grid. If a linear symbol is made into a rectangular shape, the computer can have a simple program for measuring its area. If the linear symbol is given height, then volume can also be measured by a suitable simple program. Therefore, at this stage there is a means of measuring length, area, and volume.

None of these measurements have values, and this is where the real significance of computing begins to assert itself. The more information the computer can extract from simple lines the more economic the process becomes. Clearly, a library of information which related to these symbols and measurements would provide a valuable tool. If the manhole symbol had a price or the linear symbol had a thermal-loss value, the computer could make calculations as we drew. The problem is the unit of measure, and it is here that there are problems. First, to build up a library which could cope with any possible building shape would, as already shown, be infinitely expensive. Second, to restrict the library to orthogonal shapes raises the issue of building dimensional coordination, with the attendant problems of functions and interfaces.

Therefore, one way is to program the computer as shown in Figure 66.

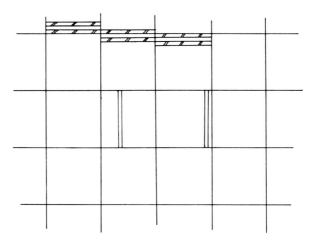

Figure 66

An external wall or internal partition, for example, need not be on a grid line to have a standard measurement length. The computer can be instructed to accept it in certain off or on grid positions, but because its relationship to the grid is known, it can be located and measured. It is therefore possible for a library of cost, performance, etc., to be built up on the basis of known lengths and, if desired, heights.

It is the intersections and corners when components have thickness, as illustrated in the last chapter, which create problems in the same way as they do in system building. If a system of zones is used, as recommended by the Dimensional Coordination papers, the corners and intersections can be anticipated and therefore put into an intersection and corner library. The danger is then that the wrong corner or the wrong intersection might be selected, and therefore a compatability program within the

121

computer is desirable. This will prevent the wrong corner or junction being used out of context.

At this stage it is now possible to create a library of symbols which are dimensionally related (Figure 67). For those who feel that this is getting a

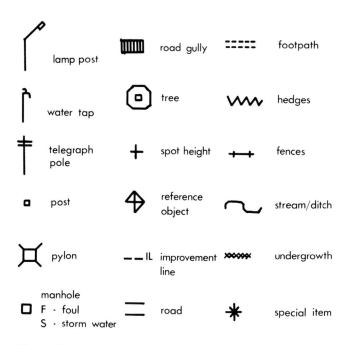

Figure 67

long way away from the art of architecture they might recall that Serlio, in his first book of architecture published in 1611, based his thesis on a development of the symbols shown in Figure 68, which he also related to a grid. However, the computer can do things with these symbols which Serlio may have wished to do, but which he was quite incapable of doing because of the time and quantity of data that would have been required. In fact it was because the architect could not quantify his drawings in terms of cost or performance that the client, in self-defence, began to employ measurers in the eighteenth century to cost the work. These measurers eventually became quantity surveyors, and other professions emerged for the purpose of measuring the performance of the other functions of the building.

Today, by assigning values to the symbols, the computer can give instant evaluation of decisions, thereby allowing the other professions to give an infinitely superior and different type of service. We can give each symbol or length of symbol a cost, or the quantity of material it would contain, or the amount of manpower expended in its execution, or plant needed, or thermal characteristics, or acoustic characteristics, etc. Once these are held in a library, the computer can then assess the information as the shapes are drawn on the screen and carry out instructed calculations to give total cost, heat loss, etc., almost instantaneously.

The library will be held by the computer as a full-scale model, and the

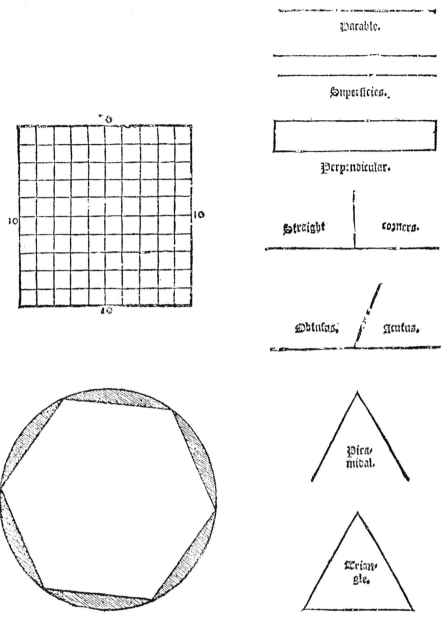

Figure 68

computer screen will represent an appropriately scaled-down version. In this it is very similar to the human brain which also holds our world as a model in the mind. Now that we have the means for holding a full-scale model of an orthogonal building in the computer it now becomes possible to give it other known rules such as those of perspective.

At this stage, we are on the threshold of handling buildings and experimenting with them as a mathematical model before they are built. But before exploring this, it is necessary to consider the third form of input/output device—speech.

123

For a long time it looked as though it would be impossible to produce cheap devices for speech input. However, it is now possible to buy a chip for a few pounds, which, together with some individual programming, provides another means of instruction to the computer. The reason for the difficulty in producing computer speech input was the problem of trying to dissect how it was produced by human beings. Even now there are still some areas where problems can arise.

Continuous speech	words are run together in ordinary speech
Multiple speech	different people say the same words differently
Limited vocabulary	error in recognition rates increase with the size of library
Noise	the transmission media corrupts the signal

However, in spite of these problems, speech is sufficiently far advanced for simple conversations with the machine. It may be useful to have some idea of how this is done. In English there are approximately forty basic types of sounds and these are used to construct the entire vocabulary. A code in the brain is translated by the central nervous system into neuromuscular signals which activate our articulators and speech-making apparatus. Speech is then produced from two sources:

(1) The voiced sounds made by the vocal chords producing periodic bursts of air
(2) The unvoiced sounds or fricatives made by forcing air through constrictions in the mouth

If the air is completely blocked for a moment the sound is called a stop.

Speech is composed of constant frequency components, which are the vowel formations, and noise bursts combined with frequency transients, for the consonants. With this knowledge the investigators into synthetic speech found that time differences of milliseconds of sound silence could be detected by the computer, as does the human ear, and it thereby was able to differentiate between different vowels and consonants. It is interesting to note that *intervals* are again such an important factor, as also noted in music and vision earlier. We constantly return to the point where visual and aural languages, and probably thinking, are based on a digital measurement of intervals which are measured against a learned standard. This shows an interesting comparison with

(1) the proposals suggested earlier for a grid as a basis of a library for evaluation and measurement and
(2) the philosophy of Wittgenstein.

It is now necessary to consider the output devices, or the equivalent of the secretary and the draughtsman. The equivalent of the secretary in her typing capacity is clearly the alphanumeric printer, which is in effect a very fast typewriter of varying degrees of technical complexity. The computer equivalent of the tracer/draughtsman and his drawing is a printer or plotter, which can locate the coordinates of the drawn line or symbol and produce a copy of the original which usually contains a mixture of letters, numbers, and drawing symbols. Apart from speed there are a number of differences between these two items and their human counterparts:

(1) Output devices are not normally confined to ordinary working hours and can continue through each twenty-four-hour period if necessary.
(2) They are very much faster.
(3) They are able to produce the output in a different format from the input.

The last is of particular importance to the construction industry. Because of numerous restrictions, such as time, the architect produces a drawing which is not necessarily his ideal, nor the measurement surveyor's, nor the engineer's, nor the contractor or subcontractor or craftsman. Because of the limitations of time and resources, he tries to produce a drawing which will on the average, be not ideal, but suit each one.

In addition to this, the architect produces drawings of a building as though it was already built, rather than as assembly drawings, even though they are often called assembly drawings. Perhaps this is partly due to the past heritage of training by measuring existing buildings for examination, but this must also be partly due to the heritage of the architect seeing himself as an artist and thereby leaving the responsibility for the construction of the building to the contractor. There is a long tradition of walking a delicate line between telling a contractor what to do, but not how to do it. Even design and build firms and consortia maintain the old conventions, even though it is adding unnecessary cost for them to do so. As the architect's responsibility for the design of a product is increased by law, the form of communication and drawings will have to change. This should be borne in mind when writing expensive programs. One change which can easily be accomplished is to program the computer to re-package the chosen input for personalized output. An architect may wish to draw all of the fixed and moveable furniture and fittings in a laboratory on one drawing; in order to do this, he scales up that portion of the building, but at the same time he confuses the plumber's needs with a lot of information which is useless to him. The plumber then has to hunt through a lot of drawings and a lot of useless (for him) data to find out his overall plan of work. But the architect cannot be expected to produce a drawing especially for every profession and trade. However, the computer, with appropriate instructions, will continue to re-sort the information and will instruct the plotter to produce all the appropriate drawings.

Just as the dyeline printer changed the architect's approach to drawing, as earlier the invention of paper, tee-square, set-square, carbon pencils, etc., had done, now the computer will undoubtedly have its effect. That is, of course, if a two-dimensional drawing is still to be used. It is rather extraordinary that a three-dimensional building is designed in two dimensions anyway, without even the use of traditional projections. Commercially produced third-dimensional inputs will no doubt be produced in which the x/y axes grid has the third grid (z) in depth, measured by aerials projecting from the two-dimensional surface. This three-dimensional input may well be developed with a three-dimensional hologram output, which will give the client, as well as the architect, a

125

better impression of the finished building than the present perspective or elevation.

Another device which is strangely underused is an optical reader, in which the computer is able to read off data for itself. For example, a statistical survey may involve the completion of standard forms by ticks and crosses. It is a long laborious task for an operator to type the data into a computer for further manipulation. An optical reader can process the information at a great rate by reading off the 'answers' in their known positions. Another form of this type of input is the use of laser beams in supermarkets which can not only 'read off' the prices on the packages to produce a bill for each customer but also enter the sale of the product into a management system which will send off a re-order instruction when stocks get low, as well as applying the data for other uses. Telephones can be used with the previously described speech-synthesis systems to provide input, and the computer can also produce speech-synthesized replies. The advantages and dangers in these systems will be dealt with later.

So far, the power of computers has not been mentioned because of the difficulty of doing so without using technical jargon. However, it might be possible to give some guides. The position at the present time is so fluid that it would be impossible to even suggest the different alternatives and potential available, but it may be helpful to recognize that, without going into more complex systems, it is possible to walk into a shop in most cities and buy over the counter a microcomputer which will have a power of 16 K or 32 K or 48 K, and with it a 116 K disk drive attachment. Up to ten of these disk drives can be operated from this one machine, thereby giving it a capability of 1,160 K continuous storage and a 48 K processor. The K = Kilo = 1,000 bytes of information, where each byte (8 bit in this case) consists of eight bits of information and where a BIT = BInary digIT is a binary coded information system, i.e. 0 or 1. This is more powerful than the larger computers many large organizations kept in huge air-conditioned rooms only a few years ago. This type of machine is not only no bigger than a typewriter but can also be connected to a television set for black and white or colour graphic input or output.

This is a considerable oversimplification of the situation for the specialist enthusiast with some special application, but may be a guide for architects, contractors, and other professionals who want to get started for the cost of a very cheap car. With the write-off value over five years it would be very difficult to lose money on such a purchase. Even the larger organizations can now break down their computing into local components rather than centralizing all their work, with the consequent effect that staff do not necessarily have to travel to a central point. Furthermore, it reduces the risk of centralized power, because this power should not be underestimated. There is a lot of concern about privacy of information, which is in any case already held on manual files, but there is little concern for the enormous centralization of a power which few can understand. It seems extraordinary that there has been such little concern for this aspect.

Groups of microcomputers can be linked together for multiple uses; the implications of this will be described later. Whilst there will be a long and continuing need for mainframe and minicomputer installations carrying out large processing operations, many large organizations will increasingly use a complex of smaller processing elements, each of which being dedicated to a particular task and yet being coordinated by a central computing resource. Many of these local users will have no more knowledge of the computer than they have of the telephone system at present. The important thing is for them not to abdicate their responsibility for making their requirements of the 'black box' known.

With regard to total computing power, it has been believed that we are limited in the ultimate power of computing by the internal signal flow, on the basis that no closed computer system, however constructed, can have an internal signal flow that exceeds mc^2/h bits per second (m is the total mass of the system, c is the velocity of light in vacuum, and h is Planck's constant). The microprocessor and other fundamentally new approaches may reduce this data highway problem. It will be recalled that the brain does not carry out all of its processing in one central computing centre, but delegates a lot of the processing to that part where the information is held. In this it has accomplished two things:

(1) Extreme miniaturization (being achieved by modern technology)
(2) A reduction of the data highway problem (being copied by modern technology)

It is interesting to see how microprocessor systems are now also replicating the activities of the brain. Fry Richardson, a mathematician, once suggested a fantasy in which the problem of using computers for weather forecasting was like taking over a theatre, but making the circles and galleries go right around the space, with the walls painted to form a map of the globe. In each seat a computer would work on the weather in that area in which it sits. The work of each group would be coordinated into regions which would then be coordinated at higher and higher levels, the results of computations being continuously shown. In the centre a conductor would keep all the regions at the same pace. This gives some 'picture' of the size of the problem for a central computer. In 1978, the European Centre for Medium Range Weather Forecasting at Reading predicted that a computer six times more powerful than an IBM 370/195 would be needed for accurate forecasting up to only ten days ahead. In the future, microprocessors in micro- and minicomputers might be considered for such models much in the same way as Fry Richardson envisaged.

Even at this early stage of microprocessor application it is possible to have interesting conversations with the computer in a number of different ways, and this raises the problem of man-machine interaction. There has been a lot of discussion on this point, and often arguments are raised against their use on this point alone.

But the issue is not as simple as it is often made out. Most people generally enjoy their interaction with their motorcar. Is this through indoctrination, usage, or (extremely unlikely) that someone designed the original cars with man–machine interaction in mind? Again it tends to raise the old issue of absolute values. Is equipment, or even a building, to be designed for what a person is now, or what he is expected to be and then allow him to grow into it? The old issues are constantly raised.

Another aspect of man–machine or person–machine interaction is what it teaches us about ourselves.

Evans of the National Physical Laboratory and Card of Southern Central Hospital, Glasgow, produced a system in which patients were interviewed by a terminal connected to a computer and their problems diagnosed. As with the art of architecture, we might expect that as the art of the consultant was missing the patient would be getting inferior treatment. Many tests were carried out to examine this point. One of these tests involved thirty-six patients in an alcoholic unit in which each patient was interviewed three times: once by computer, once by a registrar, and once by a consultant. The patients on average admitted to the computer that they drank 14 per cent more than they admitted to the registrar and 32 per cent more than they admitted to the consultant. There are many examples to show that we are more frank with a computer than with another human being, and in some cases there is a psychological relief similar to that of the religious confessional.

Although the example given is a medical one, there is clearly an application for eliciting the brief and client/user requirements or evaluating new building designs. If a series of such interrogation units are linked together through microcomputers, there would then be a potential for interactive brief and evaluation of design between several users.

Another tool, which is similar to one of Young's necessities in his comparison of the human body with a factory, is a computer diary program. With a real-time clock incorporated, it is possible to program items into the machine for some years into the future; the use for this will be seen in future chapters.

The computer is often blamed for producing large quantities of useless information, but the computer only carries out human instructions and so, clearly, care needs to be taken in the management of systems. For the most part, data are best contained within the machine for specialized output as it is required.

Earlier systems were often clumsily analysed and programmed without the involvement of senior management, who saw themselves in the position of critics. This is the worst possible situation, for management is the only group who can impart the policy of the organization and coordinate the whole. It is easy to computerize the parts and yet produce a chaotic whole. Although there are still failures, a lot of progress has been made in the construction of systems for efficient and economic use in the commercial field. They have also learned to turn their own research ideas into reality.

Architects have rarely achieved this situation. But it is in the area of stochastic and other types of models that much future work may lie.

These models may be at the project level, or even, as in the case of the weather forecasting model, at the local, regional, national, or international environment level and may be used on micro-, mini-, or mainframe computers. As described in Chapter 2, mathematics has been at the root of architectural creativity in the past, but there have been limitations in the scope of the mathematics itself as well as in the scale of the data that can be absorbed by a single human brain. Both of these are now at the point of change and will have as great an effect on art and the environment as the 'new' mathematics had on an earlier period. Just as the mathematics of perspective changed visions and stimulated creativity, so can and will computer models.

But first some general principles.

Complex problems such as those of chess, described earlier, produce an ever-increasing number of alternatives as the effect of each step creates an ever-increasing number of permutations. As this problem is rather like that of the 'fork roads' described in Chapter 3 it is necessary for one or both of two things to happen:

(1) To confine the search area by tightening the rules of the game
(2) To base actions on probability rather than examining each possible outcome sequentially

As we have seen, the human brain does both, and so therefore we come to the area now known as artificial intelligence. Some would argue that such work is a long way away from use by architects on cheap computers, but the same was also said of speech only a very short time ago.

There are many interpretations of artificial intelligence such as that of Minsky: 'Artificial intelligence is the science of making machines do things that would require intelligence if done by men.' However, this does not move the problem very far forward. Probably a better approach is to remember that a computer does not crunch numbers, as often stated, but that it manipulates symbols, just as we do, and so far we have proved that we are unable to compete with computers on this simple level of brain working. Just as we cannot compete with birds at flying or dolphins at swimming, we cannot compete with computers in those areas where the rules can be clearly defined. Whilst we are making the rules, we shall always ensure that we have further rules up our sleeves to keep ahead of the computer. Turing once said that it would be easy to make a computer behave like a human being if man would not keep changing the rules. Now we are beginning to teach computers to make up their own rules as well.

Symbols only become meaningful to both computer and man when meanings are assigned to them. Examples are badges, road signs, words, and drawings. Symbols do not necessarily need to have a similarity with that which they symbolize. The word waterfall does not sound like a waterfall. Similarly a computer symbol does not have to look like the object it is representing as long as we can agree on a standard interpretation. Another fundamental of artificial intelligence and models is the interaction of suites of programs which may be combined in the following forms:

Serially	pass orientated—each program taking over the results output of its predecessor
Hierarchically	one program in overall control and the others as subordinates or subroutines (bearing in mind, of

| | course, that the subordinate programs need not be *directly* accountable to the master program) |
| Heterarchical | responsibility for control more equally distributed throughout the system and internal communication much increased. |

The first is like a chain of slaves passing the product of their work to the next, and so on. The second is like a simple society working individually but under the control and instruction of a master. The third is like a group of specialists interacting with each other with questions, answers, and comments in a continually changing environment.

Processes so far described in this chapter, as with most applications developed up to the present time, come under the first two categories.

It is not possible in a book of this nature to describe a wide range of the third type of program, but a simplified description of a program suite of this third kind may help as an illustration. Michie and Chambers (1968) produced a suite of programs called BOXES at Edinburgh University, which was to drive an earlier pole and cart program by Donaldson (1966). This pole and cart problem assumes a motor-driven cart which must be kept running backwards and forwards on a straight track of fixed length in such a way as to balance a pole (Figure 69). The motor of the

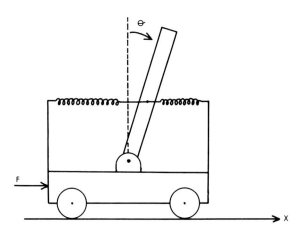

Figure 69

cart produces a fixed driving force, and the only control is a switch which determines the sign of this force and so indicates when the cart will be driven towards the left-hand or right-hand end of the track. The pole itself is pivoted on the cart and can fall only towards either end of the track. In the program, the simulator and controller pass information to each other in turn in a decision loop which is repeated every one-fifteenth of a second. Each time the loop is traversed, the controller receives the current state values of the simulated apparatus, and calculates and passes on a control signal to the simulator, which then acts on that decision to calculate a new set of state values to pass back to the controller. Failure to keep the system within certain limits causes a 'fail' signal which is noted by the program, and another is then started. Facilities were introduced to

130

enable a human subject to undertake the role of controller. This meant that the system as expanded by the BOXES suite of programs could operate as follows:

(1) Remote mode: the light-pen is disabled and every decision is generated by the BOXES program.
(2) Manual mode: only manual signals are accepted.
(3) Interactive mode: manual signals are accepted when generated, but in the absence of manual signal the remote signal is obeyed.

The BOXES controller is allowed to 'observe' all decisions taken by a human controller as well as its own. In this situation the human controller was slower at learning than the program. In the early stages the program tries to form a summary of the human's strategy but later takes decisions based on past experience whilst occasionally making 'experimental' decisions to gather information to improve its control strategy.

They went on to construct a system which was to test the validity of playing many easy games rather than one complex game—in other words, a heterarchical system. The problem was decomposed into a number of mutually independent subgames with a 'demon' in charge of each, operating within a three-dimensional matrix. Just as the chess player lumps a large number of positions together as being similar to each other and neglects the strategically irrelevant features in which they differ, so does each subgame contain a sort of model of the large game (Figure 70). Each box contains a demon who is armed with a left/right

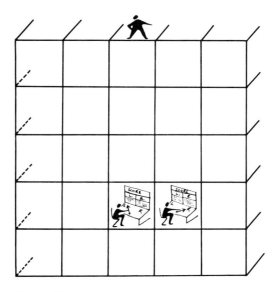

Figure 70

switch and a scoreboard, and his job is to set his switch from time to time in the light of data which he accumulates on his scoreboard. Each decision demon inhabiting a given box must learn to act for the best in a changing environment which he can only observe by the outcome of playing the subgames which have involved his box. Each demon can now operate the hawks and doves rule of trying to achieve stability.

The value of the outcome is measured not from a standard or optimum outcome but relative to a past average outcome. In other words, a draw is considered to be a good result when defeat has been the rule, but a bad result when there has been a winning streak. The program not only showed up the limitations of absolute optima in a changing environment but also showed that a computer program could obtain a better performance than a human being as well as being innovative.

Suppose, therefore, we considered the possibility of an environmental model for a house on the same basis. First, we must create a three-dimensional matrix which may, for example, contain a single housing plot (Figure 71). The demons in the outer boxes would be handling the

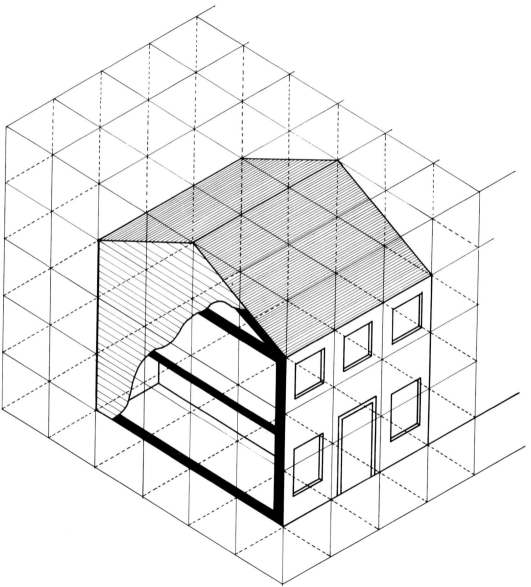

Figure 71

132

external environment. (In the case of a terrace house, two sides would, of course, be another house.) The demons in the first row of boxes inside the outer ones would be responsible for the external envelope of the house, whilst all of those demons in the boxes still further in will be handling the internal spaces and environment. These internal demons can be given the rules of the game such as temperature levels, lighting levels, and even spatial requirements and their interrelationship. The outer row of demons will be given the range of environmental conditions for the site. Clearly, the external envelope layer of demons now has to create a balance between the happenings on the outside (the external environment) and the needs of the inside (functional specification). Into this model may now be injected the accommodation and environmental needs and, in the case of the external envelope, a visual language and a set of design rules for the envelope. If a coordinated library is used in which cost and performance are specified, these will obviously be available for model evaluations (as described in Paterson, 1977).

Second, there are rules of adjacency for rooms and other spaces. The rules for doors and windows are obvious, as previously stated. There are minimum floor and window areas, and known rules of adjacency. It would now be possible for the program to keep experimenting, either by itself or with the interaction of the architect, with the continually changing solutions appearing on the screen. At worst it might stimulate ideas for the architect and at best give the user a choice from a vast number of solutions. At this point, it might be argued that this completely ignores aesthetics and that it is the design of the components and their disposition which is the most important factor. Also, this might become even more important when applying the system to larger projects. It is therefore necessary to reassess these aspects of architecture.

The first point is that openings have not necessarily been constrained by materials and indoctrination but often by mathematical concept. Even in such cave civilizations as those of Cappadocia where we would expect, for reasons of economy of effort if nothing else, entrances to caves to have been made in the shape of a person, they are nevertheless made rectangular. With the Romans, and later the mediaeval builders, a series of shapes or symbols were produced based upon known geometries (all of which are capable of being handled by computer) (Figure 72).

Variations and combinations

With these shapes, a design such as the Doges Palace at Venice, illustrated earlier, is built up. It will be noted that by using the same building which has given a great deal of pleasure to many tourists, the connection between design, method, and computing can be more easily recognized (Figures 73 and 74).

Apart from the work of a few radicals creating non-rectangular designs, modern architects have tended to use their own chosen set of rectangular symbols with perhaps a free shape only for, say, an entrance canopy. The total range of potential symbols has been ignored in order that endless identical units can be used, not for the benefits of prefabrication but for the basis of a philosophy that all men are equal—and therefore put into

133

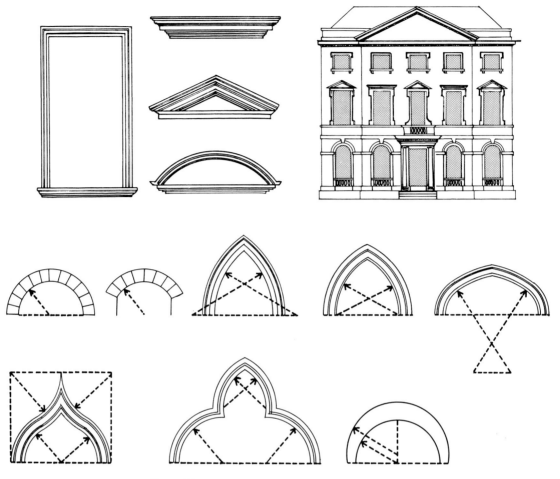

Figure 72

identical compartments as in beehives. The early work of Niemeyer, for example, was exalted because of the similarity of the *brise soleil* with the beehive. The computer can be used very easily and cheaply to produce such simple regularity. But is it what we want? We are beginning to understand that equality is not only unattainable but undesirable and that individual expression and freedom are more important. It is probable that apart from the egalitarian philosophies which caused much mindless repetition, it was also a reflection on the ability of the architect to be able to deal with such complex data-handling problems with only manual methods and Euclidean geometry available. Therefore, if computer models are to be used, it should and could have a much wider vocabulary than architects have used for a long time. It is strange that so-called architectural freedom has in fact created less variety than was created by the traditional architect using a permutation of standard symbols. It is also strange how this compares with the earlier illustration of the supermarket, where mass production of standard products can actually give a greater variety of choice than one individual craftsman can produce.

134

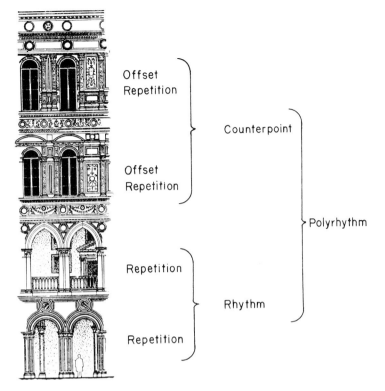

Figure 73

Figure 74 Palace of the Doqes, Venice

Unfortunately, architecture appears to be getting the worst of all worlds at the present time, as happened to the British motor industry in the immediate post-war period. It clung to hand-made methods as long as possible, only going into industrialization when it became absolutely necessary. Therefore, mass production came about in a negative way.

The American and Italian industry, for example, set about it in a positive way and in the end were better able to support research and the development of new car designs. But in America as well as Europe, the progress in the industrialization of building has been slow. Ehrenkranz (1971) stated:

> I think the key is the ability to develop an approach which would enable us to use mass-produced, standardised products which we can compare freely and economically. I think this is a major direction in which we have to go. It can only come, however, from developing information and a management system which is going to enable us to produce predictably and on time. If we do not do this, our rights to survival as professionals who provide clients with appropriate physical facilities will not be sustained.

The danger is that design guides, metric shells, standard components, etc., whilst having virtues, are oversimplistic because architects have not interested themselves in creating a more sophisticated game. Many games such as noughts and crosses, tic tac toe, or solitaire have remained unchanged for centuries, but even children are now given three-dimensional versions as presents. Even computers are sold as toys. A new generation is growing up with change, just as Renaissance generations grew up with change. But where is the architect's concept of a new model? Should we still rely on Euclid for the solution to our problems? In this open situation we can consider many scenarios and one of these is that the construction industry will move into three categories:

(1) Special buildings designed by the best creative brains which create new game rules or fashion
(2) The majority of the national building programmes which includes housing, hospitals, schools, factories, and offices on open sites
(3) Infill and conservation

The use of computers in each of these categories will be discussed later, but it is in the middle band of building where computers will initially have their greatest effect. The quality of the games and the computing will depend upon the quality of the new young architects who are prepared to become involved at all levels.

It will need as much brilliance as any architect has had in the past to conceive the dimensional models which would allow the insertion of the enormous variety of mass-produced components that could be produced with the use of microprocessors. It also needs the involvement of all architects to prevent the design of the systems, and therefore control, from falling into the hands of a few systems analyst/programmers. Architects have allowed this to happen so often in the past. Will they do it again? The microprocessor makes it possible for mass-produced components to have much greater variety than ever before. Not only does it liberate the machine but it also liberates the management control, which is as big a factor as any in standardization.

This potential variety of components can either be directed towards a closed system or, if we are to have an open architecture, a whole new concept of dimensional coordination. If the former, the system building and design and build firms clearly have an enormous advantage which will be enhanced by the microprocessor. If the flexibility of the latter is to be established, then we have to learn to control the visual scene and at the same time provide opportunity for expression by the individual. Michie and Chambers (1964) suggest:

(1) Search is endless or ubiquitous.
(2) Knowledge and therefore education reduces search.
(3) Using knowledge is intelligent.

We have seen the first and second to be true. There is a world of infinite knowledge and therefore infinite creativity, but architects, as well as everyone else, through education, indoctrination, administrative expediency, and time/effort, have limited their search area. Perhaps, then, the microprocessor will help with the third proposition by helping him to expand and speed up the search area within a much more sophisticated game than the one which is so obviously failing at the present time.

As shown earlier, the brain uses well-trodden data highways where possible to conserve energy, but this can lead, in the lazy designer, to unthinking repetition of old habits, long after their use has become outdated. The computer, apart from its other potential uses, may provide a stimulus to our search for solutions to complex problems. Architects, in the present regressive mood, may bury their heads in the sand in the hope that a lot of small solutions will become a big beautiful one, but it is not as simple as that. Whilst it is true that problems must be broken down to give more logical and personal solutions, if the overall strategy is ignored these solutions will find themselves dominated and possibly destroyed by national and international forces which cannot possibly be avoided. Hope will not turn a global communications system into a village craft system. Hope will not turn mass-production component manufacturers into local craftsmen. Hope in finding the ideal man with his navel in the right place will not produce a dimensional system of the complexity we need.

Researchers into artificial intelligence are already working on programming systems for cheap computers which will allow the computer itself to act as a consultant. Work on advanced levels of medical consultation by computer are already well advanced in the United States of America.

There can be no absolute messianic solution for all time. As the speed of change increases and the permutations increase this becomes more obvious. The slow change in the development of new materials and technology in the building industry during the seventeenth and eighteenth centuries made it look as though some ideal could be obtained, and the symbols that were produced came to be associated with that idea and an ideal taste. But the rapid changes at the present time only indicate ignorance for anyone who holds such views today. Symbols are being created, popularized, and rejected within a very short time in most aspects of society, whilst in architecture it can still take a very long time. Take, for example, the framed window. The use of vertical sheeting for economy in the pre-war period created a problem when windows had to be inserted. A DPC at the head had to be projected (Figure 75). The sides

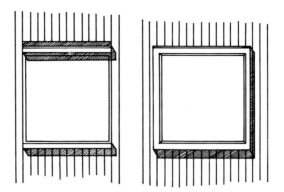

Figure 75

and sill also had to be stopped. As the head needed a gap for the DPC to protrude, it seemed a good idea to carry this right round and *articulate* the symbol. The box around the window, now established as a symbol, could be used in walls where there was no sheeting, and the articulation could also be used independently as in the Royal Festival Hall, London (Figure 76). This is only one of the many illustrations that could be given for the emergence of modern symbols.

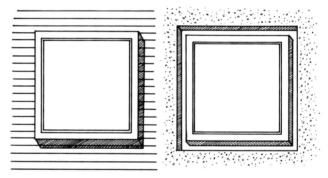

Figure 76

Two of the questions which lead on from these propositions are as follows:

(1) Can building continue to be designed and built so slowly?
(2) Should we still be designing all buildings for a very long life?

Before these questions can be considered in the following chapters there are two other aspects which must be considered. One is the use of national resources to provide special and costly facilities which cannot be supported at a local level. Two of these are Teletext and Viewdata (Figure 77).

In Teletext, the two redundant lines of signal in television transmissions are used to convey up to 800 television 'pages' of information. The

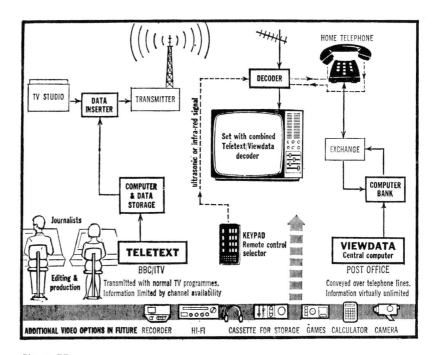

Figure 77

limitation on pages has been made to keep access time to an acceptable 12 seconds.

Viewdata, on the other hand, not only has much greater 'page' potential but also has, in theory at least, the potential for connection to any on-line computer in Europe. In time, this system may eliminate up to 50 per cent of all United Kingdom mail, which gives some idea of the effect it will have on general communication. This will come about by the connection of word-processing and computing equipment to television sets, which will also be capable of receiving these types of transmissions and their data. These data will be manipulated and sent down the telephone lines for storage or immediate action by the recipient. In this way, letters can be sent without the need for post, information can be stored without the need for filing, and so on. All of this with just a cheap computer and a modem for telephone data transmission. Furthermore, developments such as that at the CAD centre at Cambridge giving central storage for organizations means easy and fast retrieval of any information in that organization. But such systems are not just confined to one organization, or even one country. The EEC, for example, now has its own Euronet–DIANE system for international data handling, whilst the United States has continental systems such as Arpanet and Telenet. Development is now so fast that the International Standards Organization is already having to lay down standards.

The other aspect is new developments. These are occurring at such a fantastic rate that it is impossible for any book to be produced before new developments have occurred. However, there are one or two areas which are worthy of comment. One is the phenomenal developments about to take place in cheap memory storage—bubble memories, etc. The other

139

is, not surprisingly, similar to the way the brain's memory appears to work. Instead of the traditional computer system of holding data in memory according to their label or address, Semionics Associates of California are now developing memories in which the computer records data in terms of subject of interest. Another development which might confront architects sooner than they might think is the production of computer-output information as characters apparently floating in the air. The image is caused by a wand which projects an image directly on to the retina of the eye. This could be developed for what would appear to be designs in space. Furthermore, the system is very cheap. These are only two examples of the new potentials now emerging.

Before examining the possible use of the various systems described in this chapter, it would be advisable to recaptiluate on some of the ideas proposed so far:

(1) The continual decline in the size of the labour force and the declining number of traditional craftsmen which is unlikely to be reversed as standards of education improve: 470,000 (nett) jobs have been lost to the United Kingdom construction industry alone in the ten years between 1967 and 1977, most of which was a 'boom period'.

(2) The facility in the future for industry to produce cheaper and yet a greater variety of products as microprocessors come to be used.

(3) The increased use of microprocessors will almost certainly create social change which will emanate from the further reduction of working hours.

(4) Social change will also come about by the increased use of data transmission services. Whilst organizations will probably continue to get larger, the need for all their workers to be in one place may reduce.

(5) Increased leisure time and increased education, as well as the change in work pattern, will have a great effect on architecture as people expect to participate more in their environment.

(6) Increased knowledge of the working of the human brain and of society may affect our views on
    (a) equality,
    (b) property,
    (c) education
    (d) work/leisure, and
    (e) computers.

(7) Computers will play an increasingly important part in our lives as they become cheaper, more powerful, self-programmable with more complex memory systems and more sophisticated peripherals.

(8) As the art of architecture is increasingly understood and modelled by the computer, architecture may in fact become more, rather than less, important.

(9) All the items in part 6 above within the leisure-orientated society will throw increasing demands upon the environment of the community, as is already happening.

(10) A lot of the parts of the built environment will become product

orientated instead of patron orientated as at present, and this will cause organizational changes.

(11) The microprocessor will give the design and contract organization a greater potential for fast economic production with other great advantages over the traditional processes.

(12) There are great dangers if the architects do not become involved.

Chapter 6

APPLICATIONS—UNI- AND MULTIPROFESSIONAL ORGANIZATIONS

No matter how much we might hope for the success of the 'small man', there can be little disagreement that the smaller organizations have come under increasing pressure. This not only applies to professional practice but also to the corner shop, increasingly taken over by the supermarkets, the smaller countries, dominated by the superpowers, and so on. However, whilst the large organizations have expertise and capital resources, like the dinosaur a large organization has less flexibility and is therefore more vulnerable in a changing environment. It is worth recalling that any animal larger than man only stays alive by man's permission. Whilst he can exterminate, if he so wished, all life larger than himself, he has so far been unable to exterminate a single species of insect or bacteria. It is the small basic units which have the greater flexibility for changes and adaptation and, in the case of a practice, sometimes the supreme dedication necessary to create new ideas. But they do not have the capital and the resources to develop them in a world which for most enterprises requires large capital investment. Therefore there seems to be a very real need for a symbiotic relationship between large and small organizations, and an understanding that there is a need for both large and small in ways which have not yet been worked out in the construction industry. It is a symbiosis, not a competition, between small is beautiful and big is powerful.

As already mentioned, most industries are like the clothing industry in which couturier designers produce highly creative designs, some of which emerge from the evolutionary battle for survival in the world of ideas. The successful ones are rapidly absorbed by society, and the manufacturing industries produce economic versions of the style as quickly and efficiently as possible. In building, the successful ideas of creative architects are generally not accepted into the manufacturing industry, but if they are, not until they have almost become unfashionable. Any designs which are accepted are often interpreted by designers who have not been trained to translate these ideas into production terms because no such training exists. This is probably due to both the education and the attitude of architects to resist any association with industry, which is usually seen as a threat rather than an ally in the means to create environments.

If the same processes were developed in architecture as in clothing and other industries, major clients such as government and major organizations would have to adopt the role of selecting projects in which truly creative and dedicated architects could exploit their ideas, whilst manufacturers would have to become more aware of the need to react quickly and effectively to changes in architectural ideas by using good architectural consultants, not just to produce building projects but to assist in the design of systems and components. In the implementation of the systems already described, these consultants would not need to work within that building organization or for a single organization. They would be in a position to compose designs from the components made available through broad-based information systems.

The smaller organization, in its traditional form, is often overlooked because it does not have the tools which are available to the larger multidisciplinary practices. But with the use of micro and minicomputers there is now no need for this to be so. If we take, for example, the energy-conservation programs which are now being sold for use with microcomputers, large and small firms alike can have the same tool at low cost. This will also be the case with many other aspects of work, that is, of course, if the small firms take the trouble to become involved. The important thing for the smaller organization in the future will be the links it forges with other units. As each specialist in the design team reduces his response time by computer techniques, it will become more important for small units to link themselves to multiuser computer systems which will not only make them look like larger organizations which have decentralized, but will help them with an interface with the user.

For some time to come, there will be a wide variety of ways in which architecture will be practised and produced. Therefore, whilst there will be a mainstream direction, many applications of microprocessors will be needed to cover a wide range of activities within the industry. The industry is divided into public and private organizations of which there are large, medium, and small architectural practices. Some of these practices are uniprofessional and others multiprofessional, sometimes working in an interdisciplinary mode and sometimes working as part of a complete design and build operation. Furthermore, apart from the traditional relationships within the industry which are at present changing, there are also the changing relationships between the client and the user. As suggested earlier, the creation of such new methods has lagged behind the demands of the public, in spite of sincere efforts by a number of architects to devise a number of differing relationships. Some of these new relationships have been mentioned earlier, but as pointed out in the *Architects Journal* (1977):

> It isn't much good being a radical 'community architect' without being able to get a building up soundly and efficiently. But the conventional skills of producing presentation drawings to sell a scheme to a council committee or corporate client are hardly relevant when it comes to explaining the

effects of the yardstick on housing estate layout to a meeting of prospective council tenants. A whole new approach to graphics and jargon is required as well as a more humble attitude to one's own design ideas and willingness to offer alternative solutions.

It is here that microprocessor applications can help. Apart from changing relationships with the client/user, there are a lot of new types of clients and users. These include cooperative housing, coownership housing, and equity sharing groups, as well as trade-unions acting as quasi-clients. With this extraordinary complexity, it is obviously impossible and undesirable to pose discrete finite solutions, but some possible applications will be described in the major areas in this and the next chapter on the basis of the following process (Figure 78). This process starts with a policy for building and designing, the design process, the communication of that design, its construction, and finally maintenance. As the computer and information handling are synonymous, the two have been put together to emphasize their interchangeability.

On the basis of the foregoing, the uniprofessional architectural practice can take many forms and work for many different types of client, but substantially these may be considered in two categories:

(1) The architect operates in the traditional manner of taking the client's brief and budget, and creating the sort of building he believes that the client needs, even though the client himself may not have even considered the solution he is given.
(2) The architect participates with the client(s) or user(s) to elucidate their needs and act as a sort of midwife to their own ideas.

There is a very real need for very talented creative designers in the first category to produce the new mutations from which society is able to make its selection. The problem in recent times has probably been that too many architects see themselves in this role, rather than that the role exists at all. The use of the microprocessor for this category will probably be seen in two major ways and will be partly dependent upon the architects themselves applying their own creative talents to the problem. They are needed for searching out and refining the sort of tools mentioned in earlier chapters, or in other words influencing the computer manufacturers, rather than leaving the problem to a small number of academic research teams and the industry itself. Practice must become much more involved. The best creative brains are also needed for creating the 'games'.

The world's need for building is enormous. In the United Kingdom alone there were 50,000 homeless in 1979. In the United States of America 2.6 million housing units are required annually and yet the housing industry has been producing about half that rate due to shortages in labour and materials. In the meantime, the mobile home industry, with

145

CLIENT/USER   DESIGN TEAM   INFORMATION/ MANUAL COMPUTER

CLIENT/USER INPUT

AGREEMENT OBTAINED

EXAMINE
A) IF BUILDING REQUIRED
B) IF NEW BUILDING REQUIRED
C) RESOURCES REQUIRED AND AVAILABLE
D) TIMESCALE
E) POLICY ON PROJECT

EXAMINE OFFICE RESOURCE NETWORK AND
PRODUCE PRELIMINARY PROGRAMME AND
ENTER INTO DIARY PROGRAM

INPUT DECISIONS ON ABOVE

OBTAIN SITE DETAILS
COLLECT RELEVANT REGULATIONS, CODE, ETC.
PREPARE FOR DESIGN NEEDS
PROCESS SITE DETAILS
ACTIVATE LOCATION / METEOROLOGICAL SEARCH
AND COMPATIBILITY PROGRAM

ALLOCATE PROJECT WITHIN DESIGN TEAM

INTERACTION WITH THE CLIENT USER TO DEVELOP
BRIEF AND PROGRAMME

DATA ON ACTIVITIES, LOCATION AND SITE
OBTAINED FROM INFORMATION

INPUT NUMBER OF PEOPLE AND THEIR ACTIVITIES

PROCESS AND PRODUCE SORTATIONS

COMPUTER SORTATIONS EXAMINED AND VARIOUS
PERMUTATIONS EXPLORED IN TRADITIONAL MANNER
AGAINST BACKGROUND OF FUNCTIONAL
REQUIREMENTS OF LOCATION

INPUT DESIRED SORTATION

CLIENT/USER +

DESIGN TEAM CONSIDER BUBBLE DIAGRAM AND
DISCUSS WITH CLIENT
AGREE BUDGET
    FUNCTIONAL STANDARD
    NEED FOR ESTABLISHING CONTRACTOR AND CRITERIA

PRODUCE BUBBLE DIAGRAM

      ''

CLIENT/USER +

DESIGN TEAM OBTAINS DETAILS OF CONTRACTORS TENDERS &
GETS CLIENTS AGREEMENT OF CONTRACTOR

INFORMATION SENDS OUT MpAMPl DETAILS TO
CONTRACTORS AND OBTAINS PERCENTAGE AND
INFORMS DESIGN TEAM

      ''

DESIGN TEAM PREPARE PROVISIONAL LAYOUT

ACTIVATE COMPUTER TO ANALYSE FUNCTIONAL
CRITERIA AS OUTCOME OF PLACING GIVEN
ACTIVITIES IN RELATION TO EACH OTHER AND
TO THEIR LOCATION

CLIENT/USER +

DESIGN-TEAM CONSIDER DATA SUPPLIED & MAKE HYPOTHESIS.
AT THIS STAGE, DESIGN TEAM, CLIENT/USER & COMPUTER
WORK TOGETHER INTERACTIVELY. IDEAS ARE INPUT TO MACHINE
BASED ON DATA SUPPLIED AND THE COMPUTER GIVES IMMEDIATE
EVALUATION OF PROPOSED BUILDING SHAPES IN TERMS OF COST,
COST IN USE ITEMS SUCH AS ENERGY CONSUMPTION, MAINTENANCE ETC.
AND ALSO PERFORMANCE SUCH AS ENVIRONMENTAL PERFORMANCE.

INTERACTIVE COMPUTING

      ''

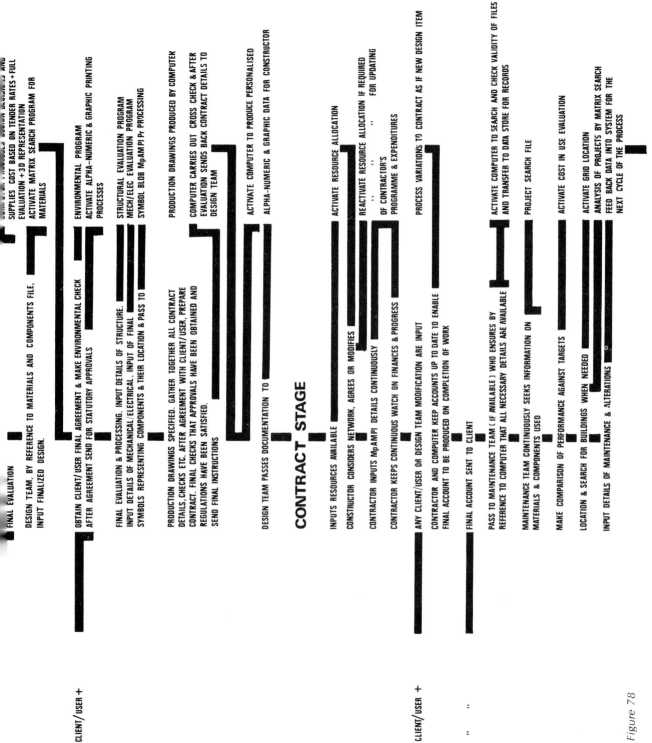

Figure 78

which architects usually dissociate themselves, achieved the following results in the United States of America:

10.7 per cent of conventional-style family starter homes in 1960
20.3 per cent of conventional-style family starter homes in 1964
36.1 per cent of conventional-style family starter homes in 1968
52.0 per cent of conventional-style family starter homes in 1969

Critics may say that these are only for the young starting couples, but in 1969 mobile homes represented 29 per cent of all housing starts. It will be argued that it cannot happen in Europe, but anyone who travels anywhere in Europe cannot help but see the enormous impact the permanent caravan and mobile home has already made. This is only in the industrialized world. What about the desperate need for building of all descriptions in the less-developed world? The pace of urban growth in developing countries means that there is a need for the production of 200 million urban dwellings alone before the end of the century. Rather than dissipate their talents on the odd individual project or some hoped-for messianic project, could some architects not use computer modelling to help design the components and develop the tools and the rules of housing for communities to help thmselves? This is the biggest task of all. The industrialized world can only maintain its standard of living whilst helping others, by exporting its ideas and knowledge. Therefore, architects in the construction industry may have to stop being passive, waiting for work to arrive, and take an active part in creating markets. The needs for this would be to create highly sophisticated models for which industry could produce a variety of components which in themselves would create further variety. This is not the old system building with simplistic modular rules but one with much richer models. The other need is for methodologies to be put on to microprocessor chips to enable communities to build for themselves with or without the help of architects. To do this they must learn to live with the computer and find out what it can do. If the architect is really involved with the *whole* environment, surely he cannot leave the mobile home industry and the computer industry to gradually take over that environment without his contribution.

The other aspect of the first category of uniprofessional architectural practice is in the traditional operation. There must remain the opportunity for the best creative talents to use the finest craftsmen for creating the symbols of society. There should be more discussion by architects and society of the morality of architecture and planning at this level. For an architect or planner to impose his will on, say, a housing community becomes increasingly morally unacceptable. However, without the symbols which act as visual signposts in the development of art and society, the environment would be a featureless place. The problem lies in finding some way of isolating those buildings where function and morality do not impose too great a restriction on the best creative talents. If this is possible, then even these architects will find that they can use the computer as a stimulant for their creativeness in the same way as Renaissance architects like Brunelleschi found their new mathematics a stimulus to creativity.

The second category of uniprofessional architects may well have to depend to an increasing degree on industry for their tools. It is beyond the realms of reason that there could be a rush back to the traditional crafts and that standards long since gone could be revived for all but a few buildings. No matter how traditionally a community desires to build they will be constrained by the components which are increasingly produced by industrialized means. The increase in legislation which has gone on for centuries is also unlikely to be reversed. It is therefore possible that some architects will have to work with individuals or communities, using cheap computers which contain programs of the building regulations (already shown to be possible by Phillips at Bristol University), together with a library of factory-produced components. The architect could try out a multiplicity of ways of designing a project whilst the user(s) is/are actually present, and by connecting these programs to evaluation programs which have been and will continue to be developed, the user(s) would be able to make judgements on the spot. If this approach were to reduce an architect's costs, as it would undoubtedly do, he might find that there was a surprisingly large demand for his services, because for the majority of people, the home and the family constitute the major part of their life interest. Whilst the architect has remained remote from all but a comparatively small number of clients and building users, the builder's merchants and kitchen, bathroom, and furnishing salesmen have increasingly created a demand to be satisfied. The old concept of patronage has unfortunately completely confused the issue. Harms (1976) has said that 'the level of *tolerance* to put up with undesirable consequences in housing or other services is *proportional* to the level of *participation* in the decisions'.

This is the key to the problem. It will never be possible for architects or anyone else to satisfy everyone's needs, but participation is not only an inalienable human right but also a recipe for greater satisfaction. The incredibly wide range of view on what is necessary, desirable, or unnecessary can be seen from the following National Opinion Poll of 2,000 householders, promoted by the Building Research Establishment.

Item	Percentage of respondents, classing items as:		
	Basic necessity	Desirable	Unnecessary
Electric light	94.6	4.5	0.9
Hot water supply	92.5	6.5	1.0
Bathroom	90.2	8.2	1.6
Refuse disposal	86.0	12.2	1.8
Internal WC	84.0	14.1	1.8
Living room heating	83.2	14.8	2.1
Power points	82.6	15.1	2.3
Free from damp	81.0	17.1	2.0
Ventilation	77.9	19.1	3.0
Daylight	71.3	26.8	1.9
Safe stairs	65.6	26.4	8.0
Refrigerator	61.3	30.7	8.0
Gas supply	61.2	19.2	19.7

Item	Percentage of respondents, classing items as:		
	Basic necessity	Desirable	Unnecessary
Street lighting	59.4	35.3	5.3
Airing cupboard	58.3	35.6	6.1
Clean air	56.1	40.3	3.6
Ventilated food store	53.8	34.4	11.6
General storage	48.6	44.9	6.5
Convenient for shops, etc.	45.9	47.9	6.2
Back garden	44.8	43.8	11.4
Safe play space	41.9	34.8	23.3
Thermal insulation	38.7	48.4	12.9
Sound insulation	37.0	47.4	15.5
Good neighbours	33.7	60.1	6.2
Privacy from neighbours	33.7	53.1	13.2
Bedroom heating	31.4	47.7	20.9
WC separate from bathroom	30.2	47.6	22.3
Well-maintained property	30.3	59.6	10.1
Garage or parking space	29.8	41.0	29.1
Free from heavy traffic	28.7	53.2	18.1
Privacy in back garden	27.3	53.4	10.3
Front garden	26.9	54.1	19.0
Informal eating area	21.6	49.6	28.8
Greenery or trees	21.2	61.7	17.1
Privacy from family	21.1	43.4	35.5
Quiet surroundings	20.9	63.0	16.1
Two WCs	19.0	44.3	36.7
Level access	16.2	45.8	38.0
Pram space	13.3	33.3	53.4
Free from parked cars	12.7	50.7	36.6
All on one level	11.1	33.6	55.3
Shaver socket	8.4	32.5	59.1

Can any architect be confident that he knows what people want after reading this?

Not only is there the problem of the need for individual choice and expression at any one time, but there are two further problems for even the most earnest participating architect. One is change. The individual or community may be clear in their minds at one particular time, but time and circumstances will almost certainly change these needs. The other problem is land ownership. At first sight, this seems to be the simplest of problems, but in fact it is probably one of the most intractable in a democracy.

To take the latter first. As the earlier chapters have shown, there has been a gradual move from the ownership of all land by the King, the Church, and a few individuals towards the control of large areas of land by the State and substantial increases in the ownership of land and property by the ordinary person. Owner occupation, for example, increased from 9 per cent in 1914 to 53 per cent in 1974. This seems to be a reasonable trend in the case of owner occupation, but as Denman (1978) points out, the controls of ownership of nationalized property are vested in a changing bureaucracy. The outcome of this is that all become trespassers except within the permitted rules of that transient bureaucracy. This can, at times, be a more tyrannical situation than individual ownership.

Even at the personal level, the merits of public and private ownership and all the other forms of tenure can be argued according to political persuasion. A simple basic morality is hard to find, and yet a morality for ownership is fundamentally at the root of community architecture. The ownership of land must have a significant effect upon the design, use, and maintenance of property, and it is therefore necessary for us to be more aware of this when talking of architectural design and planning. It is too easy to think of solving complex environmental problems by the introduction of a new style alone. The scale of the problem is enormous and the architect already has more problems than he can handle anyway by traditional methods. The problems become even more complex when applied to less-developed and underdeveloped countries and when we consider the increasing pressure to be put upon available land by future population increases. The problems of the world will not be solved miraculously by the microprocessor, but it is one way of distributing knowledge—a way which one day will be recognized to be more important than the invention of printing. Apart from social problems and the enormous political, economic, and social implications of land ownership, many areas of the world also suffer problems of land ownership and deprivation through lack of knowledge.

Whichever form of ownership or tenure emerges, there will always be a problem of interaction between neighbours or users in any society. As the population increases, particularly in the urban areas, society becomes more complex, and therefore the interaction of people's activities become more complex. An urban dweller may affect and be affected by other dwellers on either side, and above, and below him. Therefore, how can user participation be isolated from the other users? The answers to such problems are complex, but one way in which the microprocessor may play its part in this type of problem is in the use of multiaccess computing. A group of users may individually sit at separate microcomputers; as each makes a decision, its impact is recorded on other user's screens or outputs, upon which they are then able to respond. Although development in this area has been slow, there has already been enough work done in this field to prove the potential of such techniques. Now it is necessary for students of architecture to become involved with the criteria for such program systems. The use of microcomputers for giving individuals and groups of users an opportunity to participate in the design of their community environment is so enormous that speculative housing developers will almost certainly take advantage of its sales potential, even if architects do not. The relaxation of planning control over the smaller housing areas provides added scope for local choice and this type of sale. As these microcomputers can run on car batteries, it is possible that sales vans will be available on housing sites in the future. This type of approach

151

may help to overcome some of the difficulties experienced in public participation so far, in which the public have seen themselves (like councillors) as critics rather than as constructive participants. This is clearly a hangover from the past which needs to be overcome, and the microcomputer may help to do this. But not only do the public only tend to participate when they think things are wrong, and then become vociferously critical, but some factions tend to assert more influence than others. It is here that computer techniques such as the Delphi method, described earlier, can help to give a better balance.

The other problem mentioned is that of flexibility and change. This again raises the question of long-life or short-life buildings. Architects have generally favoured the former for several reasons:

(1) It is more in keeping with the tradition of architecture in its monumental role, and as an example of craftsmanship.
(2) Reducing the life of the building has so far not greatly reduced the cost of the building.
(3) Neither fee scales nor the law, as it stands at present, are an encouragement to reduce standards and capital costs.
(4) It is argued that there are insufficient resources available on the planet for the continuance of a consumer society.

However, for whatever reasons, whilst the architect shies away from the consumer society, the rest of civilization (including architects), apart from a very small number of active conservationists, continues to promote and consume more and more products which have a shorter and shorter life. Building is probably the only exception, apart from the big inroads that the caravan, mobile home, and instant building systems have already made, although many developments such as Gruissan, Cap d'Aqde, etc., are beginning to look more like temporary stage sets built traditionally (Figure 79a and b).

There is little doubt that the world market for short-life buildings and short-life components will expand enormously in the coming years, with or without the architect, with any deficiency in resources being brought in from inner or outer space. The builder's merchants will continue to expand and influence a very large market who want their needs instantly satisfied. (The skateboard craze, for example, came and went in less than two years. There was no time to design and build factories in the traditional fashion for this and many other similar industries. Furthermore, the heavy, traditionally built skateboard parks were not only too late but are now white elephants.) For those who need fast building, there is no reason why the existing computer-controlled builder's merchants storage systems cannot be connected to building system design capability on computers which can order up the necessary components.

Would the end-product be more or less standardized than the suburbs of Georgian, Victorian, and modern times? After all, they are all standard systems with personalized modifications. The personal involvement of the user in such computer-based systems may even be greater. The work at the Greater London Council on PSSHAK (Primary System Support and Housing Assembly Kit) has been rather ill fated, but valuable work by

Figure 79(a)

Figure 79(b)

architects like Kroll has provided valuable experience and may yet rise
again. The work of PSSHAK was based on that of Habraken (1977) who
has said:

> We want to shape matters because we want to live and life is
> where one can nourish the Soul by using the hands. Lifting
> stones, digging earth, putting sticks together. To combine

things, to give them a place, make them carry loads, make them surround and let them enhance our vulnerable existence. The world begins only where it depends on our action.

This sums up the reason why people want to be involved with the design of their houses, and with increased leisure this involvement may become even more important for many. Tasks which are unacceptable as paid labour become pleasure in leisure. It must be stated, however, that there will also be many who will want to spend their time in their other interests and they will see the design of their home as an insignificant part of their lives. For them, there must be purchasable packages which are either design or product orientated.

The uniprofessional practice will obviously continue to be involved with individual building design, but will find it increasingly difficult to be economic in a heavily labour-orientated profession and also increasingly difficult to compete with the larger multiprofessional disciplinary practices. Already the profitability of small practices is seen to be dropping and, if they are to survive, they will no doubt have to consort with other professional practices, and even contractors, to give themselves the same advantages as the large organizations described later. If they do not, they will be confined to conservation and infill which could, and should in any case, become a specialism in its own right. This latter would be a traditional service in every way, and is likely to find little value in the use of the microprocessor in any of its work other than perhaps accounting, word-processing equipment, and certain applications of maintenance such as the following.

If the French system of CAPEB (Confédération de l'Artisanat et des Petites Enterprises du Bâtiment) with their five regional SARTEBs (Services Artisinaux de Répartition des Travaux d'Entretien du Bâtiment) were to be adopted by practices involved with maintenance, then microcomputers would help to provide an excellent service. They could centralize the demand for maintenance work and distribute it between member firms of craftsmen. They could also carry out cost assessments and handle payment. Quite obviously, files could be set up on the matrix basis, earlier described, in which the capabilities of each firm of craftsmen are recorded. As the demand for specialized maintenance occurred, the computer would seek a match in the same way as a computer dating service. As resources for maintenance decline, the need for such a service will increase to embrace even modern buildings.

Now we must consider the multiprofessional interdisciplinary practice. These take a variety of forms. First, they are split up into private and public sectors, which are again split into those in which the professional barriers have almost disappeared and there is a completely interactive situation, and those in which each profession operates in the traditional manner but within one organization. All of these have the advantage of shortening communications and therefore, hopefully, time, but in the main the individual processes have not changed. All of these types of organization will undoubtedly be applying the advantages of the microprocessors through their use of minicomputers as well as microcomputers for their many problems.

154

One of the problems which they all have in common is the increased need to program resources, because the problem becomes infinitely more complex when not only one profession has to apply its resources to a work load but several other disciplines have to be integrated, but in differing proportions. The problem of balancing resources can be one of the disadvantages of multidisciplinary practices, whether public or private. It is, however, possible to use computer programs to ease the problem (see Appendix).

Allied to the allocation of resources is management control. Not only do the resources have to be matched to the work load as it arrives but it has to be monitored by management as it passes through the organization. This can develop into a tedious task for both staff and management, even in the most democratic of organizations. The problem can be simplified at the management level by programming the computer to produce only those projects where targets have not been achieved, rather than good and bad alike. Too often computers are programmed to produce data on everything, whether good or bad; but clearly, there is no need for management to be concerned when all is going well. If things have gone wrong, then management wants to know who to speak to and where it has gone wrong, rather than getting screeds of paper to hunt through. The only person who needs the detail is the one who is struggling with the problem.

At the input end, the targets to be monitored should, wherever possible, be a stage in the organization's computer processes, so that the computer itself can match achievement with targets. Very often, for this type of work, a real-time clock with a diary system is necessary. This type of program has a value in many places in every organization, and will be explained later.

The next potential use of the computer is at the briefing stage. The work which has already been carried out, particularly in the medical field, shows that computer programs can be developed on a question and answer basis for the purpose of eliciting needs. In some cases, this questioning has gone beyond that already mentioned and has been allied to a diagnostic system of considerable power. The same could be achieved in architecture.

It is possible for computers to be used not only for a single person-to-computer conversation for the elucidation of a brief but also for the interaction between several users to establish, for example, the activity grouping in a Bürolandschaft office, or the interrelationship between housing units. This approach can be allied to data files holding information on human needs and characteristics.

Many architectural problems involve the establishment of required activities and the grouping of these into related spaces according to their types. In other words, sometimes noisy and quiet activities are separated, while those needing daylight are separated from those which do not. These physical sortations now have to be meshed with the need for relationships of activities and circulation. This process usually goes on during a bubble diagram stage. There is never a perfect solution to such a problem, but the architect is usually the one who has to make a judgement. By using a computer, many more sortations can be presented

155

for consideration by the architect or user who would still make their own judgements, but on the basis of more sortations than could be provided manually.

The chosen relationship of spaces now has to be put into a three-dimensional shape, whilst at the same time considering the relationship between the outside and the inside. It is here that modelling programs of the type suggested in the last chapter can be of great value. The constraints for many buildings, such as housing, are very severe, but nevertheless permit a vast number of permutations in design, cost, and performance which can be modelled and evaluated on a continuous basis. The computer process need only be stopped when interesting possibilities are brought to light. There is no doubt that the architect has to consider a vast number of permutations at this stage; the number of permutations he considers must be dependent upon time and the ability to keep experimenting. Sometimes, an inferior solution is accepted because of a mental block or lack of time. A computer model can offer a continuing range of possibilities, which the architect and/or user can stop and consider, and then move on.

Without a library of design components (not necessarily actual components), the models can only consider spaces, but by inserting design components with their cost and performance details, the elevations and the building performance can be considered at every stage. For this, a library must be built up on an appropriate dimensionally coordinated basis. Once this has been established as an office discipline, then design components which are used repetitively by the organization can be built up and, with them, characteristics of their performance. These, too, have to be coordinated. For example, it is obviously extremely difficult to make comparisons at a later stage if some items are measured in metric and others in imperial dimensions. Therefore, standards are an important factor in building up a data bank. Fortunately the work of BSI, DIN, CIB, and Agrément, etc., is helping to set out the criteria for these standards.

In building up a library, it should be remembered that a basic language of numeric symbols can be built up into complex equations. To start with equations would only deny the opportunity of using the basic components for subsequently making new equations. It is the same with other data. It is wise to use simple basic building blocks for building into larger blocks at a later stage. With a library of design components, the architect need not use a model for offering possible solutions but may build up and experiment with his own possible alternatives.

Whichever approach is made, two things are obvious:

(1) All of those design components which have been put into the computer files can be evaluated to whatever degree the data have been collected. If, for example, we take a cavity brick wall as a standard design component, then any length of wall described can be measured according to criteria such as cost, weight, and so on. When used as part of a space, then its heat loss, thermal capacity, acoustical, etc., properties can be evaluated almost instantly.

(2) If only library design components can be used, then in effect the architect will be using a closed system. This may sometimes be

acceptable but for the majority this will be seen as too strict a discipline and unacceptable.

The number of offices which do not use a very limited range of solutions for a very high percentage of any building design is extremely rare. To start at the lowest level, there would be no resistance to a standard manhole range or perhaps a range of floorings and ceilings. The degree to which architects use standard solutions (not necessarily standard drawings) varies, but innovation rarely exceeds 50 per cent of the design of any building and is usually in the region of 20 to 30 per cent. There is an obvious advantage in the almost instant evaluation of between 50 and 80 per cent of any project, along the lines described above, but there is the problem of the remainder.

These personal or job design components can be created on the spot and approximate data inserted into the computer at the level normally used by the other professionals at the sketch design stage. As the design progresses, these estimated figures are gradually hardened into firm figures. Therefore, it can be seen that if some mathematical model is used as the basis of design, which after all has been shown to have happened throughout history, the computer is able to give an almost instant evaluation over an enormous range of characteristics. At first, an office may start with one simple evaluative criteria, but very quickly, as the standards for data are developed, the data files start to grow very rapidly. If these are in simple unitary form, all that is needed is an algorithm to convert them into valuable information. In extreme simplicity, once there is a file of numbers, algorithms for adding, subtracting, multiplying, and so on, can be applied. A simple file has now become part of a valuable tool.

Even the modern equivalents of the old rules of perspective can now be applied by the computer to give a perspective of the proposed design. As this is a straight mathematical calculation, the computer can carry this out very quickly, allowing many alternative viewpoints to be examined in a short space of time. This is the sort of lengthy manual problem which will inevitably become available very cheaply. Various interpretations have been made of this type of perspective program, some of which give an experience of moving in and around the design proposals. This has been particularly applied to highway design to enable an assessment to be made of the visual impact on drivers. Leeds School of Architecture has produced an extremely useful shading program which shows the effect of the movement of the sun on building shadows. Organizations such as the Norwegian firm Norconsult AS have programs which measure direct and diffuse solar irradiation, incidence of the angle of irradiation, solar height, and asimut. They also have programs measuring external shading and heat gain through windows.

At this point it may be worth noting that many manufacturers have stopped testing actual cars in crash situations and are now using computer models for this purpose because they are cheaper and more efficient. As architecture for this category of practice is often the production of one-off models, there is obviously a great advantage to be gained by using such models.

Part of the tests that can be applied deal with the degree to which a design satisfies building regulations. Building regulations at all times have had to have a basis of logic even though we may not always think so, otherwise they would not be a regulation. The fireproofing category may be expressed as a value of the distance to the boundary and the classification of material. This sort of logic can easily be expressed in computing terms; if computer graphics are used, the computer will automatically recognize the distance of the building from a boundary and will therefore be able to deduce the category of material required, etc. This is only one of the many examples that could be given. Clearly the thermal regulations are another area where great advantages can be obtained, and work on this has been carried out at the School of Architecture, Bristol University. Once the idea of a mathematical model is begun, the opportunities for testing are only inhibited by the cost of collecting and handling the data. It is here that consortia or national services will have to be encouraged; some of these services are described in the next chapter.

However, within these limitations, there is no reason why many other regulations such as those of fire cannot be applied and models for testing them cannot be developed.

The mechanical and ventilating engineers within these multidisciplinary organizations now have a basis for setting up their own data banks which will enable them to produce test solutions. For example, the three-dimensional matrix model described in the last chapter will in effect contain a number of cubes. Those cubes on the perimeter will contain the theoretical loss of the external wall, which is itself dependent upon the materials of the wall and the outside temperature range—similarly with the roof and floor. The internal cubes have no theoretical loss because they are protected by the other cubes. Heat input appliances can be selected from a library to satisfy the stated loss registered in each box, before the whole model is tested. Now that there is an environmental model, the ventilation can also be tested. If microprocessors are used for testing the performance of existing buildings in the way that computers were used at the Eastergate Primary School in West Sussex, their output can become input into the model. In this case, because it became part of a national and international test model for building evaluation, the computerized equipment cost an enormous amount of money. Today, however, the same sort of incredibly valuable feedback information could be achieved at very low cost by the use of microprocessors.

The electrical engineers are able to use algorithms similar to those developed for assessing daylight factors, and together use these for the design and testing of daylight and artificial lighting levels and performance.

If a coordinated design library is set up, the quantity surveyor can also have a basis for the establishment of a cost data base, an aspect which will be dealt with in the next chapter. The economic advantages of such collaborative working can be substantial.

It is worth noting at this point that the logic of using such mathematical models is irrefutable in terms of speed, use of resources, improved evaluation, client/user participation, etc. The only argument against such models is the fear of constraint by the designer. But so-called free design is often limited in any case, in the majority of buildings, by the restraints of time and resources, regulations, and planning approvals, apart from self-imposed limitations of style.

After the design stage comes the production stage in which construction information and costing data have to be produced.

The use of a dimensional standard against which a design can be measured enables computer peripherals, such as plotting equipment, to produce production drawings from a sketch design. It is probably easiest to explain such a computer system in terms of classical architecture. In this, the design components such as the columns and capitals and the rules of proportions and modular spacings are known to the computer, the architect being able to make any permutation or arrangement he wishes. If the column needs to be varied in height, the algorithm for the entasis is known and can therefore be applied. The grid layout of a Roman house or even a city can be laid out and the coordinated classical library is now used for modelling. If standard production drawings were to be prepared which related to the standard components, then a suite of production drawings could be produced from the particular permutation which related to the chosen plans and elevations by the plotter (Figure 80a and b).

It may be argued that with varying heights of columns, etc., there would need to be a considerable number of standard drawings. This is not necessarily true. If we take timber studding and similar items, the rules of spacing and sizing are known to the designer when he prepares a drawing. Therefore there is no reason why the computer cannot be given the same instructions. It follows that not only can some of the rules of design be programmed, such as entasis, but so can rules of construction. It is also possible to make the plotter produce the drawings by trade or process, or by many other categories.

At any desired stage of the design and production process, the details of the site as normally collected by the surveyor can be input into the plotter which will produce site plans, with or without levels and with or without contours. If desired, the surveyor and the computer can be brought together in a planned input/output suite of programs which will give not only the shape and level of the site but also details of the services, fencing, hedges, trees, and significant views, etc. To continue with the analogy with classical architecture, it is obvious that the input already proposed would give a structural engineer sufficient information to enable him to carry out structural calculations. He can see which columns are perimeter columns (i.e. have no columns outside of them), those which are corner columns, and those which are internal columns. Because the design has been prepared on a grid, a computer will know this too. The area of load falling upon each column is obviously deducible, and if the data bank holds the weight and loadings of floors and roofs, etc., it is obvious that the structural calculations can be automatically prepared as more and more algorithms are introduced. There are many computer programs available for this purpose. The same applies to mechanical and electrical engineering (Figure 81).

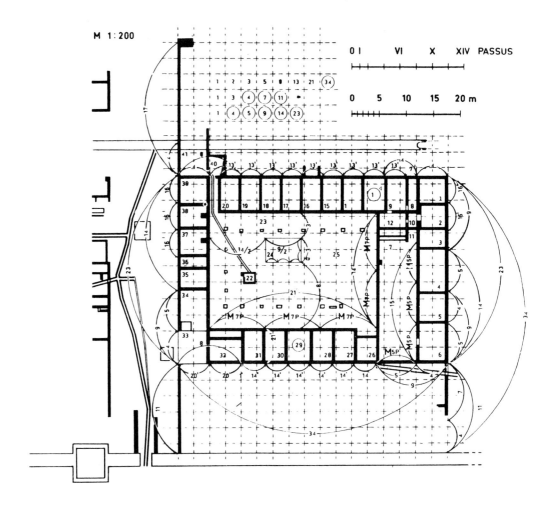

M 1 : 200

'The modular length and width of this building from Emona are multiples of 1 passus. The modular length and width of its atrium are multiples of 7 passus. The rhythm of rooms on the north side is 13 pedes, and on the south 14 pedes. Three rooms in the western and two rooms in the eastern flank of this building are in the rhythm of 16 pedes. Modules of 13, 14 and 16 pedes are deviations from the module of 3 passus (15 pedes), due to the adaptation of the type building to the size of insula (city block). In short, various multiples of standard Roman units of sizes were in use as modules for buildings'.

Figure 80(a)

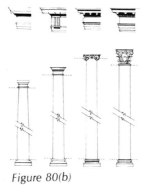

Figure 80(b)

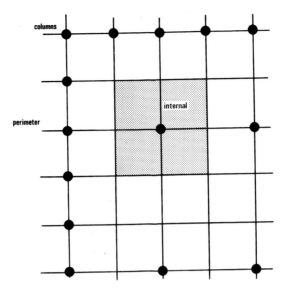

Figure 81

The requisites for making the computer carry out design tasks are clearly twofold:

(1) Is it possible to produce a logic for the activity in question?
(2) Is there a means whereby the computer can recognize the quantity and position of data to be input?

It is for this reason that it was necessary to consider those aspects of architecture called art. The answer to the two questions above is that in the case of the classical architecture example it is clearly 'yes'. Even though modern architecture has become more complex, similar principles can usually be applied, but with increasing cost, as the data either becomes greater in quantity or more difficult to find or measure. This gives an advantage to the larger organizations, which are discussed in the next chapter.

It must, of course, be recognized that the microprocessor will also have an increasing effect upon architecture, not just in the design and communication processes but also in the construction of buildings, as their power and cheapness begins to influence construction equipment. This may happen in the following ways:

(1) New manufacturing and construction equipment will be developed.
(2) New equipment will influence a designer's methods.
(3) New equipment will change the type of building needed.

In the first case, there is already emerging a new breed of equipment in which the microprocessor is used to make the equipment perform complex tasks. It is sometimes difficult to judge whether the first category influences the second, or vice versa, but clearly they have a direct interrelationship. The development of the strip excavator clearly influenced the change from pad foundations to strip foundations wherever possible. Similar influences can be expected in the future. In some cases, there may be a potential for greater variety rather than the present trend of

161

machinery to standardize into a limited range. It is almost certain that it will be possible to produce products with greater variety at no extra cost. But it may be the human who restricts the choice for management and administrative reasons unless microprocessors are also used at this level. Many products reach their peak benefits from mass production in pure production terms at a fairly early stage, but variety is not introduced because of the increased problems of storage, spare parts, management, and sales problems. Even manual craft activities impose the same limitations—take, for example, *haute cuisine* restaurants. Here would apparently be a fine opportunity to have endless variety, yet all confine themselves to a restricted menu for most of the above reasons. The traditional architect, however, in his unfortunate position of often being divorced from the processes of production, is not well placed to derive the maximum benefit of cost and efficiency from production and construction management. In large components, variety means a delay in call-off time when they are made to order and an increase in storage and management problems which increase the cost when premanufactured for a quick call-off. The penalties for non-standard products can be seen in any shop. Non-standard goods either take time or cost more. However, in the construction industry this is not so clear-cut. As already noted, most contractors and manufacturers have to work for both 'one-off' and repetitive building for their survival and therefore, often subsidize the 'one off' by increasing the cost of the standard, sometimes even holding up production lines to let a 'one-off' batch go through. The net effect of this is a confusion in knowing how the two compare. After all, if hand-made shoes could be bought at little more cost than mass-produced ones and if the mass-produced one had poor delivery dates, who would want the mass-produced shoes? Only the poor, where marginal savings are important. But everyone, including the poor, would be paying more.

In the second category, the increased use of computer peripherals in place of drawing boards, print machines, etc., will inevitably have as many influences on the design process as similar changes have had in the past.

The potential of the microprocessor in the third category is so great that it is difficult to foresee where this might lead, although some trends may be identified. The design of several generations of suburban homes have been influenced during this century by equipment. Prior to the First World War, suburban houses had sculleries and large kitchens for housing clothes boilers, kitchen ranges, knife grinder/polishers, mangles, and so on. During the inter-war years, the scullery disappeared and the kitchen reduced in size as everything was streamlined and miniaturized. Recent housing trends suggests that after a period of higher space standards, they are again tending to get smaller and take advantage of even further miniaturization. It is here that the microprocessor will play a large part. It is predicted that by 1980, there will be between seven and ten of them in every home in the United States of America. Already, few European homes have not got at least one, often in the form of a digital watch or calculator.

Large canteen restaurants will obviously be affected by microprocessing equipment, as will office design and even office furniture. Desks are still designed for an earlier age and usually have little more benefit than to give a sense of location. New computer equipment will undoubtedly have a very large effect on this whole area of design, that is, if the offices are still required at all. About this there must be some doubt in the long term.

Factories and other places of manufacture are still seen as descendants of the dark satanic mills, where a lower category of worker was subservient to the needs of the machine. It seems to have been hardly noticed that very little equipment today places such physical demands upon the human body; in fact, far from dividing workers into the blue collar and white collar categories, the two are rapidly and rightly expecting the same standards of accommodation. It is the machine which is designed to protect the human being, rather than as in earlier days the human being doing his best to protect himself from the effects of the machine. Even the computer now does not have to have a special environment, which at one time was surprisingly of a much higher standard than that provided for human beings in the organization.

One of the major areas where this will almost certainly have a considerable effect is in the environmental control of buildings. The potentials for heating, sound, and light controls are obvious; e.g. alarm systems, hotel bedroom control, etc. But there will be other developments for the protection and management of buildings which will form just part of a flood of new technology and may even include the production of the whole spatial experience.

The scope over the whole of society is so great that it would be impossible to predict the outcome of so many interacting factors, but at least there should be a realization that there will be great changes in every aspect of society and its architecture for which preparations need to be made now.

163

Chapter 7

APPLICATIONS—INTEGRATED DESIGN AND CONSTRUCTION

The advantages for the integrated design and build organizations can be so enormously improved by the use of microprocessors in their various forms that it is difficult to imagine how they can avoid taking an even larger share of the market, i.e. the market for enclosing space. Furthermore, the demand may not be just satisfied by the traditional industry, with or without its newer variations. Strangely, the industry may have to go through a period of much closer integration in order to rationalize its processes before decentralizing again to a situation which may not look too different from the traditional situation, but which in fact will be very different (i.e. integrating small units of design and of construction into larger integrated units which will then be decentralized into smaller units).

New developments have a habit of springing up quite distinctly from their traditional counterparts. The motorcar industry did not stem from the horse and carriage industry and nor did the aircraft industry stem from the motorcar industry; yet they are all transportation. New industries tend to spring up because the old industries are unable to change. The older and larger the industry, the more vulnerable it is. Is the construction industry therefore vulnerable? Certainly the rise in other industries enclosing space should not be ignored, as it has been so far. Architects would have found the question of the future of the industry unworthy of an answer a few years ago, but few would today be so confident. Nevertheless, there is a belief and hope that as the industry is so old and has taken this form for such a long time, it will somehow continue in the same way. But that is what the Guilds thought too! Clearly, conventional practice will continue for a long time to come, but, also clearly, the integrated design and build organizations will take an increasing share of whatever is going, either for political or economic reasons.

The main weakness of such organizations is the inventiveness or creativeness of their designers, but this problem is easily overcome. Their strength is the integration of processes whereby, with reasonable organization, *every symbol the architect uses for his design can become the activator for the processes which will almost instantaneously produce cost, production management information, and sometimes even the manufacture itself.* Instead of the time taken for preparation of pre-contract documents, tendering, and the divorce from the management of the contract, there is one integrated system. The time that can be saved is enormous and indisputable. The logical advantages in terms of cost and efficiency are beyond dispute.

Why then have the various forms of design and build already not scooped the field? There are several reasons. The first is that most still employ traditional processes at every stage, thereby making the process similar to the one-off system. In both public and private sectors, many organizations invite tenders from themselves in the traditional way! Second, they often try to economize on their design staff and set aside very little for research. In this again, they behave as traditional contractors, waiting for new ideas to come from outside rather than as in other industries where their full responsibilities are understood and accepted. Third, they have not understood the differences between the design-orientated and the product-orientated industry, and tend to float between the two.

This has been the salvation of the building professions so far, particularly as they can now in addition point to the building failures of the *prefab* industry. But it is not as easy as that. Both sides have made mistakes. The question is, who will win in the end? Time will answer the question eventually, but, in the meantime, the design and build organizations of one sort or another now provide a substantial proportion of the built environment. Therefore, the systems which can be used in this type of organization must be taken seriously and, if possible, married to the existing professional organizations who have so much to contribute.

Organizations will continue to grow globally in spite of desires to the contrary, and therefore in this section of the industry there will be a range from the largest public and private organizations operating on an international basis right down to the much smaller public and private organizations. It is difficult to dissociate the makers of components from this category, because their processes are similar at many levels.

This whole integrated group either obtains its work passively, as in the case of government or local government organizations which are allocated budgets, or actively, as in the case of the private sector who need to seek work. This latter part of the industry, however, is only partly active in this field, because it does not try to make a market but generally waits for one to arise or waits to be invited to tender. A small number of building and component suppliers seek and advertise for clients, but, more commonly, they expect to be invited to tender when the time arrives. The product they sell is usually responsive to their client's needs. As the client, for them, is often the architect, they feel deferential to him and his design knowledge.

The larger organizations have the capital and resources available to make aggressive selling techniques possible. The reasons they do not are again probably because of the fear of meddling with an art for which the architect has the key. It is therefore worth making some comparisons with the way the best of other industries operate. Rather than wait for events to happen, a good industrial firm will use some of the forecasting techniques, already quoted, to consider the future environment in which their products will be sold. As society changes quickly but the processes of setting up a new product is slow, it is necessary to be as accurate as possible with their forecasts. Such things as the following have to be taken into account:

(1) Potential market and the degree of forecast accuracy needed for success. The degree of accuracy needed varies according to the sensitivity of the market to be invaded.

(2) Implications of new technology. The motor industry has been planning for a long time to meet future legal requirements for clean exhaust. The building industry is still only adjusting to energy conservation after it has been forced to do so by legislation.

(3) Duration of production lines. As any product line cannot be run forever, a plan with time scales is needed for the phasing in, stable period, and phasing out of the product. Ignoring the idea of a product cycle has probably been one of the greatest causes of criticism and failure of most system building. Their design always followed a long way behind the best architect's work, and continued long after they were rejected by the public. No successful shoe manufacturer would do this.

(4) Need for research. As the production line increases, so does the need for research, because one fault is multiplied many times, the publicity is multiplied many times, and the rectification cost increases many times. This was another failure of some system building in the past.

(5) Type of marketing to be employed. Only recently have some manufacturers had the confidence to produce a comprehensive package which they can sell direct to the client. Previously, the industrialized builder would usually sell through an architect, who, because of his trained creativeness, would insist on variations and modifications. Afraid of losing the project, the firm would agree to the modifications, thereby increasing the cost because of the administration and production of specials, as well as increasing the risk of failures. Even component supplies fall into the same trap.

(6) Time for delivery and handover. Management systems must be available to ensure proper programming and scheduling. For many people today, the time factor is more important than the cost. With expensive money to borrow and a loss of return on capital during building as well as inflation, the contract period becomes an increasingly important consideration.

(7) After-sales service. Can a follow-up service be provided, because the choice of a product in our lives generally is increasingly made on the reputation of firms to provide the after-sales service.

These factors seem to be obvious needs for almost anything we buy, but how many can be found in architecture and construction?

In this process for developing a product to meet a demand some time ahead, a number of forecasting techniques have been developed, some of which have already been mentioned and many of which have been adapted for use on computers. The Delphi method is a typical and valuable computer tool for this type of work, but there are many others—for assessment of component product growth, forecasting of a steady state, etc. The techniques for industry are extremely well developed and assume that products go through definite stages which briefly include:

Research of market and product
Forecasts of market and growth
Introduction of product
Steady state of sales
Phasing out of product

It is this last phase which is of very great importance in most industries, yet does not enter the management systems of traditional design and construction. A product manufacturer, in most areas of society, has to anticipate the time when the public will tire of a given line and have a new product ready to phase in. The failure of many production companies can be attributed to failure to anticipate the end of a product's useful life—motorcycle firms, toy firms, etc. The same problem lies at the root of the public's reaction against architects and their architecture. Therefore, the traditional use of intuition instead of these management techniques could reasonably be questioned.

Information lies at the root of all production enterprises, and the advantage to the large organization is their ability to support large manual and/or computer data banks. The matrix structure of information storage can be developed by those organizations to hold, for example, information on materials. It is obvious that materials data held on this basis can be retrieved, either by name of product, name of firm, type of product, or, most importantly, by the criteria of needs which have to be satisfied. Furthermore, all of this can be done without the use of complex coding systems.

The same method can be used for holding the details of all property which may come under the control of the organization. In such cases, the entries can be found by their geographical location. A map of, say, the United Kingdom can be brought up on the terminal screen. Overlaying the map is a grid and by pointing to the desired square of the grid, this segment will be enlarged with a further grid, and the process repeated until, if necessary, by using the National Grid referencing system, one particular square metre can be identified.

The integrated design and construction organization can have a variety of structural calculation programs, which can also be linked to the location grid file for such things as wind load ratings in particular areas. The same applies to the environmental control design programs, in which the exposure of the site can be determined. Both of these types of input can be made available for modelling techniques and for testing proposed designs. If all these and many other aspects of data are nationally or organizationally coordinated, the power of the tools becomes very substantial indeed. National files can be held on the cost and performance of the resources involved in the construction process, which can then be manipulated by personal microcomputers at the desired level, together with all other resources needed, so that the cost and performance can be known at the time of design.

Files are normally held in the larger organization on the types of manpower employed and their rates of pay. Most building organizations also have bonus or target systems for which the times of various activities are required. If the cost and use of plant machinery files are held, together with the cost of materials and manpower resources, it is easy for a cost to be made on the following basis: manpower × activity time + materials + plant cost. To this must be added the profit level required. If every item of standard work related to the chosen dimensional grid is held on this basis, then the cost and resources required can be determined as the design proceeds. Take, for example, a symbol for a brick wall as already described. If this is filed in the computer with all of the MAMP necessary for its execution, then as the designer draws a plan each characteristic can be directed by the computer to a resource-levelling network. At any stage of the design the cost expended so far can be totalled; or if the resources available are input, then the length of time required to carry out the operation will be given. Cash flow, ordering times for materials, and economical use of resources can all be obtained directly from the activities of design (already described in Paterson, 1977).

Within one organization it is possible to consider the effect of different methods of production at the design stage in a way which is quite impossible for the isolated designer.

It has often been stated that this type of operation, in which the design team, and if desired the user, can evaluate a design for cost and performance almost instantly, can only be done with a closed system of building construction. This thesis has further been attached, in repeated articles and books, to the West Sussex system, for example, by suggesting that it could only be used with the SCOLA building system. This is patently untrue. Figures 82 and 83 illustrate the Old People's Home at Horsham, Sussex (1968), and the Primary School at Eastergate, Sussex (1971), which were both produced on the computer system. Not only were both designed in traditional construction and not in the fashionable style of the period, but they also contained very early experiments with energy conservation and participation not only by the user but also the community. The books of Serlio could most easily have been translated into this system to give instant evaluation and production information, but as we shall see later, this is not enough for the architecture of tomorrow.

The problems of design and build organizations using computers is not therefore the alleged one of the computer restricting the design potential, but a management one of making decisions on how far work should be

(1) repetitive,
(2) variable,
(3) repetitive, but with less working time,
(4) carried out in terms of whole operations, and
(5) complex.

The traditional architect, quite divorced from the problems of component manufacture and building management can only consider these characteristics insofar as they affect his design. But these are of enormous importance throughout the process, not only for achieving targets and reducing costs but also for the establishment of reasonable human

169

Figure 82

Figure 83

working conditions. Many of the traditional processes, not only at the building level but also at the component level, require people to work in appalling conditions which cannot continue to be acceptable for very much longer. Trades unions will force major changes in this area as well. If a Bill of Quantities is required, it can still be obtained by using the MAMP files together with a library of work items, but with a standard description written into the system so that the bill can be developed at the same time as, or instead of, a resource-levelling network. The methods of tendering are critical to the organization of a computer system at this stage.

The large integrated design and construction organizations will usually fall into three categories:

(1) Contractors who also operate in a traditional contracting situation and therefore tend to use Bills of Quantities, specifications, or similar traditional systems of costing
(2) Local authorities who sometimes carry out work with their own labour force, and at other times seek tenders
(3) The package deal organization in its many forms

Organizations in the first two categories tend to hang on to their traditional tendering systems so that they can have the flexibility to use both markets. Even in these cases, it is wiser for them to produce an integrated design and construction computer system, making the Bills of Quantities, or similar systems, a by-product rather than making it central to the system, as usually happens. The reasons are obvious. All of the traditional systems have been developed over the last two hundred years to enable the client to

(1) select a contractor,
(2) agree a total cost for the project, and
(3) have a basis for pricing variations.

When the Guilds were replaced by the new system which divorced architects from construction, considerable problems and disagreements arose over the measurement and the cost of the work, and measurers were increasingly used to measure the work carried out and negotiate payment. This led to the selection of contractors by tender, each of whom would measure the work to be carried out. As it would clearly be more economical for one man to measure the work for a number of contractors, the bills of quantities prepared by a quantity surveyor began to emerge in Britain (but in few other countries) as a basis for obtaining tenders. But this, of course, is based on the precept that tenders of this nature are required, which of course they are not in an integrated design and construct system.

The bills of quantities system is an excellent one in many ways but does have a number of disadvantages. It is a lengthy and somewhat costly means of satisfying the first need, which is to select a contractor. There are much simpler and cheaper and probably more effective methods. It only satisfies the second condition if there are no variations to the contract, for as soon as variations are made two things happen. The first is that the original total cost now becomes a hypothetical cost. The second and usually overlooked fact is that the wrong contractor may have been selected. Every contractor puts his own price against items of work according to whether he is or is not proficient at the work, or because he suspects variations will or will not occur. There is clearly an advantage in having a high rate for work which is extended by variation. Excavation is a typical example. This can mean that the lowest contractor by luck or skill is actually producing a final account which is higher than one which might have been produced by a higher tenderer. Furthermore, a higher tenderer might have completed the work quicker, thereby reducing other costs. This particularly applies in a period of high inflation.

The last characteristic, of providing a means for measuring and pricing, is clearly only necessary if there are variations.

But most products are purchased complete. If a total product is offered at a total price, as in most industries (which includes many of the items used in buildings), the second problem is removed and the third becomes unnecessary. If the organization offers a design and cost, the first problem of selecting a contractor takes a different form as well.

The prefabricated building product can be selected by comparison with other products on the basis of its suitability and total cost. A car, refrigerator, etc., is purchased on the same basis, with the time of delivery often being a significant factor. The cheapest product is very often not the one selected. How often has one purchased the cheapest shirt, shoes, car radio, and so on? Very rarely. Normally other criteria become more important and the cheapest is only selected on occasion.

In building, however, a lengthy and costly process is gone through in order to obtain what appears to be the lowest capital cost, irrespective of other qualities such as time or performance. Even then, it is not necessarily the lowest cost. Having created this attitude, many techniques have been developed which are peculiar to the construction industry and are now sadly being produced in computer form. These involve tender cost forecasting, etc. These of course become unnecessary if the building is sold as a product and the time between selection and delivery are minimal. The advantages are obvious. The disadvantage is perhaps our traditional view of architecture.

Many well-known architects in the past have supported the obvious logic of an improved production situation. Oud in 1918 expressed the view that housing should be standardized and beauty obtained by the grouping of building blocks and the manipulation of standard components. He thought that mass production had come at 'exactly the right psychological moment' for architecture. In 1924 Le Corbusier forecast that industrialization and the introduction of mechanization on site would lead to the general acceptance of standard elements which could provide greater unity. From this a style would emerge. In 1925 he was pleading for Renault, Peugeot, Citroen, Le Creuset, or one of the big metallurgists to organize the building industry. In 1910 Gropius also pleaded for mass production to overcome the need for luck in obtaining efficient and reliable craftsmen. He wanted to eliminate the craftsman and replace him with a factory-guaranteed identity of products. In 1927 he was pointing out that 90 per cent. of the population bought their shoes and other needs as ready-made products. Why not buildings? He laid down five pre-conditions for a rational construction industry to produce cheaper and better housing:

(1) Mass production off-the-peg prefabricated housing, the housing no longer being produced on the actual building site but in special factories. The wholesale manufacture of these building block units is based on standardization.
(2) Utilization of new techniques and raw materials which economize on space and bricks and mortar.
(3) Rationalized management of building using dry building methods on an assembly line following an exact timetable with the greatest possible elimination of wastage.
(4) Rationalized building plans which will be thoroughly studied down to the last detail on large-scale models before building actually begins—as with plans for assembling machines.
(5) Farsighted monetary policies from building financiers, aiming to avoid any raising of interest rates on building capital by the elimination of unproductive intermediate stages.

Even William the Conqueror brought prefabricated forts to England in 1066 as an obvious solution to a logistical problem. Brunel in 1855 designed a prefabricated hospital system to accommodate between 500 and 1,500 patients on sites of differing shapes and contours to provide for the requirements of Florence Nightingale in the Crimea. Twenty-three ships carried the sections to Renkoi in May, and the hospital were taking in patients in July.

The examples of the successes of prefabrication and the recordings of the great brains on the obvious logic are endless. So it may be asked, why has it all not happened already? The truth is that it is happening—quitely and relentlessly.

The growth of the prefabricated boxes developed for site use now continues apace. It is argued that these are temporary solutions, but will they be temporary? Many have been on static sites for a long time with renewed temporary planning permissions. The expansion of the caravan and mobile home industry has already been quoted. The expansion of the ready-made product as a means of providing accommodation is not only dismissed by architects but is also dismissed by the planners and public alike in its impact on the environment. A new standard for a type of built environment is gradually being taken for granted. Even the fact that strict and lengthy processes have to be gone through by architects to obtain approval for their designs for houses which can immediately be obscured by a caravan parked in the front garden is not questioned.

It is not only in complete industrialized buildings that the change has occurred. Take, for example, the United Kingdom. The work force in building fell from 1,839,000 in 1963 to 1,493,000 in 1972, whilst the value of construction increased from 3,257 million pounds in 1963 to 7,187 million pounds in 1972. This can only mean increased industrialization or mechanization, or both. The speed of change is likely to increase as labour in the construction industry is decasualized and therefore becomes more costly.

The anticipated swing to industrialization, anticipated in the 1920s has been slower than expected for a number of reasons:

(1) Buildings are considered as investments.
(2) The relationship between land and building ownership is complex.
(3) The financing of building.
(4) The conservatism of the industry and the professions.
(5) The traditional idea of building by the public.

Some of these factors are changing. The Community Land Act, and other acts, change the relationship of finance and property. Financing of buildings is often becoming more favourable to the hire of cheap building rather than the purchase of long-life expensive ones. Lastly, the general public is spending an increased amount of its time in prefabricated accommodation—caravans, mobile classrooms, and offices, etc. It will probably soon emerge that the problem is not whether to have industrialized building, but the scale of the industrialization which, with the microprocessor, is likely to overwhelm those who have not prepared themselves for change. The trends, already under way, will most certainly increase, and a decision on whether industrialization should be increased at component or building level will become a main issue.

In France, for example, where a post-war industry grew up to produce heavy, large-unit systems, there has recently been a move towards the greater flexibility offered by smaller components. This partly follows the universal reaction against the architecture of the 1960s but also reflects the change in the size of developments. There are now fewer large and heavily financed sites with a large repetition of units suitable for large prefabricated construction units. The industry has therefore moved towards a multiplicity of smaller interchangeable components. Whereas the former layouts were often dominated by considerations of production and crane layout, the component approach gives greater opportunities for small site development and personal choices.

Whichever course is selected, the microprocessor will give the manufacturers the advantage of speedier and cheaper production together with design flexibility within their own rules, as well as easier management control. The rapidly growing organizations of builders' merchants may also constitute an outlet not only for components but also for complete buildings. Their designs will probably be based on standard support systems of varying degree as proposed by Habraken some years ago, and will not only allow for a substantial degree of user choice in plan layout but also in the use of optional elevational treatments. Their development may create a demand for new land ownerships. They will also probably begin to encroach on other traditional areas of building. Already, research laboratories are being produced as complete building systems, attaining higher standards than their traditional counterparts often reach. They are also beginning to incorporate microprocessors into the operation of the equipment within the buildings, as well as the buildings themselves—e.g. air locks, etc.

The less industrialized design and build organizations will still find that the standardization of their data will bring down costs and improve programme time. Any reaction against such standardization will probably be overcome by marketing and participation. Advertising, or indoctrination, has a great power for overcoming prejudices against standard products.

The construction industry has traditionally waited for an architect to invite tenders, whilst the architect has traditionally waited for an invitation from a patron. No patron; no work. The void left between need and reticence will probably be filled by marketing men who will sell ideas as well as buildings. They have been sold through the ages in the middle range of building. Before expressing disgust for such open commercialization, it should be remembered that the suburbia of the 1930s was a dream of health and happiness sold by governments, railways, builders, Gibb's dentifrice, Ovaltine, and many others, which created a considerable amount of happiness for the mass of people who lived there. Whilst the intellectuals of the time sneered in their more expensive accommodation, their descendants now eagerly seek this accommodation. This speculative builder's housing, criticized at the time and eagerly sought today, had had a very long tradition, and is now seen to be nearer the desire of that section of society for which it was built than most of the architect-designed estates of the local authorities. Cox (1977), in a lecture at the RIBA, showed the course of post-war architect-designed housing and finished with a proposal for the future which was similar to that which speculative builders had been doing all the time.

The main factor therefore becomes the second characteristic—participation. Standards may be identical, but the society which is given choice, even though that choice may be limited, seems to be more contented than the society in which decisions are imposed. This is one of the differences between suburbia, where there was choice (of buying or not buying, which made the builder very sensitive to demand), and the allocated housing of the 1960s, where the architecture was often very good but there was no choice for the user. The other factor was, of course, property management.

With the computer, the integrated design and construct organization is able to give the client the opportunity of making a choice on a computer and knowing the outcome of his decisions before he commits himself. The local authority, with or without design and build integration, as well as other organizations, could decentralize their staff so that they could also work with the community for greater influence over their own affairs. In this situation, they could use several terminals for the evaluation of community needs on an interactive basis. Management and auditing, which caused centralization in the first place, could easily be handled with computer facilities. Even such methods as Flexitime could be used by people working at home or in regional offices.

The advantages of such a system are many. The design teams could identify themselves with the community, and the community with them. Each area could more easily develop its own character, giving the community greater choice even if the basic components of design were more limited, which would not necessarily be the case. There would be a premium on those areas where the team and the community worked best together, which would be self-enhancing. At the present rate of progress, it will take more than twenty-eight years in the United Kingdom to

175

improve the existing substandard accommodation alone, without even considering future obsolescence. This is without the problem of correcting and replacing tower blocks and other failures.

However, if local stimulus is encouraged, as has been done at Rochdale, Wakefield, and Pontefract, among others, the problem would increasingly reduce as confidence and self help developed. Whilst part of the problem is money, a major part of urban renewal is the need for hope. Once blighted areas begin to improve and a feeling of progress is noticed, crime rates, vandalism, and assaults are seen to drop. Very often perfectly traditional building processes are required, but the microprocessor's contribution will be to put the expertise where it is needed. There are clearly many other problems connected with urban renewal and community development, but these suggestions are made to illustrate the sort of contribution computers can, and will, make. Too often, lack of money is blamed for a lack of providing hope and initiative.

Finally, these integrated organizations will find the maintenance of existing building stock an increasingly serious problem.

As the labour force continues to get smaller, the difficulty of finding crafts, labour, and materials for maintenance will increase, as will the costs. Maintenance management will therefore play an increasingly important part in the developed world. All the buildings controlled by the organization can be held on computer files which can contain all their details for instant recall as necessary. For example, the designed heat load and anticipated fuel consumption can be fed into the computer as the building is designed, so that actual consumption can be compared later. If desired, the accounts can be encoded so that the computer can automatically record the fuel bills against the project. A maintenance manager, running through the property file, would quickly spot a rogue building where fuel consumption indicates either that there is a fault in the boiler system or that there is corruption. The same process can be applied to many other aspects of maintenance, and of course the diary system can be used for bringing forward details, specifications, etc., at the required maintenance periods. In the end, it may be the maintenance of buildings which will do most to force a change to short-life system building. Even though most people would like a vintage car, or even an old motorcar, steam engine, or anything else, it is the problems and cost of maintenance which makes them choose a short-life, mass-produced article for which parts and a maintenance system is available. The increasing difficulty of getting building maintenance carried out, together with the probability that system builders will introduce maintenance agreements, may have further effects upon the traditional system.

Many of the computer processes described in Chapter 6 are equally applicable to the integrated design and construction organizations, particularly up to the production drawing stage. *It is the economy of the use of the designer's graphical symbol as a direct input for evaluation and production, rather than interpreted over and over again by different professions and trades, that will eventually give the design and build organization the greater share of the market.* The design and build organizations also have a greater capacity to collect and maintain large data banks which enables them to strengthen and widen the search area from brief to maintenance. The filing of data in the smaller organizations is often left to low-paid, unqualified staff. As these data banks should be the memory of the organization or the equivalent of the brain in the human body, this is rather a dangerous procedure.

If a sufficiently senior person is put in charge of the collection, organization, and dissemination of information, the performance of the organization will improve, as many progressive organizations are now finding. The information manager must be part of the design and construction management team so that information needs can be anticipated. The input of data can be either in the form of surveyors taking site levels, or analysts putting in new building regulations or the input of the client's brief for a new project. The output can be by drawings or computer terminals, etc. But it is the storage of the information which is all important, and this requires a data coordination system. If this is set up in the right way, much of the data can be held in a computer, thereby bringing the input and output terminals into a direct relationship.

With the various possibilities for change caused by the future use of computers, there is clearly a need for both major strategies and local tactics. Each have problems of their own, but the greatest problems will be where they overlap.

There is a need for major strategies to agree to the siting of major roads, new towns, industrial areas, and so on, and in these areas public involvement is obtained by various forms of public enquiry. But whether the proposals come from public bodies or from representations from the public who present their own proposals, somewhere a designer or design team has to put together the proposal. A design procedure has to be used to create a proposal upon which comment may be made. But however much we may support participation, it is no more possible for this type of major strategy to be developed from a brief in which each person demands to have his own view expressed than it would be to design Concorde with public participation.

On the other hand, there is clearly a need for individuals to have more control over their own living and working conditions than they usually have at present. The major problems are likely to occur where the one begins and the other ends, and it is the organization within this category which will have to face this problem. It will not only be the official bodies who will be concerned, as it might have been in the past, but also the major commercial design and build organizations.

In the past, the success of a commercial organization could be measured by a single aspect—profit. Today, it is very different. Not only are there many interpretations of profit, but also no organization can afford to ignore public opinion in its myriad forms. So, therefore, both official and commercial design and build organizations will find themselves following closely parallel paths, as they have often done in the past. Government and local authorities, for example, will have to develop methods of keeping the public informed as decision making proceeds from one step to the next, rather than presenting a grand plan for acceptance in toto. For them, the most advanced developments in information handling will have to be used by their design teams, and these systems may not be very different from those which commercial organizations will have to develop in order to market their products. Teletext and Viewdata are only two of the communication systems which will be increasingly used in this area. At the local level, it has already been shown how modern technology can help the interaction between the user and designer. Where the major difficulties will occur is in defining the middle ground and devising means for the architects and design teams to exploit their education and dedication for the benefit of the community and society as a whole.

Chapter 8

HOW WILL THE MICROPROCESSOR SHAPE OUR ENVIRONMENT?

No matter how far we roll back the carpet of knowledge to expose more and more areas which we once thought of as art and which we can now reduce to logic, we still feel an instinctive and inexplicable affinity with some things and not with others. How and why do we feel such pleasure in some pieces of architecture which we have never seen before? Is it all based on indoctrination? It may be as Rochefoucauld has said (or as suggested in the Roman de la Rose), that few people would fall in love if they had not read about it, but it does not explain the whole range of emotions to which we are subject, very often against our will. Some of these experiences can undoubtedly be related to Berlyne's (1971) hedonic value. For example, the place where a couple fall in love will be associated with the emotion of falling in love. How many people, looking at a Constable painting, are not influenced by happy times spent in landscapes such as those he illustrates? There is also the association of activities with architecture. The first theatre or opera house visited has a special emotional appeal because of the association with the activity rather than the building. Skinner (1970) has suggested that people could be conditioned in their reaction to buildings by such associations. It is not only the whole of buildings or their activities which can affect us emotionally; parts of buildings can also evoke memories in the same way as a small facial characteristic can identify a loved or hated one, even though that detail may only be, say, Hitler's moustache or an oriel window. As well as the great subtlety of interplay between indoctrinated, half-remembered, associative visual components, there is also that part of us which is inherited. No longer is there the tabula rasa, but the recognition that large areas of experience and knowledge are inherited. Apart from drugs, hormone levels, etc., there are also the vast number of influences upon our minds and bodies from external sources which affect our senses and thoughts. Some of these influences, like hypnosis, were once seen as mystical arts to be held in the power of a few people, but now seen to be a part of medicine. How much else is waiting to be explained and to be rationalized in the area we call art? It is probable that there will always be new frontiers to explore, new games to be made and played; all the time there is, there will be a subject known as art.

Hopefully we shall become less arrogant about its absolute qualities. As we produce a logic for what we see, hear, smell, and feel which we can then computerize, we also find that these senses are based on an extreme subtlety of input. Even smell, which architects see as something to be negated, has, through research into ferromones, been seen to have a considerable effect on human behaviour even though we may be quite unaware of their existence. If we consider the possible permutations of the interactions of such subtleties on all of the senses, and then add to these the other influences such as the effect of negative and positive ions, magnetism, telekinesis, gravity, and so on, the potential world for the exploration of the emotions is enormous. Even the effect of heavenly bodies, as the ancient astrologers maintained, may come to be seen as an influence on human emotions and human society. After all, we know that the moon has a substantial influence on the earth as well as human beings, so why should not other bodies such as the planets? As we begin to understand the effect of minutely small power sources, the potential for such influences becomes increasingly apparent. Scientists in the USSR, for example, have been particularly interested in research into some of those areas, which have tended to be considered unscientific in the West; such work is described by Ostrander and Schroeder (1970). More recently, their proposition that thoughts are carried on waves of gravity has caused interest, particularly as there now seems to be some evidence that gravity waves might exist. Therefore, whilst we are able to produce a logic, and therefore computer programs, for much of that area we now know as art, new frontiers will almost certainly always be found which will then become known as art.

We can rationalize the position as follows:

(1) A tremendous amount of that area of human understanding known as magic and/or art is now being brought into the field of science and logic, and put on to computers.
(2) There will be for a long time to come, if not for ever, frontiers to be explored which for the time being will be called art.
(3) The course of society will continue to be a journey based upon innumerable forces and counterforces, gradually seeking ever-changing stabilities.

The history of architecture, as with most other human activities, is the story of these action and counteraction forces. The game of the hawks and doves has been continuously played out against the strongly held beliefs of a person or small group of people trying to impose their ideals upon all people everywhere.

The good side of the modern architectural movement was, for the people of the time, the hope and enthusiasm for a bright new world. It was a dream, and many people capitalized on the mood. Nevertheless, society also enjoyed it while it lasted. It would be difficult to say who started it, or why it started, but the dream survived a world war to continue into a post-war architectural concept. The sunshine schools of the 1930s became the sunshine homes in the sky of the 1950s. Whilst architects rose to this theme, thunderclouds were already being predicted by all the other forms of art, as well as by a society which was seeking more personal control of its destiny and which was already beginning to react against idealistic solutions. Architecture was not only continuing an outmoded theme (at best, making a few artistic concessions to styles such as Brutalism) long after the mood of society had passed on to new concepts but it was also using such a slow system of design and construction that the work appeared even more anachronistic when it was finally built. Lastly, when it was eventually erected, it was in such a solid form that it could not be put away in an attic until the fashion returned, as with all the other arts.

Some may feel that the scale and facelessness of London could now never be loved, but a visit to the Old Curiosity Shop is a reminder of the scale of London before the Great Fire, and how gross and faceless the new Renaissance architecture must have seemed at the time. Modern architecture will eventually be praised and treasured, but what happens to the society who has to use it in the meantime? This has been a problem in all human societies except those nomadic societies who built, and still build, of naturally disposable materials and then just move on. But as more and more long-life buildings are erected, the morality of the situation must begin to cause increasing concern—particularly with housing.

The problem which caused such public criticism would appear to be less the modern architectural style itself but more the class of building to which it was applied. All through history, architecture has been an exploration of new spatial and philosophical concepts applied to the symbolic buildings of society—palaces, cathedrals, public buildings, and even, to some extent, the great Renaissance houses. Society needs, and will always need, such aesthetic signposts.

This is, however, the first time in history that mass housing has been turned into an architectural symbol. Even factories and offices have been designed as architectural and social symbols. Whilst it was acceptable to change religious services to suit the poor acoustics which emanated from the spatial symbolic concepts of the Middle Ages, people are not prepared to distort their everyday lives to support an architect's symbol who is to them probably anonymous anyway. In fact, how many architects have wished to live in such monuments themselves? Strangely, those buildings which were the traditional areas of architectural symbol-ism have receded into the background whilst mass-housing symbols stand out everywhere. It is noticeable that where the traditional position prevails, architecture is enjoyed and not criticized, and the architect himself retains goodwill. In spite of the cost and delays and all the other problems of Sydney Opera House, it is praised and enjoyed as a symbol by the community. Similar examples of society's affection for symbolic buildings, irrespective of their so-called aesthetic merit, are numer-ous—Albert Hall, London, Coventry Cathedral, Festival Hall, London, and gradually the National Theatre, London. At the other end of the scale, small housing developments are being assimilated with affection while architectural award-winning mass-housing complexes such as those in Pruitt Igoe, designed for some theoretical ideal family which does not exist, are being criticized and/or pulled down. Architects everywhere have been trying to work closely with human needs and eschewing the current fashions of the day, gradually producing a visual language which is understandable to the majority rather than the few. Journalists and academics often describe architecture in a sort of poetic language (which is not always evident in the real environment) but poetry in words or architecture is not for everyday use. Largely unknown and unnoticed by the architectural press, the appeal and value of the work of architects in the community, as well as many speculative housing developers, can be assessed by the care with which it is maintained. Personal involvement is noticeable by both the architect and user. This is not the case with the monumental mass-housing schemes which try to make a political point or a social statement. There is no doubt that *given time*, many of even this type of building will be used, adapted, and even loved, which raises the very old issue of whether buildings should be designed for human needs or whether humans should adapt to the buildings.

This then again raises further issues as to what is design and what is human need. There is in these questions, which usually devolve into unhelpful syllogistic statements, the germ of a major threat where computers are concerned. Both design and human need are based upon the need for decision, but the way in which we make our decisions determines our freedom. We may be asked a series of yes/no questions which can each be answered in turn with honesty, and which may yet lead us to a solution we do not want because the order of the questions was giving a bias towards a given solution. In other words, the order is giving a weighting to our choice. Take, for example, the selection of a house at an estate agent's office. If he were to take all the houses he has for sale and we ask for four bedrooms (he then throws away all those with more or less), two bathrooms (ditto), two garages (ditto), etc., and then he asks for the desired location last, those houses which are left might be in the places we do not wish to live, whilst one with an acceptable change (such as five bedrooms) was thrown out at the beginning. Similarly with those programs in which a design is seen as a specification to be input for the computer to propose a single ideal solution. Many computer applications employ such techiques or, even worse, expect the parameters of a design to be inserted according to some set of rules. Whilst the new techniques can be interesting and even look attractive and elegant, they can also be exceedingly dangerous when the implications of the methods of use are neither questioned nor understood. Architects, who know from years of experience that design is a creation which needs development backwards and forwards, iteratively, towards a solution, may find themselves with but one choice of route to a solution. We should be grateful to such critics as Jamieson, Cooley, and Cross who have questioned the direction of both architecture and computers, because it is only by open criticism that freedom may be maintained. Hopefully, the microprocessor, particularly with its application through the cheapness of the microcomputer, may bring an awareness to all architects of both its potential and its dangers; this is preferable to the direction of computers in architecture being experienced and dominated by a very few people. The Modern Movement got out of hand because the ideas of a small group became self-indoctrinating through the media and quickly reached a stage where criticism was swept aside as being philistinistic. The same could happen again with computers, only more so in this case, for whilst they intrude more and more into our lives they are understood by only a few. Furthermore, the very act of computer programming and its need for precision and absoluteness creates a false feeling of righteousness. The dangers are very real and very considerable. As Koestler (1978) states:

> Critical reasoning played, if any, only a secondary part in the process of adopting a faith, a code of ethics, a *Weltanschauung*; of becoming a fervent Christian crusader, a fervent Moslem engaged in Holy War, a Roundhead or a Cavalier. The continuous disasters in man's history are mainly due to his excessive capacity and urge to become identified with a tribe, nation, church or cause, and to espouse its credo uncritically and enthusiastically, even if its tenents are contrary to reason, devoid of self-interest and detrimental to the claims of self-preservation. ... Man's deadliest weapon is *language*. He is as susceptible to being hypnotized by slogans as he is to infectious diseases. And when there is an epidemic, the group-mind takes over. It obeys its own rules, which are different from the rules of conduct of individuals. When a person identifies himself with a group, his reasoning faculties are diminished and his passions enhanced by a kind of emotive resonance or positive feedback.

The Modern Movement would have been less criticized if there had been a greater interest taken by the individual, as an individual, together with an understanding of the technology required by the whole industry for its interpretation. The same problem applies to computers. It is more important for architecture to retain its freedom than almost anything else because it is buildings which dominate the lives and activities of human beings. If building designers, whoever they may be, are dominated by computers (and there is no way they can avoid their use) which have been programmed by a small group, the dangers for the built and social environment are great indeed.

It is essential that we recognize that change is with us and that computers are here to stay. If we are not to jump into yet another black and white simplistic situation, we must, on the one hand, give a great deal of consideration to the problem and, on the other hand, understand what is happening in the world of the microprocessor. This must be particularly relevant to young architectural students and to the public alike. To do this, it may be advantageous to reconsider those aspects of our lives in which the microprocessor may have an affect on the future. These aspects are

(1) the new knowledge of ourselves as human beings,
(2) social change,
(3) education,
(4) property,
(5) building methods,

(6) computers, and

(7) art in architecture.

1. The new knowledge of ourselves as human beings

The development of our knowledge about the physical working of our bodies has been fantastic, but even that seems small by comparison with the conceptual leaps that have been made by philosophers and those carrying out research into the working of the human brain. Unfortunately this book is not the place to expand upon the language of vision and the concepts of the mind, but as Vitruvius has said, architects must be knowledgeable of philosophy and modern philosophy should provide us with a lot of questions which do not even appear to be considered at present. Oversimplified, almost to the point of absurdity, we have a problem in which the visual data, which we use as an input to our brain, needs a concept within the brain in order to make sense of the data. But these concepts themselves need a language because many of our thoughts only exist because the language exists. What therefore is the mind? Vitruvius appeared to be wrestling with these problems, but with infinitely less knowledge available to him, when he was asking whether we saw by rays emanating from the eyes, and he related the art of architecture to measured intervals—*harmonia, chroma,* and *diatonon.* It is with the use of these intervals that we make our games. Such intervals can be described in a number of ways, but most art seems to have been described on the basis of analogue intervals. Increasingly these are now being translated into digital intervals. The difference in concept of the same set of intervals, but in these two forms, can most easily be seen in the difference between a digital and a traditional analogue watch. The mind sees the same interval in two completely different conceptual ways. Art, as exemplified in the paintings of Lichtenstein and Vasarely, also uses digital as opposed to analogue intervals. However, the problem of intervals is more complex in architecture than in other aspects of our lives such as music and painting because we are not fixed in space. A building like the Parthenon is designed on the basis of a set of intervals, as might be a piece of music, but in the case of the building it is almost impossible to see those intervals as they were drawn or measured because of our constantly changing viewpoint. This occurs with any of the rectangular buildings we design, which can never be seen as orthogonal shapes. Do we translate what we see into a different language of shapes and intervals? There is a further interesting comparison with the watch which may have relevance to architecture. Until recently, a craft industry in Switzerland was based upon the production of analogue watches in which accuracy and reliability was largely a factor of cost. The more diamonds and the better the craftsmanship, the higher the degree of accuracy and the level of cost. Almost overnight, a multimillion-pound craft industry was lost to the silicon-chip industry, who mass-produced digital watches based on microprocessors in which it was almost impossible to produce *inaccuracy* and *unreliability.* Now, the only difference in cost is due to the casing. This in itself should be a lesson to the construction industry, because now the requirements of time and accuracy can be produced in a cheap product which is thrown away rather than repaired. What would happen if we were to be confronted with a cheap disposable environment industry?

The question would usually be regarded as too absurd to be considered, and yet we live with design for eventual disposability even if that is related to sixty-year loan periods. What would happen to the industry in general if it was not related to such length periods? The microprocessor may force industry to change that period and thereby change our concepts of long-life building in all but symbolic architecture. The signs can be seen all around us. This concept, or potential change of concept, should remind us that our lives and our concepts have been transformed by the development of machinery which started in the Renaissance. Now that we are simulating our mental processes, how will these simulations affect our concepts of the built environment in this new revolution?

2. Social change

Casual observation shows that we are living in a consumer society, using short-life products in which the only exceptions are architecture and civil engineering. Even ships are mass produced for a short life. The first question that has to be asked is whether architecture is 'the only one in step'? This seems unlikely. Will it change? If it does not, it will almost certainly be supplanted by other industries, as the craft watch industry was replaced almost overnight by the silicon chip. As people in the industrialized countries have more and more leisure time available, they will almost certainly spend more and more time upon their personal environment because there is a limit to the amount of travel and entertainment most people can tolerate. This process is already well under way with the enormous growth in do-it-yourself shops. A reduction of working time means an increased scarcity or disappearance of already scarce craftsmen, which in turn means rising costs of labour with the consequent use of mass-produced components and one's own labour.

There is probably an even greater reason why architecture, together with everything else, will become part of the disposable society. The pattern of social change through the centuries in its relationship to power and education with the mass of people has been shown in earlier diagrams. When the present pattern in the industrialized countries is superimposed upon that of the world in general, a very different diagrammatic picture emerges. The poorest person in the industrialized countries is now very rich compared to the poor of the world in general (Figure 84). Over half of the planet's population is living on an income below £250 per head per annum, and about a quarter below £100 per annum, which are one-fifteenth and one-twentieth of the *norms* set by North America and Western Europe. Improved communications and education in recent centuries has moved power to the mass of people in the developed world; the same is now happening in the less-developed world, only at greater speed. The microprocessor is now about to have a bigger impact on the education and power structure of the world than printing did in the Renaissance.

As the world population will not be prepared to stay in a state of

185

Developed

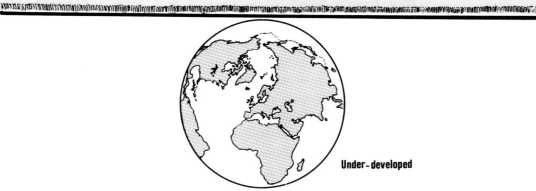
Under-developed

Figure 84

starvation and deprivation indefinitely, there are only three choices:

(a) The developed world will share its resources, and therefore standards, with the rest of the world. This would have practically no effect on the world's poor but would have an almost unimaginably dramatic effect upon the living standards of the developed world.
(b) The developed world will increase its productivity to provide for the rest of the world, without reducing its own standards.
(c) There will be a measure of both (a) and (b).

If choice (c) prevails, which is most likely, the world structure will then begin to look diagrammatically as shown in Figure 85.

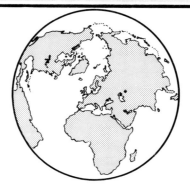

Figure 85

Even the greatest critics of empires in the developed world still enjoy the fruits of those past empires. Minerals and food were all produced at very low cost because of low labour rates and low expectations of the labourers. When these expectations are raised, as in the case of the oil countries, the drop in the standard of living in the developed countries can only be offset by technology or must fall to unacceptably low standards. But the developed countries have frightened themselves out of using technology. As the almost negligible aspirations of the under-developed world begin to rise, the developed world will have to rexamine their situation and do two things urgently:

(a) Create new technology to maintain their own living standards and to help the underdeveloped world.
(b) Find ways of improving conditions for people in the underdeveloped world.

If they do not begin soon, they will face the situation which faced other aristocracies of the nineteenth and twentieth centuries, when the build-up of the effects of printing and education caused the masses to rise in revolution against them as the people realized the unfairness of their plight. Western architecture cannot continue to pursue the alleged role of Marie Antoinette without reaping a similar *reward*.

It will be argued that political changes must come before other changes, but the climate of opinion *is* politics, not just political parties which are often more concerned with their own power. The masses of the world need help, and part of that help must come from the construction industry of the developed world—not in the traditional grand manner of the ideal cities of the architect/planner, but in just providing components and knowledge. When people criticize the slums surrounding new cities such as Brasilia do they understand the hope that some of these ramshackle buildings represent for the people who built them? Such people do not have time to wait for the idealistic dreams of others to be built. Their lives are too short to wait for great architecture. They just need somewhere to keep dry today! The same hope that was provided by suburbia, or even the converted railway carriage dwellings at Pagham and Selsey, Sussex, and elsewhere, is apparent in new struggling com-munities everywhere. They need urgent help for the simplest raising of standards. Not everyone has Western middle class standards, but everyone has hope. When the food shortage developed in nineteenth century Britain, the Australian sheep farming industry expanded rapidly to meet the demand. The consequent demand for housing was partly met by the export from Britain of corrugated iron sheets which were easily transportable and provided good shelter. Gradually, the wealthy society we see today emerged. The same sort of symbiotic relationship has to be developed everywhere. Is it not immensely arrogant of the developed world to swing from patronizing people, either with unsuitable Western architecture or in disillusionment recommending them to use their own primitive solutions? People living in mud huts, particularly when most have access to the technology of such things as television, want something better. They want components, and they want 'know how' and management. The developed countries, with the help of the microprocessor, can help to provide both. If this is done, the loss of jobs in industrial countries may not become such a threat. It should be remembered that at one time 80 per cent of people in Britain worked in agriculture whereas today, with mechanization, it is only a few per cent. The balance has moved into industry and commerce to raise the standards of all and to give everyone shorter working lives. The same can apply to the whole world now. Societies have to make a start with little more than hope, but with a little help the pace can grow. For this, the 'rhombicosadodechedra' of Drop City, Colorado, made out of odd components, is much nearer to an understanding of the problem than the megastructures that Western architects of a different financial and social background believe that they should have. The Habitat conference recommended that the appropriate support of the government should be devoted

(a) to promoting actions which motivate people to decide and act for themselves,
(b) to decentralizing planning institutions to the maximum possible extent, to enable local communities to identify their own needs and fields of action, and
(c) to determining the area of government by defining what the people can decide and do better for themselves.

This recommends that people throughout the world, whatever their status, should now obtain the benefits that the middle class wrested from the aristocracy in the Renaissance and subsequent revolutions. Ideally, there should be an architect to help every person individually or alternatively everyone should be his own architect. As neither is possible, new systems have to be devised to provide that service. Less than a hundred years ago, many people in Western Europe had to wear the uniform of their calling or of their master's choice. Less than fifty years ago, some organizations still held the same power. Architects, by tradition, served these patrons because they were the client. Today, the client is the individual in the organizations, not only with a vote but also expressing himself either individually or collectively through his community or trade-union. The architect has to recognise that he has a new client in the West. Very quickly, similar changes are occurring in the less-developed world, and so the architect will soon find himself with a new client or patron everywhere. *The Guilds, it will be remembered, finally backed the wrong client.*

3. Education

Is the present method of architectural education and research suitable for these coming changes? No doubt the existing schools of architecture, even though they tend to be divorced from the construction process, will be able to cater for the specialist type of architect. But there do seem to be areas which need much greater reconsideration. As more and more of the building process becomes industrialized, where are the industrial designers coming from? Are architects able to play a full part in the design and build organizations or will they just become design technicians? How much will architectural education have to increase its awareness of manufacturing processes and construction? Just as there are aircraft simulators to help pilots learn to fly, so computer models are emerging to give students building design and management experience. Fine (1979), for example, has produced computer games which enable students to appreciate the problems of building a row of houses. From these programs, new insights into management problems are emerging. Also, at the University of Reading, other types of educational computer programs for familiarization are being used. Can architectural education cope with the education of architects as well as that of laymen by giving an understanding and personal awareness in individual creativeness, rather than by being used as a basis for changing from the international style to the Languedoc-Roussillon style. Are we not more creative than is suggested by the slavish following of styles? Educationalists may have to deal with these questions, but the professionals may have to consider their own position in order to give them guidance, because the microprocessor will not only dramatically change the processes of design, and the processes of communication of that design, but also its manufacture and construction. It would seem likely that many aspects of architecture which at present need lengthy teaching periods, will now be available in computer program form. If most of the more mundane tasks are developed in this way, it is obvious that the balance of educational courses will have to change, if not the whole of the educational process itself. In this, *it will be as well to remember how critical education was to the future of the Guilds*. A major factor in these changes will of course be improved communications, creating new circumstances. It is probable that the microprocessor will not only make knowledge of building construction available to architectural students but also to laymen in general. If components are available, how much will the traditional architect be needed in his present role?

Finally research: in the past, academic research was almost the only area in which new ideas, requiring resources, were developed. The universities, which during the Reformation took over the role from the Church, were the only places with the knowledge, the money, and, most of all, the desire to carry out research which did not have an immediate and obvious return. Today, the universities and polytechnics, even with the national research grant systems, have minute resources for specific tasks by comparison with the research laboratories of the large organizations. When individual multimillion pound computer organizations are spending more money on research than all the national research grants put together, the academic research teams can only hope to throw up new ideas. Whilst this is valuable, it must be recognized. For example, in the case of computers for architecture, which often involves large data-handling problems, the academic institutions usually suffer from a severe lack of real workaday data and the necessary design team back-up. It is possible, therefore, that just as the universities took over research from the Church and the Guilds in the Renaissance, commercial and government organizations will take over research in these areas from the universities and polytechnics.

4. Property

Architecture must be considered, with or without microprocessors, in relation to landownership and property. Hegel contended that the general will found corporate expression in the State, but each person's personality was expressed in his possessions. He believed that the denial of private property could cramp and fetter human personality by denying the freedom to have, to hold, to give, and to share. This still seems to be true, and yet at the same time there seems to be an increasing demand for community and national ownership of land. It is not within the scope of this book to discuss the merits or demerits of various planning or land-ownership strategies, but merely to highlight the fact that land ownership cannot be divorced from the problems of architecture of which society as a whole does not seem to be aware. Designers of computer systems must also be aware of these and other problems, such as the requirements of loan periods and their influence on the life of buildings, the requirements of building societies and their influences on the design of building, and the requirements of building owners and their concept of building. Even the individual's relationship to the ownership of the property affects his needs. For example, housing tenants are not only disinclined to alter or maintain their own dwellings but are often forbidden to do so while house owners often carry out a lot of alterations and improvements. These changes are not necessarily the changes they would want for themselves but strongly influenced by the effect they will have on the value of the property if they wish to sell. Squatters, on the other hand, are neither restricted nor influenced by the capital value and therefore tend to alter the accommodation to their direct need. It is obvious, therefore, that much discussion on participation can be grossly oversimplified unless such factors are taken into account.

One argument for State housing was its theoretical ability to help in the mobility of labour. In fact, whilst it is usually easy to sell one house and buy another in the desired area, it is usually impossible to exchange accommodation from one authority to another. The mobility in people's lives has continued to increase enormously, and the question for the future will have to be whether housing will have to give an even greater flexibility of movement or whether the microprocessor will reduce mobility. Whether we are in favour of State control or market influences controlling land and property, an understanding of the future problems and their interaction with architecture must be understood if we are to help the coming generations.

Of the total surface area of the earth, 70.88 per cent is covered by water. Out of the 29.12 per cent of land available, 14.9 per cent is readily usable, made up of 4.18 per cent pasture land, 6.72 per cent forests, 2.55 per cent arable land, with a minimum potential addition of 0.76 per cent. Only just over 0.08 per cent is used in built-up areas at present, but this will increase to 0.36 per cent by the year 2000 and could easily reach between 1 and 2 per cent or more by the year 2060. That is a very high encroachment on present land areas.

Clearly, as we can now see, it is no use taking one simple facet of the problem and suggesting that we put up buildings a mile high. Whilst solving one problem, it only creates others. Like all other modern problems, there are a vast number of interacting factors involved which require complex models if we are going to be better at forecasting the outcome of decisions which could be of such fundamental importance to the lives of future families. We need to develop building designs and urban spatial models at least as complex as those for weather forecasting, and the microprocessor might allow us to do this within acceptable costs.

We should remember that the 'natural landscape' and the urban scene of our older cities was partly a product of a change in the concept of land ownership in the Reformation. Architecture, as opposed to other 'arts', cannot be divorced from capital and property. The change of land ownership from King and Church to aristocracy, and aristocracy to bureaucracy so far seems to have given little improvement in the personal freedom to build.

5. Building methods

There is a tendency among architects to grasp at any straw which looks like a return to crafts or even a primitive method of building, but whilst they have reflected and hoped over the last hundred years or more, industry has removed more and more of their traditional craft sources. In the world as a whole, the incontrovertible facts are that even the poorest races in the world are quite rightly trying to avoid the drudgery of manual labour and also that everyone is seeking a higher standard of living. As mass-produced plastic shoes and utensils, bicycles, coca cola, and even television can be found in even the most primitive parts of the world, it is no use ignoring the problem of industrialized building for the under-developed world. Imposing Western standards, which are not necessarily always in themselves very good, is not always a solution either. There must be a variety of solutions to the problems of societies which are at various stages of evolution. All nations came through a period of 'do-it-yourself' building, using the cheapest components available from the industrialized world at the time. Today, the developed countries can use the microprocessor to develop cheap self-build components for the billions of people yet to come.

In the richer nations, mechanization and industrialization must continue to increase to help the poor nations, even if those who decry the use of modern technology can continue to survive without it—which is doubtful. Even apprentice recruitment fell from 11,336 to 10,249 in the United Kingdom in 1976, further weakening the traditional position. The decasualization of building labour, which must yet come, together with the inevitable shorter working week, will cause further problems. Now there is a new danger in the construction industry for which we must be prepared. Even though manufacturer's products such as doors, windows, ironmongery, etc., are reduced to limited ranges to help with the economics of batch production, the choice is still enormous and the possibility of simple junctions between components is remote. This means that a lot of resources are used for making joints in traditional ways. But it may be anticipated that the microprocessor will offer the opportunity to produce almost infinite choice at no extra cost, and therefore we could be facing a situation of utter chaos in the traditional industry which will only further assist the closed system organizations. Again it seems to be essential that the dimensional rules we have must be developed into a system of great subtlety which can be used as the basis for mathematical design models. A system of notation must be developed to which manufacturers can produce a wide variety of products and upon which they can base their administration, whilst offering architects and users alike a wide range of choice and flexibility together with a structure for data assembly and instant evaluation.

There are, of course, other constraints on building which also have to be considered. As Bernhardt (1971) has said:

> Yet the Industry's potential is still inhibited by a number of external constraints. These constraints, largely a consequence of public policy, include the erratically fluctuating impact of fiscal and monetary policies, the fragmentation of demand, zoning constraints, differential building codes, restrictive union practices, lack of a viable system of nationwide standardisation or modular and dimensional coordination, a practical non existence of building research and lack of a system of dissemination of information. The result is that . . . America, Europe and Japan have been confined to mere rationalisation of the historically formed crafts. . . .

As the industry inevitably moves away from a craft base to manufacturing base (contrary to the often-imagined belief that we are returning to a craft base), a number of factors begin to emerge. An industry which had grown up on the basis that practically no capital was needed to start or run a practice or building firm now begins to need capital in ever-increasing quantities. Whereas a builder could operate with a small loan and be paid by the client in instalments as the work proceeds (an incredible situation which has become ritualized), the industrialist, on the other hand, has to have the capital to support the purchase of raw materials, plant, labour, and stock for a long time before he gets payment. These differences are reflected in the profit margins which are incredibly small in the case of the traditional builder. The traditional system tends to be self-perpetuating insofar as a situation is created in which the cost advantages we would expect from industrialization, as in other industries, do not seem to be apparent, particularly when the traditional components are used to subsidize the 'one-off' components mentioned earlier. But once the industrialized side of industry passes the point of balance, the industrialized component and building manufacturer could be expected to capture the market fairly quickly, leaving only a small couture market, as has happened in almost every other industry.

Can architects afford to be left out of this change? Already they ignore the large-volume building industry springing up all around us; it is to be hoped that they will not deny their talents to other growing aspects of the construction industry. Must they not also become more involved with design/construct themselves—even advertising as, for example, is now beginning in the United States of America.

If the microprocessor has the almost certain effect of giving greater advantages to the industrialized side of the construction, unless dramatic steps are taken, *we can anticipate as great a change to the role of the professions in the industry as happened with the Guilds in the Renaissance.*

6. Computers

We must of course recognize that we are not only at the beginning of the use of computers, but also that, as far as architects are concerned, the influence upon them will not just be confined to computer-aided design, computer-aided building design, computer-aided architectural design, or any other variations on the same theme. Computer-aided architectural design has always been a dangerous term, and as misleading as calling architecture tee-square-aided design. Not only is it misleading, but it has probably held back the use of computers by architects because of its implications. We should be thinking about architecture and the construction industry in a world in which there is new technology—telephones, televisions, and electric typewriters, to which is now added an extra dimension of word-processors, data-handling devices, and so on, based upon microprocessors. To argue about the relative merits of a particular piece of hardware or a particular computer program is as irrelevant to the profession and the industry as a whole as to argue the merits and performance of any other particular tool. For whilst we are watching carefully for the development of something special like 'computer-aided design' the computer will enter our lives in an insidious but nevertheless relentless manner. For example, the laser code-checking system in supermarkets, mentioned earlier, which not only adds up the bill for the customer, keeps the store's accounts, and even orders more goods to replenish stocks, has, on occasions, even been used to monitor the behaviour of staff. An unglamourous piece of common-sense computing equipment has now suddenly taken on a 'big brother' aspect. The balance between efficiency and personal freedom is, and always will be, a delicate balance requiring constant watch. Education rather than ignorance is the best watchdog.

It is essential that architects, if they are to survive, must recognize two things:

(a) Whilst the cost of computers is dropping at an incredible rate, the cost of producing computer programs does not reduce significantly at the present time. Therefore, as the costs of developing new worthwhile tools for practising architects is usually expensive, an architect either has to buy those provided by the manufacturers or software houses based on their ideas of architecture or consort together to specify his own. If the profession as a whole, however, could learn to specify its requirements, there is no doubt that industry would respond to that

193

need. The problem is to decide what is wanted. To do this, it is a matter of defining future architectural policy, not writing programs, for which there are many skilled software houses available.

(b) The introduction of the cheap, but nevertheless powerful, microcomputers make it possible for creative brains everywhere to begin to understand the problems involved and to learn to specify needs, not as computer specialists but as practising architects.

Both aspects will be affected by future developments in computing which include the following:

(a) Multimicroprocessor systems. This is the construction of systems from a set of interconnected microprocessors to give lower costs for the same capability as large systems, to reduce maintenance costs, and to give better fault detection at no extra cost. The implications for the development of complex models at low cost is considerable and should be examined on the widest possible base.

(b) Multi-user computing. This has already been mentioned, but the development of new microprocessor techniques will cause rapid developments in this area.

(c) Programming. Two of the many developments in this area will include the following. First, mainframe and minicomputer programs have usually needed large teams working together to produce systems, but the microprocessor project by its nature is often small in scope and time scale. In many cases, the project can be broken down into one-man teams where the productivity is substantially improved—perhaps twice as much debugged program as in the past for the same resource input. Second, the self-programmable computer. The industry is working towards the production of computers in which the layman can develop his own requirements without using a special language. This will be welcomed by many, even within the computer industry, who are concerned at both the power held by analyst/programmers and also at the creation of huge culture gaps between the user, the programmer, and the chip manufacturer. Cross assemblers will also speed up programming as this development both enables programs to be written in one language and compiled in another, as well as enabling an interchange of programs between mainframe, mini-, and microcomputers.

(d) Increased power. It is likely that the introduction of 32-bit chips will be introduced in the next few years to increase the power from 4-bit to 8-bit to 16-bit microprocessors, already achieved in a short time. When this happens, the capacity for creating complex models will be further advanced at low cost.

(e) General development. The Arthur D. Little Corporation, which carried out an exhaustive evaluation of the future of microprocessors, sees the following pattern of development for microprocessor technology (see Figure 86).

Finally, the breadth of the implications of the microprocessor for the construction industry might be considered as follows. The looms and other similar machines which have been developed by man can, and

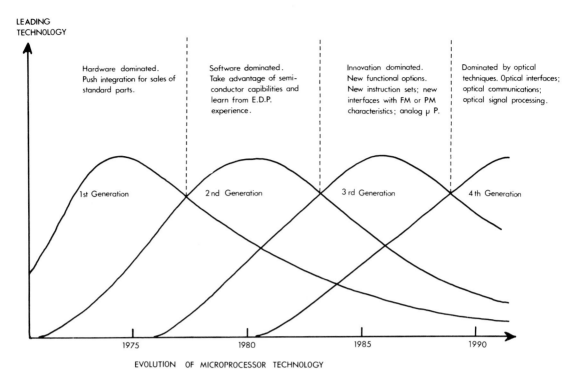

LEADING TECHNOLOGY

Hardware dominated. Push integration for sales of standard parts.

Software dominated. Take advantage of semiconductor capibilities and learn from E.D.P. experience.

Innovation dominated. New functional options. New instruction sets; new interfaces with FM or PM characteristics; analog μ P.

Dominated by optical techniques. Optical interfaces; optical communications; optical signal processing.

1st Generation   2nd Generation   3rd Generation   4th Generation

1975   1980   1985   1990

EVOLUTION OF MICROPROCESSOR TECHNOLOGY

Figure 86

do, simulate incredibly complex human actions to produce the great volume of goods we consume in an expanding population. These machines emerged as a result of increased understanding, over the last few centuries, of the way the body works, and its simulation by machinery eventually came to form the basis of the Industrial Revolution. It is worth noting, therefore, that a motor mower is at present on sale which incorporates a microprocessor. The user mows his garden once to imprint his mental decision upon the chip; thereafter, the mower mows the garden by itself, according to that pattern. It is not difficult to imagine that any craftsman, or even artist, no matter how subtle his ability, can have his actions replicated with absolute precision for mass production. This is not just replicating human actions but mental actions as well. How do we feel about replicas of Foster and Hockney with personal quirks (increasingly it is the imperfections which establish authenticity) in this new Renaissance in which we are replicating our mental activities? *The machine wiped out the Guilds. Who will the microprocessor wipe out?*

7. Art in architecture

It is clear that our present concept of art is not only comparatively modern but is also in the process of change. The craftsman, who held enormous power in the Middle Ages, has gradually seen not only his power but also

195

his income and status reduced as his work has been replaced by the machine. Will the same happen to the artist as his art is replicated, or will he survive by changing the rules of the game? If it is the latter, there will have to be a lot of changes made very quickly. Is this the time for a new understanding of architecture? Certainly the atmosphere of the world in general is that of waiting for some new direction. The poised elegance of van der Rohe's Farnsworth House is very reminiscent of Beckett's *Waiting for Godot* or even the work of Einstein; all contain that atmosphere of quiet before the storm or the stillness before darkness in the countryside. Could it be that we shall return to the traditional situation in which architecture, as we have come to define it in the past, is continued as a need for the creation of symbols, whether this be as a result of teleological or existential concepts? Society will probably always need these symbols as signposts for the future as well as milestones of the past. In order to obtain these symbols, which must stretch both the creator's and the observer's mind, there must be people who will apply themselves with complete dedication to the exploration of the world of the senses. Instead of dividing the world into art, science, and sport, we may see them as different facets of the same thing—the attainment of the highest level of electrochemical activity of the brain in both the creator of the game and its play (in architecture, their expression can only be made by common consent because of its impact on others). The architects and designers of the remainder of the built environment, freed from the need to create a new moral or philosophical game on each project, can work for the satisfaction of human need with their knowledge of design and construction. The question will of course be asked as to the difference between art and design. The difference between fine art and commercial art, for example, is not disputed. The one is concerned with the creation of new games and the other with the achievement of playing those games to the highest standards and in a way that is understandable to the general public. The one is influenced by the other but they are different. The need to satisfy the needs of society in this way seems to stimulate rather than depress levels of creativity, and certainly does not reduce levels of competence in other areas such as music, dance, or literature. The design ability of the architect is extremely important to society, but does it always have to aspire to be poetry?

Hopefully we are coming to the end of the grand solutions based upon one man's belief that he has all the answers to the whole of society's problems—a view of architecture in which Johnson can say that he is bored with steel and glass buildings and then sets about designing a large office block (for people) in a capricious interpretation of nostalgic forms, presumably for *his own* benefit; a view of planning in which Fuller wants everyone to live in a Dymaxion world, Doxiades in a star-shaped hexagonal world, Hecker in a honeycomb world, and so on. Sauvage, Rudolph, Taller Bofil, Soleri, and Niemeyer are just a few of an endless list who have proposed regular standard solutions for the lives of hundreds or even thousands of people. When their work formed a symbol for a city or was an individual's own needs, their work was clearly of considerable importance to the cultural development of mankind. When it became a long-term standard solution for a community or even a whole society, it was in danger of not only becoming a prison but also of stifling that society. Darwin (1859) said:

> On the average every species must have some number killed year by year by hawk, by cold, etc.—even one species of hawk decreasing in number must affect instantaneously all the rest. The final cause of all this wedging must be to sort out a proper structure. . . . One may say there is a force like a hundred thousand wedges trying to force every kind of adapted structure into the gaps in the oeconomy of nature, or rather forming gaps by thrusting out weaker ones.

Hoyle and Wickramsinghe (1978) state:

> In the complexities of urban life every way in which a person might conceivably earn a living seems to have been found. This filling out of all possibilities is not so much a tribute to the intelligence of civilised man as it is the standard format of biological evolution which works incessantly to seize every opportunity whereby life can be supported.

These statements would appear to stand equally well as a description of social evolutionary change—a vast myriad of hawks and doves carrying out a myriad of games at every level of society. To try to stop this organic growth by overorganizing and tidying up the world will only build up a pressure which will eventually explode in revolution.

We can hope to see a new concept of art developing, which gives authority to each individual's creative need at all levels of society but yet provides an understandable framework. Whilst some people like opera or the music of Schönberg, the majority enjoy pop music as they once enjoyed Strauss. Whilst some people like and can afford haute couture, haute cuisine, and so on, the majority enjoy, and can only afford, the products of mass production. Even architects themselves usually can only afford to live by the products of mass production, and yet they strive towards the creation of buildings which, because of their training, aspire towards art and traditional craftsmanship. This concept, when added to the system of production in which an architect is not only divorced from construction but also very often from the user, puts him in a most invidious position and a target for society's criticism. Many aircraft bomber pilots are extremely kind and gentle people who would not normally kill, and yet they are able to drop bombs on innocent women and children because they are divorced from them as well· as being dominated by blind belief. As Milgram at the Department of Psychology, Yale University, has shown in his much publicized experiments, which are confirmed by similar tests in Germany, Italy, Australia, and South Africa, man is prepared to inflict suffering on his fellow men with no more pressure than a belief in Authority. The implications of the tests, which showed that between 60 and 85 per cent of ordinary men and women volunteers were prepared to inflict torture even to the point of death to satisfy authority, are indeed terrible and need continuous safeguards.

197

It is easy for the designers of large building complexes to become absorbed in the mathematics and processes of designing whilst forgetting the incredible complexity of the lives and aspirations of the people who are going to live and work in their building. Is it possible for us to overcome this problem? At least it is a problem which needs open discussion without overtones of artistic invincibility. As opposed to the views of architects throughout history in which a single aspect of design was considered as the only one, we may now see more easily that the situation is a constantly changing kaleidoscope depending upon each individual's taste and viewpoint. Functionalism, which still persists in an abated form, assumes that there is one perfect functional solution and often cites the motorcar industry as an exemplar of functional production. But the motorcar industry, even in its most pure engineering form, is still subject to fashion and social whim. There are so many functions to satisfy in any design that it can only be whim which selects one rather than another. The question is, whose whim, and for how long should that decision last?

The problem is, on the one hand, a need for a framework, whilst, on the other, a need for individual freedom and expression. If everyone made up their own words all the time there would be a complete lack of understanding and communication. On the other hand, to have the words and sentences imposed would deny individuality and freedom. It is the same with visual language. Orwell (1949) in *Nineteen Eighty-Four* states:

> You believe that reality is something objective, external, existing in its own right. You also believe that the nature of reality is self-evident. When you delude yourself into thinking that you see something, you assume that everyone else sees the same thing as you. But I tell you, Winston, that reality is not external. Reality exists in the human mind, and nowhere else. Not in the individual mind, which can make mistakes, and in any case soon perishes: only in the mind of the Party, which is collective and immortal. Whatever the Party holds to be truth, *is* truth.

Might we even replace the messianic architect/planner with the messianic computer programmer?

Whilst we have pop art, pop music, pop clothes, and so on, where is pop architecture? Everywhere there is a striving by architects and planners to produce an environment of fairly uniform good taste. The nearer this is achieved, the greater is the antagonism of the people, who try to get away from it to some less-idealized world for their holidays. Perhaps architects and layman alike will come to use the microprocessor to provide that wide spectrum of human experiences possible in this human sensual experience, and at the same time make it possible for new talent to emerge from outside of the establishment, as with the Beatles, Quant, and Warhol in other aspects of art and design. After all, it might be recalled that the expensive nineteenth-century academic exercise in the restoration of Carcassonne (Figure 87) by Viollet-le-Duc, much appreciated by art historians, is only another tourist centre, equivalent to Disneyland for the layman. Both are remote from the everyday world and both promote a similar image.

Figure 87

Freed from the tyranny of an idea of what architecture should be, a situation might arise in which those architects who are talented in creating new games and new symbols are given greater freedom, once the morality of their position is clarified, whilst those individuals who wish can express themselves more freely with the architect's help. Some users can obviously express themselves with great talent, as shown by Wampler (1977), once they are given the opportunity. For the majority, there is the potential for participation with architects and the microprocessor by means of the application of some of the emerging design and construction processes described. If architecture could be 'decentralized' and released from the tyranny of international styles, we might begin to find that variations in the architecture of different environments might begin to emerge again. This would help to provide an interest in the world environment which is at present being destroyed by a standard universal training in good taste which, it must be said, could be exacerbated by standard computer packages. Instead of using the simplistic Euclidean geometrical models of ideal cities, we should now begin to develop the complex frameworks within which individuals can express themselves with the new mathematics and new tools which are available to us. To these models will be added our developing knowledge of the language of vision, dimensional structuring, and shape grammars. These will separate future societies from the present as much as the new models of the Renaissance separate us from the Middle Ages.

199

Some of the emerging problems to be solved can be seen, for example, in the new holiday resorts on the Languedoc coast of France, which have a number of characteristics which are particularly relevant to the statements made in this chapter.

(a) Need for housing a vast increase in population with increased leisure time.
(b) Capital investment on a vast scale.
(c) Fundamental requirement of designing the project to obtain maximum return on capital, i.e. maximum water frontage for housing and boats.
(d) The creation of 'scenic' atmosphere to appeal to different tastes. Each resort has set out deliberately to obtain a different character.

One of the most significant needs for sophisticated n-dimensional computer models can be seen in these resorts, not only in assisting the tests for economic viability but also in the visual control of the interacting spaces. The interrelationships of such free style architecture often becomes a visual chaos as at La Grande Motte, for example, where the scope of the problem exceeds the capabilities of ordinary geometric design. Even at this level of development it becomes obvious that the large computer models used for war games and weather forecasting are now needed. The cross impact of so many conflicting needs can only be tested by such models. Just as alternative strategies can be tested in war games, so must models be created for alternative strategies. Even the structure of the industry can be handled in the same way. By testing the alternative inputs of capital, available resources, etc., the Government might better be able to understand the effect that its budgetary decisions might have.

At the community level it may be possible to develop computer models to assist the design of large complex environments which, whilst having a cohesive framework, would enable maximum freedom within that framework and, furthermore, to be able to test the model before its implementation. In planning, there should be a greater scope for communities to develop in this way, once the main strategies have been agreed. Architects, who traditionally separate different types of activities in building design, have tended, when they become planners, to believe that old and young, rich and poor, quiet and noisy should all be put together for the sake of equality. Any suggestions of groupings because of mutual interests is classified as the production of ghettos, but a ghetto was an environment forced upon people. To force people to integrate might be as bad. Some people enjoy the noise and bustle of others, whilst others are shy and seek introspection. The grades and permutations are infinite and too great to be selected, but not too great for people to find their own desired groupings for themselves.

It is easy to fall into the trap of parcelling people and things into neat packages with low quality computer programs when there is already sufficient computer expertise available to give more subtle shades of difference than even manual systems can provide. The danger of low quality computer programs assuming all people to be like the analyst/programmer must be increasingly guarded against, as the implanting of a

Figure 88 La Grande Motte, France

single person's ideal becomes an inviolable computer rule. Le Corbusier had hygienic and sexual rules ('never undress in your bedroom; it is not a clean thing to do'). What if he were a computer-aided design enthusiast today?

If we imagine the spiral, previously referred to representing the cyclical development of society upon which is overlaid more and more spirals of varying size, we begin to see the scale of permutations which makes every person and every community different. It makes life easier for designers and administrators alike to make tidy packages which the mind

201

can handle, but with the assistance of the best modelling systems now available in other industries this should no longer be necessary (consider, for example, how personalized computer-based travel systems have become).

If Orwell's threat of 1984 becomes a reality, it will be our own fault because the choice is our own. Either we become involved or we accept the consequences. As Orwell (1947) points out:

> But it was also clear that an all-round increase in wealth threatened the destruction—indeed, in some sense was the destruction—of a hierarchical society. In a world in which everyone worked short hours, had enough to eat, lived in a house with a bathroom and a refrigerator, and possessed a motorcar or even an aeroplane, the most obvious and perhaps the most important form of inequality would have already disappeared. If it once became general, wealth would confer no distinction. It was possible, no doubt, to imagine a society in which *wealth*, in the sense of personal possessions and luxuries, should be evenly distributed, while power remained in the hands of a small privileged caste. But in practice such a society could not long remain stable. For if leisure and security were enjoyed by all alike, the great mass of human beings who are normally stupefied by poverty would become literate and would learn to think for themselves; and when once they had done this, they would sooner or later realise that the privileged minority had no function, and they would sweep it away. In the long run a hierarchical society was only possible on a basis of poverty and ignorance.

Can we achieve a non-hierarchical state, or more precisely a multi-hierarchical state of equal opportunity, or will computer programmers become the 'privileged caste'? The only hope must be the spread of knowledge about computers, rather than allowing it to become the province of a few.

Society will move into the future with microprocessors, with or without architects, and the comparisons with the events which occurred in the Renaissance are too great to be ignored. This is not due to the microprocessor alone, but to its position of crystallizing the events that have been developing. We therefore have a number of choices:

(a) Hope that the microprocessor will either go away or will not affect architecture and the construction industry.

(b) Try to forget the *1.9 billion people* to be added to the existing world population between 1979 and 2000 alone. Ignore the fact that to increase the income of everybody in the world at present to that of Bulgaria or Portugal alone would require a global output half as big again as the present entire output of America and Western Europe put together. And this needs to be achieved in less than *500 weeks* if we are then to tackle the problem of the new 1.9 billion people yet to arrive.

(c) Ignore the changes that have taken place in society almost everywhere in which not only the majority of mankind has freed or is freeing itself from one form of bondage or another, but women have freed themselves from bondage to men. Forty years ago, only a small percentage of the population of the United Kingdom had been abroad or even received holidays with pay. In 1956, one and a half million English people travelled abroad, and in 1966 five million people went, whilst today that figure has multiplied and is still increasing.

(d) Close our eyes to the existence of mobile homes, caravans, and instant volumetric building and ignore the industrialization which has taken place not only in every aspect of society but also in societies of every political inclination.

Anyone in a position to ignore all of these changes must have a very protected environment indeed. But can even he ignore the future and the moral implications? In fact, for everybody, the moral implications of architecture and planning must become a matter of increasing concern. Properly used, the microprocessor can help, but there must be a realization that it can also constitute a considerable threat, mainly through allowing it to be ignored.

Whilst society talks about the threat of central computer banks, they go on being constructed. The problem is not the computer, or even the data banks, but the right for people to know what the banks contain. That, strangely, is seldom demanded even of manual systems. Whilst society talks about the threat of computer surveillance and 'big brother', they take for granted that much of life is carried out under the surveillance of closed-circuit television cameras in city centres, stores, and shops. Large computer systems have and are being developed which centralize power in a small group of people, but society does not question how they work or what they do to freedom. Will architectural computer systems, based upon outdated ideas, also be developed to dominate our lives and our environment? If we are not careful, we shall find that whilst we are hoping the problems will go away, we shall not only miss the advantages of the microprocessor but, even more frighteningly, miss the dangers which they could so easily bring.

The Modern Movement was supported by a very small group of people for many years until, suddenly, half-understood ideas swept through nations. Now we are paying the penalty. Could the same happen with computers, where a few people without necessarily the experience needed by practising architects will write programs for the industry using views which they think that architects ought to have. The dangers are far greater than they ever were with the Modern Movement. It must be seen not as the universal panacea that the enthusiasts claim; nor is it the threat to art that most people fear. It is just another tool, and the sooner *everyone* starts to use them for the development of a new architecture for each and every condition of man, and think of them as they do their tee-squares or telephones, the safer will be our freedom to design and understand what is going on. Those who abhor the thought of these coming changes should remember that the people who lived through the Renaissance also had to live through dramatic change. Now we look back and see them as fortunate people! Can any of the new threads be woven together to suggest a pattern and therefore hope for the future, in the same way as we have been able to unravel, in retrospect, the threads of the Renaissance which have gradually brought us to the pattern of today?

Whilst it is dangerous to forecast the future, it might be worth doing as scientists have always done, which is—to create a hypothesis based upon existing evidence and then search for evidence to support that hypothesis. On this basis we may take the following as irrefutable trends:

(a) Increasing knowledge and therefore power of the individual
(b) Increasing demand of the individual to fulfil his own destiny
(c) Increasing industrialization of all human activities
(d) Increasing demand for disposable goods

Either we may assume that architecture will stand apart from these trends, or perhaps *should* even stand apart to become a select group as with the Guilds, or consider a new role. If we look for possible directions for that new role, there are two examples which are outstanding as possible signposts for the future.

The first is the work of Kroll at the Faculty of Medicine, University of Louvain, Woluwé, Brussels (Figure 89). As one approaches the La Meme block, the first emotion is one of outrage as one's architectural pre-indoctrination is contradicted. Within minutes, however, as with any true work of art, a new vision of society and its architecture is exposed, and immediately the whole history of Architecture (with a capital A) seems to have become a history of authoritarianism. The so-called democracy of Greece is exposed as is all architecture right through to Jacobsen's St. Catherine's College, Oxford, in which he designed everything down to the cutlery and assumed that he could also design the activities of the students. The way the students used the building from the moment of take-over was certainly not how he had intended and clearly exhibits the fallacy of such assumptions. How much of the work of the Modern Movement falls into the same category? Too often it seemed that it was architecture for a special breed of people, rather than ordinary people who go to the pub and the club, who are married, single, or divorced, and who all carry out multifarious activities.

Kroll was requested by the students to be their architect and he in turn asked them what they wanted. Out of this dialogue emerged a need to satisfy three major categories of students, but with endless personal permutations within these categories. The three categories are described as fascist, anarchist, and the barn section. The first is for those who feel the need for a formal architectural framework in which to live, a framework which gives them a feeling of security. The second is for those who are strong within themselves and would find such a framework inhibiting, and therefore have a need for fluid changes and adaptability to changing circumstances. The last category, the barn section, is for those who wish to live in interacting communities of varying size. One part of

204

Figure 89(a)

Figure 89(b)

this, the barn, for the large group, has proved to be the least successful, but it is perhaps the faults which are violently exposed, like raw nerves, which are its greatest value.

The administration understandably hates the whole thing, not only because of the encouragement to individual student expression but also because of the problems of administration and maintenance. Cleaning individual 'spaces', for example, on a multiplicity of levels is almost an impossibility. But will general cleaning in society as a whole become an impossibility anyway? Perhaps everyone will have to do their own servicing in the future with disposable furniture, carpets, etc., to join the existing disposable sheets, handkerchiefs, underclothes, dresses, etc., already sold. The maintenance of the building fabric is also a problem. Could this be helped if we had a vocabulary of industrialized components to fit into a linguistic framework in continuance of the work of Ehrenkranz and many others? Here again Kroll is already overthrowing the old language (not as in the facile old Langue d'Oc modernism) by using windows as doors and holes in the roof as windows, and so on.

What is emerging here is an architecture which tries to mould itself to the changing activities of the individual or the group and which leaves the architect as a midwife to the creative expressions of the students where it is needed or as a structuralist where it is not. Instead of movements, quasi-political dogmas, and pseudo-intellectualism, here we have an architecture which is as negative and yet as exciting as the organic and pragmatic developments of the past where human expression has created the interest.

The other example is the work of Piano and Rogers at the Centre Georges Pompidou, Paris, which they describe as having 'no facade, so transparency and scale has more to do with the activities within the external open steel framework. The building reveals its internal mechanism to all who look up at it. It is a flexible, functional, transparent, inside-out building.' Here again is a building which is only alive when human activity brings it alive. It is not an object to be maintained in elegance and viewed from selected viewpoints, as with so much architecture, but is a building to be used and adapted.

Both of these examples show not only how exciting this type of architecture can be, but also how the microprocessor may come to be used in forming a creative living environment by

(a) holding the rules of change which may be extensive but can never be limitless,
(b) helping the manufacture and integration of the multiplicity of parts needed, and
(c) helping with the use of multidimensional models to explore the potentials for human habitation.

If this is the future, and after all the future is the only place we have to go, we may find that instead of the currently fashionable view of architecture going through a menopause, it might be that the microprocessor will one day be seen as the acne of adolescence before we reach the maturity of a *truly* democratic understanding of society and its spatial needs.

APPENDIX

The following pages give a guide to some types of programs which are available to architectural practices or which can be developed in-house. They range from the simple types of program for small practices to the more complex types of program for the integrated organization. Similarly, the range of cost of installation will vary. Nevertheless, it may stimulate a search for programs which may be useful in helping to get started, some of which may be found in books such as *Computer Program Description for Architects*, published by the Department of the Environment, *Information Methods for Design and Construction*, published by John Wiley, and *Computer Programs for the Building Industry*, published by the Architectural Press and McGraw-Hill.

Simple advice to architectural practices

Buy a cheap microcomputer for little more than the cost of an electric typewriter. Buy one that either has a video screen or the capability for connection to a television set and also has programs available at low cost. (The cost becomes very small when written off against tax, as equipment.) Do not be put off by apparently complex ideas in magazines or lectures, but let the staff play with the machine. Let them take it home for their children to play games and their wives to work out recipes.

First, this will bring the whole mystique of computing into focus. Suddenly it is not an ogre but a tool, and then the ideas will roll in as to what it could be useful for. Then somebody may volunteer to write a simple fee-costing program and gradually, by learning a simple program language like BASIC (probably in a day), a few simple programs will emerge.

At this stage everybody will have a better idea of what they might want to use it for than all the lectures in the world would give them. Also an office strategy might begin to develop for the implementation of more sophisticated programs. Here it may be necessary to consort with others to finance them or put pressure on institutions to provide packages. In the United Kingdom, an MAP grant for up to 2,000 pounds in consultant's fees might be obtained.

For a small outlay, the ability to discern needs and discriminate before investing large sums will have been gained.

Diary programs

Programs are produced and sold as standard software by some computer manufacturers. These allow a daily search of its diary files for items which may have been input days, weeks, months, or even years before. Programs can have a fifty-year calendar and enable a user to request presentation of the following types of information on any date in that period:

(1) A reminder note
(2) A document such as a maintenance specification complete and ready for checking
(3) Letters or documents ready for signature

The uses of such programs can be considerable and can obviously have even further advantages when used with word-processors.

Typical applications are those which contain repetitive data used on a regular cycle, such as insurances, maintenance items, reviews, etc., those with known forward problem dates, such as the ends of guarantee periods when some further action may be necessary, and also, of course, those with general reminder dates.

This program can also be related to the resources program, described overleaf, for progress checking.

Site survey programs

There are many programs of this nature available and usually involve only small changes in the surveyor's normal practice. His level book can be replaced by a computer input form, which will enable the computer to reduce the levels and, if necessary, prepare the contours which can be plotted direct (plotter required).

If a range of symbols is prepared which covers the characteristics normally to be found on sites, then the surveyor can indicate their location and the plotter will reproduce these as well. An example of some of the symbols is given in Figure 67.

In more ambitious suites of programs this information can be held in the machine for manipulation at later stages of the process, when instant evaluation of cut and fill or even perspective can be achieved.

Resources network programs

This is a network program which will not just make an analysis of the shortest path through the network, usually for the purpose of giving the shortest time, but can also carry out similar examinations of other resources such as manpower on a number of separate activities. Many computer firms sell this type of program as standard software.

The uses of this type of program are many and varied and are largely dependent upon the type of practice or organization. An example is one in which a network of varying degrees of complexity is made for the work carried out on a project—say brief, sketch design, production drawings, quantities, etc. A programme is prepared for each project and all of them are then put into the computer. The availability and types of resource, architect, technician, quantity surveyor, etc., are also input into the program for the lengthy problem of trying to make the resources and the programmes meet the required dates. Having established a work program, it can now be monitored at regular intervals by substituting actual for programmed dates.

This type of program can be related to the diary program and also such accounting programs as may be used for office accounting. In practices involved with the total design and construct process, this type of program can, of course, be invaluable for the estimation of contract periods and the allocation of construction resources. (See Paterson, 1977.)

Pre-design brief and analysis programs

There are many different aspects of briefing and computer programs which have been produced for several of these aspects:

(1) The collection of the client's needs by questions and answers such as the medical type program
(2) The assessment of activities against data banks of human requirements and physical attributes
(3) The sortation of activities into bubble diagrams
(4) Assessment of area, sanitary accommodation, etc., in buildings for which there are established criteria
(5) Cost forecasting and targeting
(6) Analysis of circulation and timetabling
(7) Management control

Most of these are self-explanatory, but together they mean that if an adequate data bank is provided the client can give his requirements to the computer which will then analyse these rquirements for both performance and cost. Cost targets can be produced and the activities manipulated, with the aid of the architect, into bubble diagrams, analysed for relationships, circulation problems, and, if necessary, the movements of people within the proposed building. Brief data can also be used for the evaluation of various criteria at this pre-design stage.

The efficiency with which these types of program can be used is not only dependent upon the quality of the programs but also on the organization of the data.

Materials and property file programs

All of this type of program follows a similar format and are ones in which the collection of data is important. Data collection and organization can be a very costly affair, and so it is necessary to arrange for this to be done in the most economic way possible. For this, it is wisest to take time and care in setting up the criteria of the data before rushing into programming, as too often happens. Standards need to be laid down, such as the measurements to be kept (metric or imperial), the areas involved (includ-

209

ing or excluding internal partitions, etc.), and a definition of terms (good or bad can mean different things to different people).

Once the criteria are laid down, the collection can often be done by preparing new proformas with these included. In this way the data are collected in the normal routine at no extra cost. The savings made by this rationalization can support the next development, and so on.

A property file can be built up by maintenance surveyors filling in proformas on their regular inspections, for example. Reexamination dates can be logged into the diary program. Material files are more difficult as the manufacturers and/or their representatives seldom have evidence of the behaviour of their materials or components. However, brochures are increasingly providing the sort of information necessary for building up good files.

It seems likely that some form of this type of file will be available on Teletext or Viewdata for access to materials and manpower costs, etc.

The program is prepared on the basis of sorting information into the form of a matrix and selects property or material, or whatever, in the same way as a computer dating program.

Management programs

The range of these programs is probably greater than any other, as the choice does not have to be confined to ones specifically prepared for the construction industry. As it is impossible to cover this wide range, even in principle, it is worth considering some factors when making a selection:

(1) Is the input difficult and/or lengthy to obtain?
(2) Is the input costly to obtain?
(3) Is the available information in a compatible form, or does it need costly translation?
(4) Is the means (terminal) of input/output easily accessible?
(5) Is the means (terminal) of input/output user compatible?
(6) Is the means of computing under management's own control?
(7) Is the output in the form needed? Can it be taken away and studied if necessary?
(8) Is the output personalized or does each member of the staff have to struggle through everyone else's data as well?
(9) Is the program organized to give (a) only information when required or (b) only information which is necessary?
(10) Are there sufficient inbuilt self-checks in the program?

Regulations programs

These have been one of the greatest needs and yet one of the slowest to emerge. However, some useful programs are now becoming available. Most of these take the regulations which have emerged from the legislation for energy conservation, and to varying degrees enable the architect to examine proposals against these regulations.

Alphanumeric input through a keyboard or graphic input through a cathode-ray tube can be used. In the case of the latter, the principles already described are used for registering the location of the components which then enable not only heat losses, etc., to be calculated but also other allied characteristics, such as floor-to-wall and window-to-wall ratios, for checking against regulations.

These can also be associated with degree day programs to forecast fuel consumption in any particular design. This fuel consumption forecast in a building should be held in the computer files for checking with actual performance (e.g. property file). Programs are also being developed for other characteristics such as sound transmission in buildings, acoustic performance, structural stability, and ventilation.

It can reasonably be anticipated that software houses will prepare and sell cheap computer programs covering this area, as it would be of great value to all building designers. There have also been proposals discussed in which those responsible for regulations can use these types of program to check submissions made.

Production drawing programs

These come in a variety of forms.

One type of program uses information allocated by a digitizer (a means of gathering graphical data in digital form), which is run over an existing drawing. The advantages of this type of program can be small unless connected to evaluation and other production processes. There is little gained by producing a drawing in one form which is then translated into a similar form on a digital plotter.

However, graphical input through a television or cathode-ray tube can be used not only for the production of working drawings of high quality but also as the input for the production of bills of quantities and/or construction management information. It is this use which provides enormous financial benefits.

When a dimensionally coordinated library of parts is available, production drawings can be developed from the original layout drawings, as these can be pieced together by the computer. Also the layout can be produced by layers as required. The computer accepts instructions to reshuffle the drawing information it has into a variety of desired outputs.

The problem for some time to come is likely to be that the cost of computer peripherals such as plotters will not reduce in price in the way that the processor has done. This means that it is the cost of the peripheral which may inhibit the use of computers in this area in the smaller practices.

Cost evaluation programs

If standard work units or components are brought together on a dimensionally coordinated basis, they will constitute a library from which repetitive aspects of building can be chosen. The units can be drawn and measured, and a symbol can then be attached to them, i.e. a brick wall (Figure 65). Attached to the symbol and the drawing can be measurements and the specification. It can be measured in terms of cost, but it can also be measured in terms of materials, activity time to build it, the type

211

and cost of labour to build it, and the plant. It can also be measured and described in the terminology of the standard method of measurement.

Therefore, as the building is being drawn a variety of actions can be carried out by the computer. The area, length, and volume of spaces can be measured. The Standard Method of Measurement description can form the basis of bills of quantities (if required). The manpower, activity, materials, and plant characteristics can at the same time be allocated to a network or listed. If the MAMP files are kept up to date by the information section with times and prices, then costs can be immediately available to the designer. If these updated files are produced in schedule form by the computer and sent out to contractors as a basis for tendering, then they should be able to give a percentage (plus or minus) of what they would require for constructing a design in accordance with these rates. As this can be done at the very earliest design stage, it means that the designers can have a set of tender rates to design with, merely by inserting the successful tenderer's percentage into the computer.

This can give a uni- or multiprofessional team separated from the contractor the same advantages as the design and construct organizations. As the designer is preparing a design he can find out the amount he has spent at any stage. He can also evaluate any of the other criteria which have been included. In this way, organizations where design is separated from construction begin to achieve the same advantages as the design and construct firms Paterson (1977).

Design models

These can take two forms. The first is more common in which information on a certain design is gradually built up in the same way as a conventional model might be built up. Then the model may be modified according to those findings and another test made.

The other and less common variety is that in which information is made available to the computer programs which gradually develop their own model or even a series of models.

In both cases the model can be made up of theoretical or actual components. In the former, the use of the model is not only limited to schematic testing but also prevents their use for the transfer of data to the construction team, as already discussed. Those architectural stochastic models which can hold real-world construction data are at present very rare. Those of any magnitude are even rarer, but where sufficient resources are available, such as for war games, the testing of differing strategies is of unlimited value. Desirably, the model should include the surrounding space rather than limiting itself to the building only. Architecture must be seen as spaces relating to spaces, and computer programs which inhibit this view only aggravate an existing problem.

One of the major deficiences in both types of model is in the form of input, often through some type of cathode-ray tube, which is very unsatisfactory. Not only architects but also laymen find it easiest to use a soft pencil and paper for the exploration of ideas, but little work on a form of input compatible with this has yet been done.

The greatest problem of all with any large suite of programs comes in the problem of updating the data base. If data are continuously being updated, no one can tell where the base line for, say, tender prices is. The whole data base becomes a floating sea of information without location points unless some sort of control system is set up at the beginning.

REFERENCES

Architects Journal (1977). Issue 19th October 1977. Architectural Press, London.

R. Arvill (1967). *Man and Environment*, Penguin Books Ltd., Harmondsworth.

R. V. Ayres and A. V. Kneese (1972). *Resources for the Future*, Reprint No. 99. New York.

H. Beck (1976). *Architectural Design*, 11/76.

D. E. Berlyne (1971). *Aesthetics and Psycholobiology*, Appleton, New York.

B. Berenson (1952). *The Italian Painters of the Renaissance*, Phaidon Press, London.

E. Bernhardt (1971). Dietz and Cutler (Eds.), *Industrialized Building Systems for Housing*, MIT Press, Cambridge, Mass.

G. D. Birkhoff (1933). *Aesthetic Measure*, Harvard University Press, Cambridge, Mass.

G. Broadbent (1973). *Design in Architecture*, John Wiley and Sons, London.

N. Chomsky (1976). *Reflections on Language*, Temple Smith, London.

N. Chomsky (1968). *Language and Mind*, Harcourt, Brace and World, New York.

Le Corbusier (1947). *The Modulor*, Faber and Faber Ltd., London.

L. Cottrell (1960). *Enemy of Rome*, Evans Brothers Ltd., London.

O. Cox (1977). *RIBA Journal*, July 1977, RIBA Publications, London, pp. 298–303.

C. Darwin (1859). *The Origin of Species*, Mentor Edition, New York.

R. Dawkins (1976). *The Selfish Gene*, Oxford University Press, Oxford.

J. M. R. Delgado (1971). *Physical Control of the Mind: Towards a Psycho-civilised Society*, Harper and Row, New York.

D. R. Denman (1978). *The Place of Property*, Geographical Publications, Berkhamsted.

P. E. K. Donaldson (1966). *Proc III International Conf. on Medical Electronics*, pp. 173–178.

C. A. Doxiades (1968). *Ekistics*, Hutchinson, London.

D. Dunster (1976). Sign Language, *Architectural Design*, 11/76.

E. Ehrenkranz (1971). In Dietz and Cutler (Eds.), *Industrialized Building Systems for Housing*, MIT Press, Cambridge, Mass.

H. J. Eysenck (1968). *Journal of General Psychology*, 1968, 3–17.

P. Feyerabend (1975). *Against Method*, N.L.B., Bristol.

B. Fine (1979). *Occasional Research Papers*, Fine and Curtis Ltd., London.

E. Fromm (1978). *To have or to be?*, Jonathan Cape, London.

S. Giedion (1941). *Space, Time and Architecture*, Harvard University Press, Cambridge, Mass.

J. Gipps (1971). *Shape Grammars and Their Uses*, Birkhauser, Basel.

R. L. Gregory (1966). *Eye and Brain*, Weidenfeld and Nicolson, London.

R. L. Gregory (1974). *Concepts—Mechanism of Perception*, Duckworth, London.

T. Gold (1977). *Relativity a Time Encyclopaedia of Ignorance*, Pergamon Press, London.

N. J. Habraken (1972). *Supports—An Alternative to Mass Housing*, Architectural Press, London.

N. J. Habraken (1977). Inroduction to *All Their Own* by Jan Wampler, John Wiley and Sons and Schenkman Publishing, Cambridge, Mass.

215

H. Harms (1976). Limitations of self-help. *Architectural Design*, XLVI, 230–231, April 1976.

R. Heilbroner (1975). *An Inquiry into the Human Prospect*, Calder and Boyars Ltd., London.

Hillier, Leaman, Stansall & Bedford (1976).

W. Hogarth (1753). *Analysis of Beauty*, J. Reeves and Clarendon Press, Oxford.

F. Hoyle and N. C. Wickramasinghe (1978). *Life Cloud,* J. M. Dent & Sons Ltd., London.

C. Jones (1970). *Design Methods*, John Wiley and Sons, London.

A. Koestler (1964). *The Act of Creation*, Pan Books Ltd., London.

A. Köestler (1978). *Janus, A Summing Up*, Hutchinson, London.

R. A. Lyttleton (1977). *Encyclopaedia of Ignorance*, Pergamon Press, Oxford.

E. N. Marais (1937). *Die Siel van die Meis* (trans.), Jonathon Cape and Anthony Blond, London.

E. N. Marais (1969). *The Soul of the Ape*, Anthony Blond, London.

E. N. Marais (1971). *The Spirit of the White Ant*, Anthony Blond, London.

J. Maynard Smith (1976). 'Evolution and the theory of games'. *American Scientist*, 1976, 41–45.

D. H. Meadows, D. L. Meadows, J. Randers, and W. W. Behrens (1972). *The Limits to Growth*, Universe Books, New York.

D. Michie and R. Chambers (1968). *BOXES an experiment in adaptive control*, University of Edinburgh, Edinburgh.

W. Morris (1882). *Hopes and Fears for Art*, Longmans Green, London.

W. Morris (1962). In Asa Briggs (Ed.), *Selected Writings and Designs*, Penguin Books, Harmondsworth.

I. Murdoch (1977). *The Fire and the Sun*, Clarendon Press, Oxford.

C. Norberg-Schulz (1971). *Existence, Space and Architecture*, Studio Vista, London.

G. Orwell (1949). *Nineteen eighty-four*, Martin Secker & Warburg, London.

S. Ostrander and L. Schroeder (1970). *PSI Psychic Discoveries behind the Iron Curtain*, Sphere Books Ltd., London.

J. Paterson (1977). *Information Methods for Design and Construction*, John Wiley and Sons, London.

Sir K. R. Popper (1972). *Objective Knowledge: An Evolutionary Approach,* Clarendon Press, Oxford.

Sir K. R. Popper (1974). *Conjectures and Refutations: The Growth of Scientific Knowledge*. Routledge & Kegan Paul, London.

T. Poston and N. Stewart (1976). *Taylor expansions and catastrophies*, Pitman Publishing, London.

K. H. Pribram (1971). *Language of the Brain*, Prentice-Hall, London.

R. J. Proudhon (1898). *What is Property?* W. Reeves, London.

M. Quantrill (1975). *R.I.B.A. Journal*, 8/76.

A. Ray-Jones (1968). Computer development in West Sussex. *Architects Journal*, 21st and 28th February 1968. Architectural Press, London.

M. Rowan Robinson (1977). *Encyclopaedia of Ignorance*, Pergamon Press, Oxford.

J. Ruskin (1855). *The Seven Lamps of Architecture*, Smith Eldes, London.

S. Serlio (1611). *The Books of Architecture*, Robert Peake, London.

B. F. Skinner (1970). *On the Future of Art*, Viking, New York. pp. 61–75.

J. Summerson (1964). *The Classical Language of Architecture*, Methuen, London.

C. M. Turnbull (1976). *The Forest People*, Jonathan Cape, London.

United Nations (1974). *Yearbook of Construction Statistics*, 1963–72, United Nations, New York.

E. E. Viollet-le-Duc (1884). *Discourses on Architecture*, trans. B. Bucknell, Allen and Unwin, London.

J. Wampler (1977). *All Their Own*, Schenkman Publishing, New York.

C. J. Willis (1978). Presidential Address to QS Div. RICS 18/10/78.

R. Wittkower (1978). *Ideas and Image: Studies in the Italian Renaissance*, Thames and Hudson, London.

H. Wooton (1624). *The Elements of Architecture,* Longman Green, London.

V. C. Wynne-Edwards (1962). *Animal Dispersion in Relation to Social Behaviour*, Oliver & Boyd, Edinburgh.

A. L. Yarbus (1967). *Eye Movements and Vision*, Plenum, New York.

J. Z. Young (1978). *The Programs of the Brain*, Oxford University Press, Oxford.

217

BIBLIOGRAPHY

C. Alexander, S. Ishikawa, and M. Silverstein (1977). *A Pattern Language*, Oxford University Press, New York.

M. A. Boden (1977). *Artificial Intelligence and Natural Man*, Harvester Press, Hassocks.

R. G. A. Boland and R. M. Oxtoby. *Computers for Management, Language and Concepts*, Hodder and Stoughton, London.

M. S. Briggs (1927). *The Architect in History*, Oxford University Press, Oxford.

E. C. Carterette and M. P. Friedman (1978). *Handbook of Perception*, Vol. X, *Perceptual Ecology*, Academic Press, New York.

The Catalogue (1974). *Index of Possibilities*, Clanmose Publishers, London.

N. Cross (1977). *The Automated Architect*, Pion Ltd., London.

D. Crystal (1971). *Linguistics*, Penguin Books Ltd., Harmondsworth.

R. Duncan and M. Weston Smith (1977). *U.N. Handbook*, Pergamon Press, Oxford.

Her Majesty's Stationary Office (1968). *An Introduction to Dimensional Coordination*, HMSO, London.

Infotech International (1977). *Microprocessors*, Infotech International, London.

C. A. Jencks (1973). *Le Corbusier. Tragic View of Architecture*, Allen Lane, London.

C. A. Jencks (1977). *The Language of Post Modern Architecture*, Academy Editions, London.

S. Kostof (1977). *The Architect*, Oxford University Press, New York.

F. Muir (1976). *The Frank Muir book*, Heinemann, London.

V. Packard (1978). *The People Shapers*, Macdonald and James, London.

A. Rosenfeld (1972). *The Second Genesis, The Coming Control of Life*, Pyramid Communications, New York.

H. M. Sapolsky (1972). *The Polaris System Development*, Harvard University Press, Cambridge, Mass.

M. W. Schein and M. H. Fohnman (1955). Social dominance relationship in a herd of dairy cattle. *British Journal of Animal Behabiour*, **3,** 45–55.

R. Venturi (1977). *Complexity and Contradiction in Architecture*, Architectural Press, London.

T. Winograd (1972). *Understanding Natural Language*, Academic Press, New York.

L. Wittgenstein (1953). *Philosophical Investigation*, Blackwell, London.

NAME INDEX

SUBJECT INDEX